The Calling

THE
CALLING

3 FUNDAMENTAL SHIFTS
TO STAY TRUE, GET PAID,
AND DO GOOD

RHA GODDESS

Founder and CEO of Move The Crowd

ST. MARTIN'S
ESSENTIALS
New York

The names and identifying characteristics of some persons described in
this book have been changed and some persons are composites based on the
stories of more than one individual.

First published in the United States by St. Martin's Essentials,
an imprint of St. Martin's Publishing Group

THE CALLING. Copyright © 2019 by Rha Goddess. Foreword © 2019 by Gabby
Bernstein. All rights reserved. Printed in the United States of America. For information,
address St. Martin's Publishing Group, 120 Broadway, New York, NY 10271.

www.stmartins.com

The Library of Congress Cataloging-in-Publication Data is available upon request.

ISBN 978-1-250-20469-1 (hardcover)
ISBN 978-1-250-20470-7 (ebook)

Our books may be purchased in bulk for promotional, educational, or business use.
Please contact your local bookseller or the Macmillan Corporate and
Premium Sales Department at 1-800-221-7945, extension 5442, or by email
at MacmillanSpecialMarkets@macmillan.com.

First Edition: January 2020

10 9 8 7 6 5 4 3 2 1

For you, Daddy . . . may I always make you proud

Contents

Acknowledgments

This book has been inspired by so many people. People who have touched my life with the way they live theirs. People who move with such courage and grace as they pursue their callings. When you show up in the world you are poetry in motion, and I am so grateful for you.

To my mentors, thank you, Eve Ensler, Gail Staub, David Gershon, MaryKay Penn, Barbara Huson, Queen Afua, Lisa Nichols, Susie Carder, John D'Aquila, Lynne Twist, Bob Proctor, Jay Abraham, Charlee Sutton, Rosemary Blake, Dr. Devika Singh, and Brendon Burchard. To my lifetime collaborators and co-creators, Lori Hanau, Raphael Bemporad, Nathalie Molina Niño, Jodie Evans, Reshma Saujani, Claudia Chan, Gabrielle Bernstein, and Paula Abreu, I am inspired every day by you and all that you are bringing to this world.

To my soul sisters, Kimberly Greene (biological), Ghana Imani Hylton (BFF), Kyung-Ji Rhee, and Brooke Emery. To my beloved Move The Crowd clients and all those who have engaged in our trainings, it has been such an honor to serve you!!! To our rock-star leadership circle: Heather Box, Anurag Gupta, Phakiso Collins, Amina AlTei, Jesse Johnson, Anasa Troutman, Randi Zinn, Michelle Maros, Barb Schmidt, Eren Ozmen, Deepa Purushothaman, Anna Claussen, Rodney Lopez, Ella

Turenne, Diana Gasperoni, Taij Moteelall, Cheryl Derricotte, Z Griss, Anna Glass, Theresa Coleman Wash, and Piper Anderson—thank you, for all you do to change the game!

To my beloved Move The Crowd team both past and present, there is no way that I could have ever done this without you, Rolando Brown, Eve Smith, Dana Balicki, Joselina Fay, Danny Skinz, Lillian Koenig, Marisol Ybarra, JLove Calderón, Monika Moss-Gransberry, Josh Van Vliet, Nikki Orzel, Ursula Burden, Barry Girsh, Ben Gruber, Micah BlackLight, Shalonda Ingram, Pat Manuel, Stacy Pobatschnig, Dana Podgurski, Annette Naif, Regina Dowdell, Katrina Frye, Chris Kazi Rolle, Karen Dellaripa, Sue Freeman, Connie Vanderzanden, Calgary Brown, and Anietie Ekanem, thank you, for all the ways you've helped me every day to Empower the Dream!

To my brilliant agents, Celeste Fine and Jaidree Braddix, and the awesome team at Park & Fine Literary and Media, thank you, for your genius always. To my awesome attorney, Nancy Wolff, and the team at Cowan, DeBaets, Abrahams & Sheppard LLP. To my phenomenal copy editor, Kristina, "say it plain, sister!" Grish, thank you, for all the love and dedication you brought to these words. ☺ To my wonderful editor at St. Martin's Press, Monique Patterson—thank you so much, for seeing the vision and helping me usher it in.

To my beloved family, the Greene, Fletcher, Bell, Butler, Davis, Allen, Kupfer, and O'Leary clans. Thank you, for loving me and encouraging me to always keep it real!

Last but never, ever least, to my phenomenal husband, Corey S. Kupfer, you are my rock and my reason. Thank you, for being my partner in all things and for helping me create such an amazing life. Your love encourages me every day to answer the call.

A Word About the Stories in This Book

Some of the stories in this book describe the life circumstances and experiences of individuals I have worked with who have chosen to be identified by their real name. Some stories are inspired by the circumstances and experiences of individuals who chose not to be identified. I have changed identifying details and events and given them fictitious names.

Finally, some of the stories in this book are composite accounts based on the circumstances and experiences of a number of individuals who had similar challenges. For these composites, any resemblance to any real person or persons with similar names and/or circumstances is purely coincidental and unintentional.

Foreword

I believe that God works through people. I believe that we're guided to the people who will support us in our development and we're guided to them exactly when we need their help. This has happened many times in my own life, but one in particular stands out. That's the story of how I met Rha Goddess.

In 2008 I was struggling big-time with codependence. I'd been in an unfulfilling relationship, jumping through hoops for my boyfriend's attention. I was terrified of losing him and of being alone. Finally, I hit bottom. I was desperate for relief, so I stopped pouring all my effort into making him interested in me. Instead, I started praying.

The more I asked for guidance, the more I received. I was led to many helpful resources, from books and meditations to a group for women healing codependent patterns. I began experiencing a lot of beautiful synchronicities that blew me away.

One day my neighbor suggested I set up a business meeting with a woman named Rha Goddess, who, like me, worked to empower young women. A week later, another friend independently suggested I meet Rha Goddess. I accepted the universal memo and emailed Rha to schedule a meeting. She responded to my email by saying that she couldn't meet right away because she was going on a spiritual retreat. I was shocked, because it turned out I was going on the same retreat! I flipped out over this synchronicity, but it didn't seem to faze her.

We didn't end up meeting at the retreat. But on my flight home, I connected with the woman sitting next to me on the plane. I told her about my work and that I lived in New York City. She said, "You must meet this woman." And then she handed me Rha Goddess's business card! I laughed as the universe hit me over the head yet again.

The next week I traveled to New Orleans for an event for Eve Ensler's V-Day, a global movement to stop violence against women and girls. When I got there, I looked over the lineup for the first day. Following talks by Rosario Dawson and Jane Fonda was a performance by guess who? Rha Goddess! Clearly I needed to meet this woman. The guidance was so apparent that I felt overwhelmed with joy.

Finally, we met. I was moved by her powerful energy and her loving presence. After her performance, we gave each other a big hug and laughed about how a power greater than ourselves was working hard to get us together. We agreed to set up our long-awaited meeting later that month.

The day when I was set to meet Rha for a dinner meeting in Brooklyn was dark and rainy. The gloomy weather mirrored my state of mind: I was tripped up about my romantic relationship again, experiencing a lot of fear around being alone and feeling like I wasn't good enough. But I wasn't about to miss my dinner with the woman the universe so clearly wanted me to know, so I pulled myself together and went to Brooklyn.

Even though we'd set up the meeting to discuss business, Rha and I began talking about our personal lives from the moment we sat down. She told me about her spiritual beliefs and her coaching practice. She also told me about her magnificent husband and how she had manifested the relationship. She explained how she'd gotten over her negative relationship patterns and become clear about what she wanted in order to free up space to call in her man. Rha exuded light when she spoke about her husband and their relationship. As she spoke, I heard an intuitive voice say: *Ask her to be your coach!*

I listened to the guidance. "Do you still coach people?" I asked. She responded, "In fact, I do. Each year I coach a handful of people who are already deep into their spiritual journey. My work is to take them to the next level. I coach people just like you."

From that day forward Rha worked with me as my coach. It was clear to me that my prayers had been answered: I'd been led to meet the perfect guide for releasing my romantic illusions. I was ready to get to work. Rha helped me understand how I was limited by my belief that I was incomplete without a man. She helped me feel past wounds and honor all my feelings as equally important. Then she guided me to become honest about what I wanted in a romantic partner.

Within six months of working with Rha, she'd helped me heal my codependent addiction. I had more clarity than ever before. For the first time in my life I was unapologetic about what I wanted in a romantic relationship. Rha's guidance supported me not just personally but professionally, too. She helped me own my self-worth and guided me as I manifested the early visions I set for my businesses, from landing my first book deal to growing my audience. Most important, she taught me to follow my calling and honor my inner guidance system.

Thanks to my work with Rha, I became crystal clear about what I was here to do. Rha helped me turn my visions into a movement that has had a major impact on the world. It's my mission to help people crack open to a spiritual relationship of their own understanding—to live as happy, inspired Spirit Junkies! This movement has grown in ways I never could have imagined before I began working with Rha. Millions of spiritual seekers have joined this movement in different ways and become beacons of light in the world. And in my own life, I've experienced miraculous personal growth, too. Once I released my romantic illusions, I could bring my authentic self into relationships. Seven years ago I married my amazing husband, and now we have a beautiful son.

Today, eleven years after meeting Rha for dinner in Brooklyn, I'm thrilled to be writing this foreword to her book. In *The Calling*, Rha will do for you what she did for me. She'll guide you to become aware of what holds you back, and then she'll help you take responsibility for your life while cultivating immense self-compassion. She will help you forgive yourself and others so that you can feel truly free and design the life you dream of. With Rha's wise and loving guidance, you'll crystallize your vision for your life so you can take inspired action on it. And most important of all, you'll have fun and celebrate this process of change and growth each step of the way!

This book is both grounding and inspiring. It's exactly the book we need right now, in a time of massive societal change. You'll discover how to stay rooted amid upheaval, how to see challenges as beautiful opportunities, and how to live an abundant and authentic life while doing what matters most to you. Rha's True. Paid. Good. method will help you uncover and truly claim your calling, no matter where you are in your professional life or on your path to personal growth.

Rha has a gift for channeling divine wisdom and translating it into practical, actionable steps. When you follow her guidance you can expect transformations that will catapult your life to a whole new level! Having big dreams is a big responsibility. Through this book Rha will help you fearlessly bring those dreams to life.

—GABBY BERNSTEIN

The Calling

Introduction:
You Have a Calling

I used to believe that if I wanted to make money and be viewed by others as successful I'd better be prepared to trade for it—whether that meant sacrificing my health, life's purpose, authenticity, fulfillment, friendships, or family time. Growing up as an African-American woman in a lower-middle-class community, I believed that only certain people (namely, upper-middle-class white men) could afford to dream big without consequences, while the rest of us were destined to struggle to make ends meet in order to feed our families with dignity. And as I got older, I met professionals outside my community who validated these beliefs—those who felt that to pay their own bills, they also had to grin and bear whatever it took to keep the lights on. It seemed that no matter what your race, class, or religious upbringing, this damaging worldview had been ingrained in far too many of us, plus the generations before. To make a good living, we were told that to varying degrees, we would have to swallow our pride, strangle our creativity, bite our tongue, trade inspiration for pragmatism, and lose sleep as we wondered if *this* is all there is.

There are so many myths we've bought into that keep us on the hamster wheel of life. And "the trade" is just one of them. We've also bought into the belief that our happiness and true fulfillment live outside of us.

That our success is defined by what we have and by what other people perceive about us or believe we are capable of. That no matter how passionate we feel about what's going on in the world, we don't have the ability to fix or solve it, nor is it our business or responsibility to do so. We've been conditioned to play it safe, to avoid pain and disappointment, to take the easy way out. And along with all those tendencies come the habits of dismissing our dreams, stepping around our true potential, and denying our deepest longings. No wonder so many of us are anxious, depressed, frustrated, enraged, and ready to give up! I hear you. But you don't have to live this way. You don't have to let your cynicism rule your days. It is possible to live an amazing life—one where you get to create what you desire. A life that actually honors your passions, celebrates your contributions, and aligns with the things that are most important to you. You can have a life where every interaction is meaningful and where every day you are joyous, fully engaged, and totally fulfilled.

You don't have to swap what you L-O-V-E for a J-O-B. You don't have to barter in ways that compromise you, you don't have to stay bound to ideologies that limit you, and you don't have to remain shackled to abusive relationships, situations, or circumstances. You can break free and reclaim your own destiny. And you can do it now. A meaningful career, robust compensation, and soul fulfillment are yours for the making, and I'll show you how to get there.

This lesson has been hard-won for me. I've studied and worked in the worlds of political participation, racial equity, juvenile justice, youth and young women's empowerment, education, mental health, economic justice, and spirituality. I've been an artist, coach, corporate consultant, nonprofit leader, professional mentor—and at times, a healer, teacher, facilitator, and guide. I've worked in the United States and abroad, right alongside CEOs, celebrities, and even convicted felons. And what I've come to know with every ounce of my being is that *all* of us, no matter what our story is, want to be true to ourselves, be well compensated and acknowledged for how we serve others, and contribute to the greater good. These are fundamental human needs. And they are unalienable human rights. On a personal level, I've learned that it wasn't until I pursued my deepest calling, which is to create profound experiences that help others pursue *their* purpose, that I began making satisfying money and working from a loving place within me. In other words, it wasn't until I embraced the philosophy that I'm about to teach *you* that my life transformed in the most incredible way.

This philosophy and curriculum are the culmination of knowledge and insights I've amassed over the last thirty years from vastly diverse stakeholders all pondering the potential of a better life and world. These ideals and perspectives have met the challenges and opportunities of my own experience and been transformed into a core set of principles and strategies that enable people to pursue their passion, purpose, and profit. I've successfully applied it across various contexts, industries, and temperaments. And now, finally, I am ready to share it with you!

Why Now? Why This? Why You?

My primary aim in writing this book is to show you how to get free. Free from all of those expectations that are consistently placed on you by others and society at large. Free from all the inner chatter that constantly tells you to dim your light and guard your heart. Free from the limiting conditions and conversations that tie you down and bleed you dry. If you are stuck in a never-ending loop of hyper-achievement or driven by the quest for external validation, I want to show you that it is possible for you to live a meaningful life on your own terms. There is a process that I'm going to teach you that has been battle tested on the concrete of thousands of lives, with people from various backgrounds and multiple persuasions. From multiple *New York Times* bestselling authors to multi-million-dollar venture CEOs, to residents in a battered women's shelter and everyone in between. This process truly puts your life back in your hands and enables you to create a step-by-step blueprint for how to express your truest self and pursue your highest calling.

And it begins with three core commitments: *Stay True. Get Paid. Do Good.*

Staying true means honoring who you really are, your deepest values and grandest visions; *Getting paid* means being well compensated for sharing your unique combination of talents and gifts in a way that adds tremendous value in the marketplace; *Doing good* means creating positive change in the world by making a profound difference in the lives of others.

Every single one of us has a calling. No matter who you are or where you come from. Your calling is that thing that only you can do. For most people, it is the thing you have to force yourself *not* to do. When you ignore it, it is the thing that weighs on you, pulls at you, and consumes your conscience until you give it its due. It is the thing that both terrifies you and brings you the most joy. Unless your path and purpose are nurtured from a young age, you may have no idea what's calling you. You may meander about for years, searching for "the thing" that will give your existence meaning. You may get glimpses of inspiration along the way or have life-changing magical moments that show you something else is at work, but you may not feel the level of clarity and conviction that points the way. The call may be rooted in your profession; it may show up in the dynamic with your children; it may wrap itself in the middle of a health crisis or another traumatic experience. Regardless of the path, the call is still the call. And it will always compel you—but it will be up to you to decide whether or not you're going to answer.

Through the coaching and consultation agency I founded, Move The Crowd, we help thousands of people every year to find and follow their calling, from *New York Times* bestselling authors, to world-renowned storytellers and technologists, to spiritual and movement leaders and even a global peace negotiator. Move The Crowd invests in creating breakthrough changemakers, cultural visionaries, and social entrepreneurs who are shaping the future of our economy and culture in real time.

Just as we do in our acclaimed True. Paid. Good. Academy, I can teach you too how to find your calling, how to *Stay True* to your deepest values and core beliefs, *Get Paid* for sharing your unique talents and gifts, and *Do Good* by creating positive change in the world while you're at it. At Move The Crowd, we call it "bringing your whole self to the party." It means defining your goals and establishing practices—both in business and in your personal life—that are always in alignment with your most deeply held values, your unique talents and gifts, and the profound difference you want to make in the world.

You can achieve this level of success no matter where you begin. I know this is true because I myself did not come from wealth.

My father, born in 1927, survived over two decades of Jim Crow segregation and worked tirelessly beside my mother to raise, clothe, feed, and educate four rambunctious children. Growing up in Albany, New York, he experienced the kind of racism that ranged from blatant to subtle, and like most people of that generation, he would tell you that he preferred the blatant kind. But living in the North lent itself to the sort of cloak-and-dagger isolation that left you scratching your head wondering if you had imagined it. Yet the effects were real. Opportunities that seemed ripe over the phone would vanish into thin air when he arrived. In 1941, he moved to Brooklyn, where he attended integrated schools and worked side by side with men from other backgrounds. He fostered friendships and built bonds across racial and cultural divides. Yet, for all of his scholarship and brilliance, and reverence for democracy, he struggled with the culture of capitalism. Specifically, with the way the conflation of the free market and civil liberties became a central driver for inequality. My father did not just see the denial of opportunity to certain people as offensive; he saw it as unpatriotic. During his lifetime, he fulfilled only a handful of his dreams.

I believe part of my calling has been to heal my father's legacy by helping others pursue their deepest passions, make a profit, and make a difference in their communities be they local or global. I want those I serve to experience the kind of personal freedom and success my father could only imagine.

The happiness and fulfillment we all seek already lives in a unique expression that we each possess and are on this earth to share with others. It is found in our purest selves and highest contributions. You can't turn on the television or flip open a magazine without being told to "just be yourself," "get real," and "show them what you're made of," but where do you actually begin such an exciting (and scary) exploratory journey of finding and staying true to you?

You might be surprised to learn that being smart, capable, and highly talented isn't enough to get there. You might be masterful at pleasing others, playing the game, and checking off boxes related to typical success milestones, but these factors don't guarantee happiness. Because, at some point, the call will come knocking—and you'll have to consider all of the ways you've been conditioned to sell out on your own wants, needs, and desires.

Often when I meet someone new and I explain what I do, they want to tell me all about their life story. This isn't because I ask, but because they know that on some level, they're hiding out, or not living up to their full potential, and just a glimpse at the opportunity to "come clean" gets them going. It is natural for us to aspire to more, but the more we're seeking doesn't live in the number of cars we drive or houses we occupy. The more that keeps us awake at night is the profound connection we seek to have with our most authentic selves and greatest offerings.

So what enables you to take that leap? *The Calling* combines all of the strategies, techniques, and insights that have proven to be most effective in helping build the courage and fortitude to move toward the things you desire most. It integrates spiritual guidance with structure and accountability, tools for visioning with strategies for implementation and plenty of case studies to demonstrate just how impactful these concepts can be when you apply them to any walk of life.

Six Steps to True. Paid. Good.

I've created a six-step True. Paid. Good. process that has the ability to transform any limiting conversation and corresponding habit(s). Whether you are an emerging, established, or experienced entrepreneur or organizational or community leader, the True. Paid. Good. philosophy can be beneficial at any level. If you feel stuck because you know you're here to do something greater, but stepping outside your comfort zone makes you want to pee your pants, True. Paid. Good. is for you. If you are hiding behind everyone else's expectations of what you could, should, and would be doing in order to be successful and well liked, True. Paid. Good. is for you. If you feel more comfortable rooting for everyone else's dream as you abandon your own, then True. Paid. Good. is for you. And finally, if you can't shake this burning desire to do something with your life that will actually make a difference in the lives of others, it's time we get started:

Step 1: Recognizing that it always begins with awareness. If you can't see it then you can't do anything about it. You've got to take the time to see what's actually happening and where your choices and behaviors are contributing to any form of limitation in your current reality.

Step 2: Accepting, embracing, and telling the truth. It means taking responsibility for yourself, your life, and the things that you want or need to be changed. In order to create something new, you must make peace with where you are; you must also give up the urge to fall into the traps of denial and critical self-judgment.

Step 3: Forgiving yourself and others. This is where the rubber meets the road. Forgiving yourself and others for any situations that have led to your limiting beliefs and behaviors is the difference between living at the mercy of your circumstances and creating a life you intend by design. On a universal level, your ability to cultivate compassion for yourself and others is also what invites a wealth of possibility into your future.

Step 4: Redefining and visualizing (reimagining) your new future. This is where conscious creation really takes hold. I will teach you how to articulate your vision as a new belief, as you're making a decision to replace the old one with a new one. I teach my clients that any time you extract a limiting conversation, you must put something new in its place or, just like an aggressive weed in that garden, it will grow back.

Step 5: Aligning through right actions. Nothing supports how a new belief takes hold quicker than taking actions that are consistent with that new belief. Consistent, aligned right actions—no matter how big or small—give life to that new decision and inspire you to keep going.

Step 6: Finally, you must celebrate! This sixth step insists that you bring some joy to the process of rebuilding your belief system. Celebrating encourages you to acknowledge your efforts, pay attention to your progress, and affirm to yourself that you are making the beautiful, powerful changes you need to make.

Even at this stage in my life and my work, when I encounter any limiting conversation or habit this six-step process is my go-to. Some of the most rewarding work I've done with this six-step process has been with trauma survivors. As more individuals are stepping forward to give voice to severely distressing incidents, like what we've been witnessing with the #Metoomvmt, #Blacklivesmatter, #Marchforourlives, and #Immigrationreform, many others are finding they too have been affected. In these instances, having the ability to speak your truth, redefine your life, and take charge of your own experience can be game-changing.

The Journey—How This Book Is Organized

I've organized this book into three parts to purposefully mirror the three fundamental shifts I've seen my clients make over the years toward *Staying True, Getting Paid, and Doing Good.* Each aspect of liberation comes with its own set of challenges and concerns and I address these key areas through the six-step process for each part of the journey. Each transformation process builds on the one before it, and the progression is designed to give you the clarity and confidence you need to step into a more joyful and fulfilling existence.

In part 1, when I teach you to *Stay True,* you will begin by recognizing your creative strengths, accepting responsibility for your current reality, forgiving any self-imposed and societal limitations and giving voice to your vision, mission, and purpose, aligning your actions with your dreams, and celebrating a new level of clarity, authenticity, and self-love.

In part 2, when I put you on the path to *Get Paid,* you'll begin by recognizing your relationship with money and capitalism, accepting responsibility for your current financial state, forgiving any constraints in your financial past, redefining and revisualizing your role in your personal economy, aligning your business propositions with your values, and celebrating a new way of doing business.

In part 3, armed with the clarity of your true calling and a passionate values-aligned financial strategy, you'll leverage your capacity to *Do Good* by recognizing your full potential, accepting responsibility for being part of the solution, forgiving any judgment around not doing more sooner, revisualizing what good means to you as you identify your highest contribution, aligning your actions with your movement, and celebrating your newfound meaningful contribution.

At the end of each chapter I've issued Your Call and given you homework, which includes specific practices and assignments drawn from the tools, concepts, and stories I've shared in the preceding sections. The best way to maximize these teachings is to get on the court and start applying these concepts and theories for yourself. You can access a downloadable version of the worksheets and tools I reference throughout the book at: www.movethecrowd.me/TheCalling/resources.

What Is Your Calling and
Why Should You Pursue It?

There has never been a better time to answer your calling. We are living in a world that is both ripe for entrepreneurial success and desperately in need of positive social change in every corner of society. We may not be facing the same challenges that my father did in 1941, but I don't need to tell you there's been a never-ending tirade of social, political, and economic upheaval lately, and you can find it either inspiring or, let's be honest, a little terrifying. The establishments that we once felt we could count on for stability and guidance, such as government institutions, blue-chip stocks, moral and faith-based institutions, friendly librarians, and even a welcoming corner bakery, no longer exist or are no longer as stable as they once were. Like it or not, we're in the rolling rapids of an era of disruption. You can choose to be instrumental in creating change or allow these intense waves of change to create you.

Throughout *The Calling*, my goal is to help you un-mine, apply, and elevate what it means to be a deeply fulfilled, well-paid, and happily engaged citizen of the world. I believe that you already have the most important elements within you to live out your full potential. It's just a matter of gaining access to the knowledge, skills, and insights that will enable you to architect success on your own terms. I will give you the framework, tools, and encouragement to achieve what you're after. I will guide you through exercises and provide worksheets to help you narrow your focus and achieve your goals. I will share stories about successes and failures, so you can see how the True. Paid. Good. philosophy works in real time.

As we go, you'll do your part and put in the work, too. As Jay Abraham, a marketing genius and one of my own teachers, likes to say, "If you aren't taking action, then you're indulging in 'intellectual entertainment.'" This is why Move The Crowd is both a company and what I call a "community of practice." There's no lack of motivational philosophy and ideology floating around, but we help clients hone their mission and feel supported as they put their big ideas into action. I've successfully done this work with tens of thousands of people over the last thirty years, and now I want to do it with you.

It's time for you to put your stake in the ground for the kind of person you want to be, for the life you want to live, and for the world you want to be part of. You've got to become adamant about fulfilling your own hopes and dreams and unapologetic about thinking for yourself. On a societal level, as we continue to wake up and become increasingly aware of what's happening around us, the call is also going to get louder. You must act on your desire to do something. Embracing this time means no longer sitting by and expecting a cushy job or random world leader to make it better for you and those you care about. Success and movement need to happen on your terms. You've got to mold and shape it, because no one will do it for you.

The exciting news is that you've never been in a better position to change the game for yourself, express your truth in this moment, and do something that matters. I know you want to inspire yourself and others—and now is the time. We're in the midst of an economy and culture that, frankly, didn't exist 10 years ago. Thanks to a shifting technological and social landscape, we're redefining how we achieve success and happiness. We're putting our values first, whether they're to be more loving, collaborative, conscious, sustainable, you name it. We're digging deep to understand ourselves and then marry aspects of who we are and what we do for a living with our most soulful conscience, to pursue a high-risk, high-challenge, and high-reward reality.

By reading this book, you've joined a movement. And as a part of that movement, you have the opportunity to participate in our global community of practice with a complimentary subscription at www .movethecrowd.me/TheCalling/resources. It's my commitment to have this True. Paid. Good. process become real for you. Let's now unearth the authentic you, cultivate profitable strategies for sharing your gifts, and rock the world with *your* unique brand of impact.

Let's get to it—now's the time!

Part I

STAY TRUE

1

Step #1: Recognizing Your
Creative Strengths

A number of years ago, I was keynoting at a live event in New York City called Reveal—as I stepped offstage, I was approached by a young woman from the audience named Christine, who looked as if she were about to burst. Her chest was heaving, her eyes watering, and her upper lip was quivering. I knew that whatever she said was going to be good. The event was a hip annual gathering created by one of my beloved Alumni clients, renowned author and theologian Meggan Watterson. Meggan is a brilliant spiritual and self-love teacher, and this event was all about helping women discover the truth about what matters to them in their lives, their work, and their relationships—and helping them live from that place.

"I'm done with playing small," Christine blurted out.

Now that's my kind of confession! In fact, these words are liquid gold to a coach like me, because all we ever want to do is help people see how magnificent they are—so they can confront all the areas in their lives where they settle for less than they deserve. The catch, however, is that until someone gets fed up—I mean *really* fed up with whatever is not working, be it their job, relationship, money, family, health, or friendships—nothing will ever change.

So Ms. Christine was right on time.

If you're lukewarm about making changes to improve certain areas of your life, don't even bother asking for help. Without the right mindset, you won't take the necessary actions to alleviate your suffering. Pain, as much as we don't like it, is comfortable. We get used to it. It's *our* pain, which somehow makes it more bearable. But that kind of pain won't get you anywhere. You've got to get to a point where the pain of *not* challenging yourself feels worse than the pain of hiding out. In other words, you must hit your version of rock bottom before you're ready to move. Christine's pain was so visceral, I could practically feel it coming off her in waves—she was literally shaking as she went on to list what she felt must change in her life for it to improve. This included her deadbeat boyfriend, overbearing mother, MIA business partner, and "psycho" client (to put it gently).

No matter how smart, rich, or accomplished you are, it's frustrating when your life doesn't look the way you had hoped it would or, even worse, when it does turn out as you'd hoped, but you're still not happy for some nebulous reason. Like Christine, you may feel like a victim, caught in an endless cycle of anger, fear, doubt, and frustration. And since you feel like a victim, you unwittingly create the same disappointing outcomes over and over by feeding the emotions that put those behaviors in place. Before you know it, you're tangled up in a never-ending swirl of undesirable circumstances, causing you to feel trapped and out of control.

What Christine didn't realize at the time was that she'd been co-creating her misery. And here's the kicker: The only way out of her cycle would be to see that the common denominator in all her problems was, well, her. That's no easy task. Before this gutsy young woman could even be capable of creating the positive change she craved, she had to first see that she helped create the drama in her life, too. Now I knew that if I told her this, one of a few things would happen. She could argue me down with a "you don't understand," or she could say, "I know . . . I know," and just keep talking. She might also use this golden opportunity to beat herself up and convince me that she's a hot mess! Trust me, I've seen it all.

However, none of these moves would help Christine make the changes she needed to make. Because even if she theoretically understood the hand she had in her reality, not much would change until she actually *owned* the idea that she was creative. Meaning, she had to recognize her ability to co-create her reality, and then choose to either use her creative powers for good or stay stuck in that same frustrating loop. This is actually your first step toward staying true—choosing to tune out all the noise in your head so that you can tune into a message that's different from your usual chatter. You see, until now, Christine had been exposed to the same "not my fault" or "all my fault" narrative that permeates our culture and allows most of us to either push blame onto others or flog ourselves senseless when things don't go our way. Yet neither holds any real power or promise of change, which is what Christine and you are after.

So before life could transform for Christine, she had to embrace her power and understand on a deep level that her reality would only be different if she was willing to envision it differently. Then she had to consciously do the work to turn her vision into a new reality. That required taking her blinders off and getting to the truth about why she sought me out in the first place.

In Order to Stay True, You've Got to Get True First!

The first thing I did was hug Christine, because I wanted her to know that I truly cared about what she'd been through before pummeling her with advice. "I hear you, and I feel you," I said. And then I asked a question: "So if you had your way, how would you resolve these issues?"

Christine paused, speechless, as if no one had ever asked her this question before. I watched her body language shift, and she went from looking battered to emanating defiance.

"My boyfriend would respect me; he'd keep his promises or tell me when he couldn't so I wouldn't rely on him when he can't do something. My mother would back off and stop trying to run my life by scrutinizing every little thing I do. My business partner would answer my emails and texts within twenty-four hours, and she'd tell me what she was going to do to fix a problem instead of leaving it all up to me . . . ."

"This is a great start," I interjected, "but all of it requires *others* to act differently first. What about you? Independent of any one of *them*, what are *you* willing to create for yourself?" Christine began to chew on her bottom lip—a clear indication that my girl was digging deep.

"I'm willing to have a boyfriend that respects me and keeps his word," she said.

"I'm willing to tell my mother that although I know she loves me, she has to give me room to make mistakes and stop projecting her fears onto me; and that may mean we don't talk as often.

"I'm willing to let my business partner know that our relationship, as it is, isn't working for me. I need to know what she's willing to bring to the table or talk about parting ways.

"Oh, and I just need to fire my client. I mean, enough is enough."

See what just happened there? And notice how fast it arrived? Once Christine realized what she was willing to have versus what she'd settle for, she could envision it clear as day.

Now she had to consider how she might go about creating it. "Awesome," I said. "That's your homework. Have those conversations in honor of what you want to create."

I gave Christine my card and asked her to email me in two weeks with a rundown of how her plans went. True to her word, her deadbeat boyfriend and MIA partner were gone, and her client was fired. Mom, however, was a work in progress; even so, Christine was so much happier.

If you're looking to turn things around and get true, which is the first step in the journey to True. Paid. Good., like our friend Christine, I've got three words for you: "You are creative." No matter who you are or where you're from, you have the ability to co-create with anything occurring in your life. *And* you have the ability to heal and transform anything that is not working for you. This is not just my opinion; it's a universal law that's been operating from the onset of human awareness. This creative principle is woven throughout many Eastern spiritual teachings, like those from Buddha, who said, "All that we are is the result of all that we have thought," and in various Bible verses like Mark 11:24 and in the book of Matthew: "Ask and it is given, seek and ye shall find, knock and the door shall be opened unto you." You have the capacity to create your reality through what you think, believe, and act on—this, in conjunction with a higher power, which I'll get into next, is what puts you on the path to getting true. This is all amazing news, because it means you have an enormous say in what goes down on your watch, not from a place of externally focused drama and manipulation, but by altering your internal beliefs and intentions.

In this chapter, I'll introduce you to the notion of co-creation and I'll show you how you can co-create your reality in both positive and challenging ways. You'll learn how to get control over your life, so that victimhood is in your past. I'll also invite you to consider how getting and staying true is the first step toward becoming True. Paid. Good. and relying on your ability to understand what it means to be a conscious versus unconscious creator when it comes to challenging the circumstances in your life that don't align with your greatest desires and highest calling.

So How Does Creation Work?

You and I are creating all the time, but most of us don't know it. Whether you manifest a million dollars or a parking ticket (yes, both are possible!), it's all creation at work. Sometimes you initiate the creation, like when you ask for something you desire like a raise or promotion, and sometimes life throws you a curveball with an invitation to improvise, like when you get fired from your day job, only to discover that your passion is to lead retreats all over the world for burned-out corporate executives, which ends up being far more rewarding and lucrative. Either way, you are in a constant dialogue with a higher power—call it God, Source, the universe, doesn't matter. Just like at a restaurant, you place orders every second of the day and are served what you "ask for." And what you ask for isn't just what you verbally say but also what you mentally and emotionally expect—i.e., what you ultimately believe is possible and feel is going to happen.

When you create, you do it through what you think, feel, and act on. And what you think, feel, and act on is driven by what you believe. Sometimes when I hear people say negative things, I cringe because they have no idea what they are creating. They are totally oblivious to the fact that they are orchestrating a recipe for disaster just by virtue of the words (spoken with conviction!) spilling from their lips. Then you have those who attempt to "fix it" through positive self-talk or forced gratitude exercises, and when I see this I get just as concerned. Granted it's a step in the right direction, but when you have absolutely no relationship to what you're saying it won't turn into manifested action. So even if you're trying to say or do the right thing, if what's going on inside doesn't line up, the universe doesn't honor it because it's just not true for you.

A perfect case in point: I encounter people all the time who tell me, "I'm broke, but I know the universe is going to bring me the perfect opportunity to make a million dollars any day now." And as they're telling me this, I can see the terror in their eyes. That is not the way to create a million-dollar reality! They're clearly scared to death, starving inside, and putting on a good face by quoting popular self-help books. It's fancy language with no money, and that's exactly what they end up with. Listen, if they can't fool me, they sure can't fool the universe!

In the early days of my coaching and mentoring career, I spent six years teaching conflict resolution in the New York City public school system through an organization called Educators for Social Responsibility. Here I used a visual tool called The Conflict Cycle (developed by the Community Boards conflict resolution center, which can be found at https://communityboards.org) to help illuminate how and why certain types of conflict occur over and over in a person's life. This helped me understand how my own ingrained attitudes, beliefs, and perceptions about conflict influenced the way I would respond to any conflict in my environment. This simple diagram perfectly illustrated how my belief system drove my conditioned responses to conflict and how those conditioned responses kept producing experiences that only served to reinforce my beliefs. I soon realized that I was raised to believe that conflict was bad, so I had developed conditioned responses that caused any conflict to be a bad situation (i.e., lying, calling names, walking out, getting violent, avoiding). Ultimately, those responses produced experiences that reinforced my belief that conflict was bad. For example, I was dating a very friendly guy at the time, who loved to flirt with other women any time we were together. Initially, I let it slide, because I didn't want to make a big deal out of it, and I was with him after all. But one day, he smiled and made some comment about a part of a woman's anatomy that was offensive, even to me, and I said something about it. He tried to dismiss the remark, and I blasted him, then got up and walked out of the restaurant and never looked back. All the way home, I just kept telling myself this would not have happened if I had not said anything. The experience just reinforced what I already knew: that conflict was indeed bad. This belief kept me stuck in a never-ending loop of bad experiences—hence my conflict cycle.

Over the years, however, I realized that The Conflict Cycle has a broader relevance not just for me and my clients, but for everyone seeking to discover how limiting conversations hold you back from your true self and true calling. This cycle is actually built on a universal principle called the Law of Vibration that says everything in the universe is comprised of energy and therefore vibrates at a particular frequency. And within this realm "like attracts like," so you bring things into your world that are similar to whatever frequency you give off.

Your vibration, aka your vibe, is the culmination of what you believe. And the way you think, feel, and act in *any* given situation is linked to

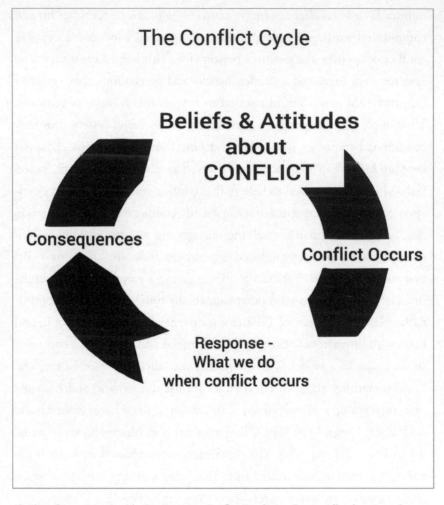

The Conflict Cycle

Beliefs & Attitudes
about
CONFLICT

Consequences

Conflict Occurs

Response -
What we do
when conflict occurs

© 2019, Community Boards, San Francisco Conflict Resolution Center. All rights reserved.
Community Boards.org

your belief system. These beliefs then dominate how you live, love, work, relate, and feel—in other words, they control what you experience in your reality, every single day of your life, from your job, to your health, to your relationships, to prosperity.

So if you really want to change the game and get true, as in True. Paid. Good., two creation-minded moves need to happen: (1) You must embrace the fact that you are creative, and (2) you must start to pay very close attention to what you believe. Cumulatively, this means that you need to become acutely aware of how your internal dialogue sounds and how that dialogue goes on to influence your perception, mood, and behavior. Only then will you come to understand how that behavior ultimately gives you, for better or worse, the experience called your life.

Creation in Action

This is how creation works:

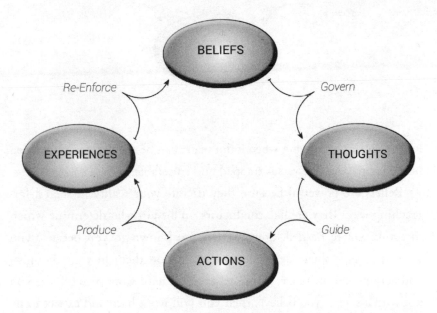

As this graphic, which is called The Mindset Wheel, shows, your beliefs govern your thoughts, your thoughts guide your actions, your actions produce your experiences, and your experiences reinforce your beliefs—and then it all begins again. When these belief-thought-action cycles become ingrained, they turn into habits, aka things you do over and over without consciously thinking about them.

From brushing your teeth to choosing emotionally unavailable partners, this kind of autopilot conditioning is great when you're developing a

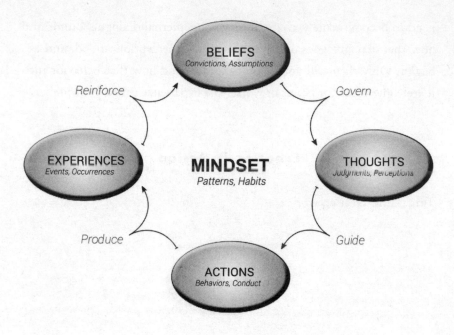

habit that serves you, but when it doesn't it can be the difference between being happy and free versus trapped and miserable.

Beliefs are powerful because they dictate your reality in such a far-reaching way. They are like conductors on a train who determine which direction you're headed. Some beliefs are known to you because you actively engage them and deliberately draw on them in your thoughts and actions. For instance, if you believe that hard work pays off and you know that's what you believe, then you will work hard and expect to be rewarded for it—and most times, you likely will be. Other beliefs, however, are not so obvious, since they have been thrust upon you through experience and conditioning. For example, if you watched your father work really hard and, though he was rewarded with acknowledgment and respect, he made very little money, then you may have an ingrained belief that respect is more important than money or that hard work doesn't guarantee you'll make more money. You may then unwittingly put yourself in situations where you're working hard and you're respected, but you're not making a lot of money.

One of the greatest opportunities you have when you embrace the fact that you are creative is that you get to challenge what is actually false and what is true for you. You can then go from being what I call an "unconscious creator," which means you're unknowingly controlled by beliefs that don't serve your best interests, to being a "conscious creator," which means you get to redefine your beliefs in a way that serves you. A conscious creator is awake and aware of what they believe, think about, focus on, and give their energy to. When you are conscious, you can practice intentional thoughts and actions in every moment, so that you can master a process that allows you to choose and have more of what you want in your life. This is the foundation for becoming true, paid, and good.

My client Anna is a great example of someone who moved from unconscious to conscious creation. When she first came to me, she was already a brilliant, strong, determined, and very successful creative producer and managing director at a successful nonprofit arts organization in Brooklyn. She was very loyal and committed to the communities and organizations she served, and it was her nature to go the extra mile. Though this was virtuous at times, it often tipped into martyrdom. Because of her upbringing, Anna felt it was her duty to take on the weight of the world, which made her feel perpetually exhausted and depleted. When Anna got pregnant with her first child, something had to give, and she asked me to help her strategize a professional transition. She loved her organization, but she knew she'd soon have two babies to care for—her new child and her old job—and she wanted to show up for both.

Enter: a perfect opportunity to introduce and apply the principles of conscious creation. Anna was fully aware of her concerns but had no idea how to address them in a way that would enable her to care for herself during her pregnancy, prepare her home for the new baby, and attend to all of the things the organization needed from her during that time.

To help Anna shift her self-sacrificing mindset, I asked her to create three potential scenarios that she'd like to see happen after her baby's birth. Scenario A was to be her ideal; B, a middle ground; and C, her least desired but still acceptable outcome.

Naturally, I wanted Anna to believe she could create Scenario A, and I was committed to making that happen. As it were, her most common organizational experience and history came from perpetually feeling obligated and put-upon. Every role she took on had required some level of sacrifice, time, energy, money, and sleep in order to produce an acceptable outcome where others felt seen, heard, and taken care of. And so, she became conditioned to accept that some level of painful sacrifice was her only choice—this was *her* truth. (I've seen this repeatedly happen in the arts world. There are too many incredible organizations that provide vital resources to communities but are grossly under-resourced, which causes those who are passionate about the mission to consistently stretch in ways that are not healthy to make up the shortfall.) I challenged Anna to consider the possibility that she would not have to suffer or trade in ways that were painful to be both a good mother and a great leader. In other words, I asked her if she was willing to challenge that belief, and after some resistance she finally said yes. Over a two-month period, we focused on this conscious creation opportunity. I gave Anna a series of considerations to help her create and envision achieving her Scenario A.

I knew that this ideal scenario had to feel believable to Anna if she was going to advocate for it with her boss. To work, she had to believe on some level that it was possible. I asked her to visualize herself being nurtured and cared for, as she got the rest she needed and prepared her home for a child. She simultaneously had to visualize her organization thriving, and her team knocking it out of the park during her maternity leave. Anna also had to imagine her finances in great shape so she could relax and focus on being a terrific working mom. I asked Anna to visualize this reality over and over, for 15–20 minutes every day, until it became viscerally real for her. She needed to see, feel, and imagine this outcome as a possibility.

Three weeks later, Anna walked into a meeting with her director and emerged ecstatic. I'll never forget her text: "Got my Scenario A at full salary *and* was given more time at home. We did it!" Because she was able to consciously envision an outcome that did not require giving up the things that were most important to her, she was able to actually create that very same outcome. It was, in fact, an outcome that was initially way outside her realm of possibility.

Once you accept and own that you're capable of creating your desired reality, your reality will start to transform, and you will experience an unprecedented level of joy and satisfaction as you watch more of what you truly desire manifest. You will understand that you are not a victim, no matter what you've been through or how many times you hear this from the media, your parents, spouse, or kids, or even well-intentioned friends who are always ready to commiserate. You will see that you're meant to envision an amazing future, then act on it. You'll begin to understand that even when very difficult things happen, you can meet those circumstances with the power of your own intentions and begin to find your own sense of personal power in the circumstances that impact your life.

Recognizing your power to co-create your reality is the first step toward staying true and pursuing your calling. If you are looking to anything outside of you to validate your existence, you're wasting your time. The external world is mostly a reflection of what you believe, think, and act on. Many of us have experienced various forms of trauma in our lives that require a special commitment to heal—and you can do it. In my work with thousands of clients over the last thirty years, I've watched too many talented and capable souls squander their skills and gifts because they could not release their grip on victimhood—even if they didn't intend to do themselves harm. The truth is, we come by our self-doubt honestly. Our society often encourages us to play small, whether by messaging or by violent force, to live according to other people's standards, to color inside the lines and stay inside the box. This is such a tragedy, because every one of us has a calling in this lifetime. We each have a purpose that poises us for unlimited and unequivocal greatness—that is the truth. No matter how victimhood has tried to place you in its grasp, it's up to you to set the intention to get free, to pursue the things you really want, believe the outcome to be possible, and then take a leap of faith to create your desired True. Paid. Good. reality. It all begins with recognizing and owning your creative strengths.

Your Call

Are you ready to really embrace what it means to be a conscious creator? Let's start with two practices to engage in daily until you finish the book, plus two exercises to complete before moving on to the next chapter. Each one is designed to help shift your mindset from any form of victimhood to one of conscious creation and help you develop a greater awareness around your current state and your desired reality. From here on out, you'll need a journal to complete some of the book's exercises. If you have one, great: otherwise, go buy one that makes you happy. I've also created an additional set of resources to support the exercises at the end of each chapter. You can download it from www.movethecrowd .me/TheCalling/resources; then get ready to buckle down and do some work!

PRACTICE 1

"I am a conscious creator, and I have the ability to create the life I most desire."

Repeat this mantra at least five times a day. I'd like you to do this once in the morning in the mirror when you first wake up. Look into your own eyes, and say it. During the day, say it three times—perhaps when you are transitioning between work projects or traveling from one destination to the other, just before your lunch break, or before you pick up the kids. Finally, repeat the mantra in the evening, after you climb into bed and just before you close your eyes.

PRACTICE 2

As you work to develop your conscious creation skills, keep a copy of The Mindset Wheel front and center to remind you of how creation works. Post it above your desk in your office or in your meditation room, or keep it on your phone—use this diagram to remind you of your new commitment to becoming more aware of what you're creating in every moment. You can download one at www.movethecrowd.me/TheCalling /resources.

EXERCISE 1

Since you now appreciate the power that beliefs hold, let's take inventory of your current belief system. Beliefs can become so ingrained that you don't really recognize them unless you're encouraged to. The following exercise will help you understand more of what's informing your thoughts, feelings, and behaviors. Once you're aware, you can decide what to do about them. This exercise will highlight what's actually going on inside you, which increases awareness and is the precursor to any form of change. Complete the following Belief Inventory exercise.

THE BELIEF INVENTORY

There are six major areas that I invite you to explore in this exercise. Use these questions as prompts to explore your current belief system.

I. Beliefs About Yourself:

- What kind of person are you?
- Do you feel good about yourself (i.e., who you are, what you have)?
- Do you see yourself as capable?
- Do you see yourself as worthy?
- When you look in the mirror, are you pleased?
- If you had to choose five words to describe yourself what would they be?
- What are the things you're really good at?

- Do you feel confident in claiming the things that you're really good at?
- What are the things you're not so good at?
- How do you feel about the things you're not so good at?
- Do you feel confident in letting others know about the things you're not so good at? Why or why not?
- Do you trust yourself? Why or why not?
- Is there anything else you see here about what you believe?

II. Beliefs About Others:
- Do you feel comfortable around others?
- Do you feel comfortable around people you do not know?
- Do you feel comfortable around people who are different than you are?
- Which differences, if any, make you uncomfortable?
- Do you believe that most people are good?
- Do you believe that most people care about others?
- Do you believe that you have more in common with your fellow women/men or less?
- Do you generally trust other people? Why or why not?
- What do you believe people are most motivated by?
- What are five words you'd use to describe other people?
- What are five words you think they'd use to describe you?
- Do you think it's important to seek the advice of others? If so, when and why? If not, why not?
- If you could choose to occupy space with other people or be alone, which would you prefer and why?
- Is there anything else you see here about what you believe?

III. Beliefs About Your Current Situations/Circumstances:
- How do you feel about the current state of your life?
- Are there situations or circumstances that currently make you

smile? If so, what do you love most about what you are experiencing right now?

- Are there situations or circumstances that are currently challenging you? If so, what's the most challenging part about it/them?
- Do you feel empowered to change the things that are not working for you? Why or why not?
- Do you find that change is easy or difficult for you? Why or why not?
- Do you believe you can create what you want when it comes to your current circumstances? Why or why not?
- Why do you believe this challenging situation/circumstance is happening?
- What do you believe would make the situation or circumstance better?
- Is there anything else you see here about what you believe?

IV. Beliefs About the World:

- How do you feel about the current state of our world?
- How do you feel about society in general? Is it safe, just, peaceful?
- What are the specific things that concern you?
- Do you believe these things can change?
- What are the things that give you hope?
- Do you see yourself as a part of the problem or part of the solution? Why or why not?
- Do you think you can affect the things in society that you don't like?
- What are the things that you believe are impossible to change?
- If you could change one thing, what would it be?
- Is there anything else you see here about what you believe?

V. Beliefs About Success:

- What do you believe it means to be successful?
- How do you define "successful people"?
- If you had to describe the perfect life, what would it be?
- How much money do you think you need in order to live your ideal life?
- How much time do you think it takes to achieve success?
- What else is important when you consider being successful?
- Do you believe success and happiness are the same thing?
- Do you see yourself as successful? Why or why not?
- Is there anything else you see here about what you believe?

VI. Beliefs About Source (i.e., God, the Universe, Love, Creativity, etc.):

- Do you believe there is a Source, i.e., something out there that is bigger than you?
- Do you feel a sense of connection and belonging when you think about it?
- Do you feel safe, secure, and cared for?
- Do you think it's operating for the good of all?
- Do you believe that your interests are included?
- Do you believe that everyone has access to this Source?
- Do you think you have to do everything in order for things to turn out well?
- Do you believe in Murphy's Law?
- Do you believe you have to "do something" to deserve this?
- Is there anything else you see here about what you believe?

EXERCISE 2

In thinking about Anna's story at the end of this chapter, consider where you may be limiting yourself from a possibility that could make you feel dramatically happier.

Use Your Journal to Write Down Your Responses to These Questions:

What have you been telling yourself isn't possible?

Would you be willing to reconsider?

Now imagine having the thing you desire. Envision it, *feel* it, experience it, as best you can. (Write about it in your journal.)

Then put it down and go about the rest of your day.

For the next 10 days, spend five minutes each day rereading your journal description, focusing on the images that come to mind, and feeling the feelings that are associated with this desired outcome. If you get inspired to take any specific, positive actions during this 10-day period, take those actions.

At the End of the 10 Days, Check In with Yourself:

In what ways did you move closer to this goal?

What new opportunities emerged for you?

How did you feel during the process?

Write down your responses in your journal so that you can reference these examples in the future.

2

Step #2: Accepting Responsibility for What You Believe About Yourself

Now that you understand what it means to embrace your creative powers and take inventory of what you believe—about yourself, your life in general, your notion of success, your view of others and the world at large—it's time to accept responsibility for those beliefs and how they may be standing in the way of your ability to stay true to who you are and answer your calling.

When I mention the term "acceptance" here, I'm not talking about settling for or tolerating a subpar image of yourself. No—this is about having the courage to face what's holding you back, head-on, and deal with those roadblocks. It's about recognizing the impact that those self-imposed beliefs have had on your choices and decisions, plus how they have influenced the way you see yourself and the way you view what may or may not be possible for your life.

Ultimately, taking responsibility for what you believe about yourself is about taking your power back from the jury of public opinion. It's about setting a new standard that comes from your own values and convictions—who do you want to be for you?—and then determining how to operate in ways that honor this new vision while maintaining a healthy degree of self-respect, self-love, and self-acceptance. In this chapter, I'm going to show you how your most prominent beliefs influence the way you perceive yourself and your current reality. You'll discover which aspects of your belief system empower you and which do not. We'll also get to the source of these beliefs so that you can choose what you want to let go of and what you want to keep as true as you pursue your calling. I'll also demonstrate how acceptance isn't always a smooth and upward trajectory. Resistance is real, so I'll talk about the behaviors that can keep you stuck and trapped in negative patterns. Letting go of limiting habits can feel like you're throwing away a piece of yourself, but you have to realize that it's less about "fixing" what's wrong and more about identifying, honoring, and surrendering to what's true for you. Accepting is about recognizing where you are and telling the truth about it, so that you can shake free from the things that hold you back and move toward the thoughts that liberate you.

How Did Your Belief System Come About?

In the last chapter, I introduced you to The Mindset Wheel and talked about how your belief system influences your thoughts and actions, but to accept responsibility for what you believe you must understand where those beliefs have come from and how they either support or hinder your truth and ultimately your calling.

Your belief system is comprised of various decisions you made while growing up—it's your overarching view of the world, but one that hasn't necessarily been formed by you alone. Just as you are creative and have the ability to shape what you experience, you are also impressionable—highly influenced by the beliefs and perceptions of others. The most potent decisions you make about what you believe are established through the messages you receive during your formative years. These come from family, close community, school, church, and other religious and foundational institutions that hold some level of authority over the cultivation of your values and ideals.

Though these influences play a role throughout your early and formative years, experts have repeatedly honed in on the first five years of people's lives as the most crucial in determining who they are and how they eventually see themselves as adults. These early experiences influence how you view your personality, physical traits, sense of safety, capacity to love and be loved, and your sense of normalcy and belonging. During these years, your brain is growing rapidly, intensely, and is most susceptible to external influences both good and bad. You are taking in messages through words, feelings, interactions, and experiences; all of these factors govern the way you ultimately view yourself, those around you, and your environment.

As you grow, these perceptions tend to become reinforced through corresponding messages and experiences. In addition to your primary influences, every day you receive thousands of messages from work colleagues, friends, acquaintances, networks, and associations on social media, television, etc., that either confirm or refute what you've been conditioned to think thus far.

Together, the beliefs you take on from a young age and their reinforcing experiences inform your perspective. They can have empowering aspects that motivate you to accomplish incredible feats, as well as limiting aspects that hinder your happiness, achievement, and growth. Either way, they cumulatively determine how you view yourself, others, and the world around you. If you come from a long line of educated intellectuals, say, you may deeply connect to this quality and take on the belief that you too are very smart and entitled to an Ivy League future. Reinforced beliefs might even have to do with your appearance. If you have a certain kind of nose that everyone in your social circle pokes fun at, you'll take on the practice of hating your poor nose, which could cause you to feel bad about yourself every time you look in the mirror.

All of which begs the question . . .

Who Are You to You?

When you consider what may be holding you back on the road to acceptance, you must address who you believe yourself to be—in other words, what's your self-image like? It's natural to feel varying degrees of self-consciousness, fear, anxiety, worry, or doubt over how you see yourself. After all, many of us have been conditioned when we look at ourselves to feel like something is wrong or missing. Sometimes it's more pronounced in different situations, in your eyes and as you imagine the way others see you, too. You might poke fun at, even bond over, any subsequent self-consciousness, plus point out similar "shortcomings" in others to help validate the way you feel. You might even tolerate similar qualities or dynamics from others that get in the way of being true to yourself, because they reflect your established beliefs.

Your insecurities come home to roost, however, when you start making changes to your life, especially if criticism so much as trickles in from others. One of the biggest fears that clients must confront while navigating the road to their calling is a fear of being alone. "If I make these changes, what's my family going to think?" they wonder. "What about my wife? Husband? Or boyfriend?" The implication here is that when you become more self-assured about who you are, the insecurities you once had that made others feel comfortable will cause them to no longer feel accepted or like-minded, and then, hello, here comes the rejection. Or perhaps you're afraid the real you isn't the wife or friend they want and they'll move on. Shaking up the status quo feels most empowering when you're secure in who you are and where you're going. This is tough since it's normal to seek validation, but you can't let external voices and opinions hold you back.

When I ask clients what they believe about themselves, they often feel confused about how to respond. After all, one day you might feel like a badass, ready to take on the world—and the next? A total failure. Why is that, and which is true? The bottom line is, so many of us measure self-worth against external standards, and we do this without questioning whether or not those standards represent what we truly value and believe is important. We trust that others know better and therefore follow their lead while giving over our power to others' perceptions. When this happens, you give over not just your sense of self but also control and agency over who you are.

And you can decide in this moment that those days of giving up your power are over for you. To identify and pursue your calling, you must own your sense of self—accept responsibility for what you believe about who you are and what matters to you—this is the ultimate test for getting and staying true. Owning your sense of self enables you to focus on what supports, honors, and reflects your healthiest view of you. No matter how many beliefs have been passed down or reinforced through the years, it's time to push to the forefront what's important to you, what makes you feel great and inspires you to be your best. When you do this, you'll experience a greater sense of self-love, trust, and appreciation. This, in turn, will enable a stronger connection to your inner creativity, passion, and conviction.

It's here, my friend, where your calling resides. It is born from honoring your unique and most authentic self, as *you* view it, and how you choose to express your values and commitments to the world.

When Your Beliefs Do More Harm Than Good

When you have core beliefs that are empowering, they encourage and motivate you to act in ways that reflect the best of who you are. This means your thoughts, feelings, and actions will then produce positive experiences that make you feel good about yourself and your circumstances. As in our earlier example regarding intellectual lineage, if you believe you're a smarty-pants, you'll pursue opportunities that challenge you and invite you to grow. You'll have a certain level of confidence when solving problems because you have faith in your ability to figure things out. However, when you have core beliefs that are hindering, you act in ways that disempower you and ignite thoughts, feelings, and actions that produce negative experiences. Those experiences can make you feel sad, angry, and frustrated with yourself and your life circumstances. Just imagine what it feels like to look in the mirror every morning at your pointy nose and confront how much you hate something that's such a central and immovable part of who you are. In both cases, these thought/feeling/action patterns have become ingrained and hindering and they require a particular kind of vigilance to see, understand, and transform.

The beliefs that hold us back aren't always obvious and we may not even be aware of them as they float into our minds and affect our behavior. This, in and of itself, makes them more challenging to address, because if you aren't aware of them, then you're probably not aware of what those negative beliefs cost you. Think about my mirror example: Sadly, in this case, you may actually become so used to your internal voice of criticism that after a while you don't even realize you're doing it. You just look in the mirror, see your nose, and feel sad all of a sudden. And sometimes even when you are aware, you have no idea how to change it. Meaning, you see, hear, and *feel* the negative self-talk, but you don't know how to make it stop. And so you beat yourself up about that, too.

One of the most challenging dynamics for any coach is trying to work with someone who is unwilling or unable to confront their own belief system. Despite our best efforts and intentions, if someone is not ready to make the change, the change will not occur. It takes great courage to do this work, and coachability is key. You don't need to know how to do it, but you do need to be open to guidance and support.

I remember in the early stages of my coaching career, working with a woman named Lydia—a very beautiful and accomplished creative producer in dire need of support as she transitioned out of an agency role and into launching her own shop. She had brilliant ideas, all of which had the potential to be very lucrative, and I was excited to help her create a strategy to bring them to life. She had had a great track record of creating and producing really impactful projects, but she had a massive falling-out with one of her collaborators and was unable to move past her own hurt and anger, which manifested as negative self-talk. Lydia knew her ideas were great, but she didn't believe anyone would fund them; she knew who she wanted to serve, but she didn't believe that anyone would pay her for it; she knew who she wanted to collaborate with, but she didn't believe they would respect her leadership—and on and on it went. Lydia was so committed to the narrative of "being alone" that she painted herself into a corner that made it exhausting for her to even get out of bed every morning. Her certainty about "how it was" kept her from pursuing anything different, even when her creative genius called. What became painfully apparent was that she needed time and space to heal and to explore the origin of this "I am all alone" belief that got reactivated through the breakup with her business partner. As much as she was hurt and angry about the falling-out, there was a much deeper, much older belief being triggered for her. She was too busy trying to make this "new thing happen" to slow down and do the real work that would allow her to see and ultimately transform it. This was more important than any of the major meetings she was setting up because if she went into those meetings expecting to be rejected, guess what was going to happen?

I felt it was important to affirm her vision while still challenging her to pay attention to her beliefs. I walked Lydia through The Mindset Wheel and encouraged her to take an inventory of what she believed before walking into each big meeting. When we identified the beliefs that might challenge her ability to be successful, I'd take her through a process of transforming her inner dialogue so that she was not unconsciously creating her worst scenario. Her homework was to practice interrupting her negative beliefs and shifting her internal conversation toward what she wanted to create. Though Lydia was able to conceptually understand the idea that her beliefs were creating her reality, she was too caught up in the "evidence" of her past to imagine anything new. I continued to challenge her to think differently about herself, her potential new collaborators, and life in general. I encouraged her to pay close attention to what she was saying to herself. Then I taught her how to create a mantra to support her most desired outcome. She'd do the work in our sessions but wouldn't apply her insights when it came to those critical business conversations.

Subsequently, even with all of the guidance and support, Lydia couldn't get even one of her new concepts off the ground and wound up having to take a job she didn't love in order to survive. Sadly, she was more devoted to her analysis of what was happening to her than she was to creating a new perspective that would enable her awesome ideas to flourish. What made this even more challenging to watch was the realization that her new concepts represented her true calling. She had the kind of clarity that many people would kill for! Her ideas were a beautiful amalgamation of everything that mattered to her, and they were definitely worthy of pursuit. Bringing these concepts to life was the easy part. Addressing the negative beliefs about herself and others that lived in the shadows was where the work really needed to happen, but it was just too painful and scary for her to confront. I think of Lydia often, and it is my wish for her that with more time and readiness that she will one day return to these ideas with a renewed sense of courage and willingness to heal whatever is in the way of her realizing this vision as a symbol of her truest self and her greatest contribution.

Lydia's example was also a tremendous lesson for me as a new coach at the time. The willingness to address one's belief system is fundamental to any form of growth and it subsequently became my number one criterion for working with others.

What Are Your Most Limiting Beliefs?

When you're struggling with an intense personal challenge like Lydia, it can be hard to identify the root cause and tease it out. Sometimes limiting conversations have multiple layers that need to be explored. They're stacked conversations that have to be peeled back like an onion, until you can get to the to the heart of the matter. For instance, if we stay with Lydia's example, I've often suspected that her fears of abandonment came from a childhood experience. Underneath the belief that she is alone is a belief that speaks to *why* she is alone. Had Lydia been willing to delve into that question, she may have discovered the root cause—a la, "I am alone because no one loves or cares about me" or "I am alone because there is something wrong with me." To get at the core limiting belief, she'd need to excavate this conversation until she figured it out.

To use a nature metaphor, this extraction process reminds me of plucking weeds from a garden. As a coach, I live for these "mother weed" (which is my nickname for core limiting beliefs) moments, because when a client dismantles a core limiting belief their whole relationship to that challenge or struggle they face changes and they are no longer battling with themselves over this issue. They have crystal clarity, and in that moment they choose to either let their issues stay rooted in the ground or pluck them right out to make room for beautiful new beliefs and, hence, opportunities to bloom. I usually see massive shifts like this occur during traumatic experiences, because it's often when someone is facing an intense crisis that their belief system comes under attack. The experience disrupts their thinking and poses a direct challenge to their core limiting beliefs. Maybe it's a sudden life-threatening illness, or the unexpected death of a loved one, or the surprising breakup of a long-term love relationship. When you are in these jarring moments, you're forced to get really clear on what's important and to evaluate what thoughts get to dominate your time and energy.

While studying the way beliefs operate over the years, I've discovered that the most tenacious limiting beliefs are those that contribute to how we define ourselves. These core limiting beliefs are the negative *I am* statements entrenched in an ideology that governs how we perceive everything. For some, they might exist as mantras embedded in their daily conversations (*I'm a very suspicious person, so . . .*), and for others, they operate like white noise, always on and whirring in the background (*Yeah, but if you come from a poor neighborhood like I do . . .*). I like to call these persistent negative conversations your Greatest Hits. Why? Because just like on the radio, these tunes are on heavy rotation and they get stuck in your head—so much so that you keep singing them over and over again!

Too bad that your Greatest Hits are anything but great. They actually pose the most significant and often debilitating challenge to embracing your true self, because they've been an integral part of your identity for longer than you probably realize. Either you've inherited them from trusted loved ones like friends, mentors, or family, and/or you've been immersed in a community that collectively shares these beliefs. Therefore, you've accumulated tons of evidence in your own experience that supports how "true" they are, which makes them difficult to let go of. Yet no matter what the cause, when these beliefs do shift, worlds of possibility open up that simply did not exist before. It's the equivalent of being born again. Everything looks and feels different when you transform a Greatest Hit.

One of my most memorable Greatest Hit experiences came from working with my beloved client Heather. Heather had been a political organizer who worked on national campaigns to increase voter engagement for the benefit of local politicians throughout the nation. And though she was great at her job, she was seriously burned out. In our first session, Heather shared an intense desire to "rescue people," whether she was rescuing the constituents she served from impending harm or the homeless man in McDonald's who needed a few bucks for coffee. Heather was always beside herself with what to do, in every moment, because her limiting beliefs—supported by her heroic organizing work—told her that she couldn't ever relax because others desperately needed her help.

At first glance, it might seem strange to position Heather's need to rescue others as a bad thing. On the contrary, her desire in its proper perspective is an awesome thing. But an obsessive need to rescue—day in and day out, whoever crossed her path—and an inability to slow down, sit down, or calm down wore her down. It also came with a lot of worry about judgment from those around her—concern that others would think she was self-centered if she didn't help out or, just as bad, that she'd appear to be an egocentric savior type if she did this too much. It was a damned if she did, damned if she didn't existence that left her anxious and wanting to climb out of her skin.

My goal was to help Heather hold on to her gift but peel away at the beliefs that fed the dysfunctional side of her belief system. I had her spend the next two weeks jotting down, in a small notebook, when the urge arose to rescue someone; then, I had her track when she gave in to the urge and when she didn't. Two weeks later, Heather told me that 24 incidents came up, plus a ton of limiting beliefs and conversations causing her to be at odds with herself almost constantly—she put these into a spreadsheet and gave me access before our session. We dug into the grid and identified the core belief that all these other conversations stemmed from and went to work on it. We created a set of criteria to help Heather determine when she operated in her gift and when she came from a place of feeling "too responsible" for others' decisions.

Over time, Heather's perspective shifted. She felt armed with a new level of clarity and let go of the notion that she had to "save" people from their own bad choices. She also realized that at the heart of her anxiety was a belief that she didn't trust herself to carefully tell the difference between when she had a real contribution to make that would be helpful and when her ideas got in the way of someone else's growth by not allowing them to learn from their own experiences. This deep anxiety came from a childhood experience where something terrible happened to a neighbor and no one stood up to prevent it. In reaction to this anxiety, Heather took on the responsibility of helping everyone, which is just impossible to do as one person. Heather's emotional excavation led to a very clean and clear realization about *how* she wanted to use her gifts to help as many people as she could. She launched an amazing venture called the Million Person Project—a global project that teaches changemakers all over the world how to use personal storytelling as a tool for fostering authentic leadership in their work and beyond. She's now putting her gift to phenomenal use and building a massive movement in the process.

The Cost of What You Believe: The Four Binding Behaviors

I wish I could tell you that every client has been willing to claim responsibility for what they believe, but as with Lydia, many tend to get stuck at the awareness level and never make it to their own truth. As a result, they never reach their greater purpose and calling—and this is not what I want for you! As crazy (or familiar) as it may sound, people will wholeheartedly argue for their own limitations. And these arguments most often show up as: complaining, blaming/judging, justifying, and avoiding. I call them The Four Binding Behaviors. I use the word "binding" here because these actions can keep you tied up in a state of victimhood—which is the opposite of where you want to go, which is toward empowerment, freedom, your truth, and your highest calling. Let's run through each of these behaviors to see if any relate to how you behave, so you can identify and then counteract the ones that potentially hold you back. Think you're above these? Think again. When any of your Greatest Hits are playing, one, if not all, of these Four Binding Behaviors is bound to follow.

The Four Binding Behaviors have a lot in common. Each is designed to keep you from owning your power and taking responsibility for what you want to create. Even though they may be chosen to "protect" you in any situation, they become awesome distractions and can cloud an issue in a way that keeps you from ever having to look at your own behavior and hence your belief system. Finally, when these behaviors are used consistently, all of them stunt your growth. So let me break these down for you one by one so that we're on the same page about the definitions. As I review each behavior, pay attention to which one(s) resonate with you the most.

THE FOUR BINDING BEHAVIORS

1. *Complaining* is when you express annoyance or dissatisfaction with what's going on, with no plan or intention to resolve it. You might do this to blow off steam or simply vent, knowing full well that your audience can't do a thing about the chaos. You might even complain to hear your frustrations validated and be told that your gripes are justified. If this is a first step toward actively resolving the issue, you get a pass. But if you are just complaining to complain, then we've got a problem. The trouble with complaining is that even though you feel better for venting in the moment, you never empower yourself to get a resolution, so the issue will likely persist, as will your frustrations.

2. *Blaming/Judging:* When you blame and judge, you point the finger at someone as the cause of whatever has gone wrong. You blatantly say it's their fault and they are the reason why the situation isn't going according to plan. And with judgment, you go one step further by expressing your disapproval of their behavior and labeling them in a negative way. They are not only the cause of what's gone wrong; they *are* wrong. There are two types of blaming and judging: a) The first is blaming others. When you blame others, you put the emphasis and focus outside of yourself and the other person becomes the reason you can't have, do, or achieve what you want. This is a total relinquishing of your power. b) The second is blaming yourself. When you blame yourself, you hyper-focus internally and criti-

cize to the point of paralysis. Because you are both the victim and the perpetrator, you've got double drama going on and, as a result, you declare war on yourself which is *pain-ful.* The other challenge with this behavior is that it automatically alienates you from others and yourself. What's more, it may give you a false sense of power and entitlement to say and do things that are harmful to yourself and others. Be careful here, because any form of abuse can be very difficult to come back from.

It's important to note that there's a difference between blaming someone and holding that person accountable for their promises. When you hold another person accountable for, say, breaking an agreement, you are asking them to address why they have not kept their word. This does not automatically make you right or them wrong. It's a request to address what has broken down in the relationship. When you hold someone accountable, you are focused on the situation and not the individual. You are also engaging with a strong commitment to resolve the problem.

3. *Justifying:* When you justify, you rationalize why something is happening with a belief that the reason should be accepted as valid. But what you are really doing is arguing on behalf of your own limitations by making excuses for the way things are or demonstrating why a limitation makes sense (even when, in your heart, you know it doesn't). Justifying encourages others to "let you off the hook" for being accountable to the promises you make to yourself or to others. Justification is tricky because it can diminish your credibility and reliability (to yourself and others) and may leave (you and others with) the impression that you aren't serious about what you say you want to have, do, or achieve. This can compromise the power of your values and convictions, and these are the central drivers for your capacity to Stay True and pursue your calling.

4. *Avoiding,* which means to ignore or mislead yourself or others so that you don't have to address what's really going on with you or a given circumstance. You may see what's happening, but you don't want to deal with it, so you intentionally shift the focus to something else or tell yourself and others that something else is happening rather than what is really going on. The problem here is that the issue does not go away. And you may create additional unnecessary challenges by what you choose to avoid. As with the other behaviors, this one can not only compromise your credibility, but it enables the issue to persist.

After reviewing each of these behaviors, do any ring true for you? I'll confess, I used to be the Queen of Justification! Especially when it came to managing my time. "Well, what had happened was . . ." was my mantra! Facing yourself and telling the truth about your limiting perceptions, even with love, is not easy for anyone. I've had to learn how to gently and humorously challenge myself any time I want to make an excuse about why I'm not pursuing something that is really important to me. But every time I catch myself, I learn something new about what I believe. And that new knowledge enables me to make new choices about who I want to be and about what I want to have and pursue in honor of my calling.

That being said, I'd like to leave you with a cautionary tale of what can happen if you don't proactively address your Binding Behaviors and just how costly they can be. The rest of this book is filled with success stories; however, I'm adding this example because I want you to recognize early on that when it comes to transforming your life no one can do it for you. Coaching is a partnership, and being willing to do the tough behavior-changing work is imperative to your success.

My client Avery was a really sweet guy who came to me through an informal network of wellness practitioners whom I knew really well. We'd attend a lot of the same events, and we knew a lot of the same people and were always friendly. Young and ambitious, Avery was the student of a prominent author who'd written lots of books on metaphysical healing. And though Avery had been working hard in the industry to make a name for himself, he couldn't seem to gain the recognition that his colleagues had earned—i.e., bestselling books, tons of fans and followers, high praise from other noteworthy influencers. Naturally, Avery was anxious and frustrated because he felt that he should be moving ahead at the same pace as his peers. He constantly compared himself to them, trying to figure out why they were able to get lucrative brand endorsements, major book deals, A-list press, and garner the kind of following that so far he couldn't manage. So, he contacted me about working together. Though Avery had a cushy day job working with a tech billionaire client who was into mindfulness, he wasn't doing what he loved full-time, which was writing, speaking, and leading group experiences. And though he had ideas about how to grow his brand as a writer, speaker, and teacher, Avery was afraid to act on them. He also wanted a relationship but was still emotionally attached to an ex who didn't.

"I'm making myself sick," he told me. "It's like I'm hiding out in this cushy situation instead of going for what I really want. I want to just go for my dreams!"

Early in our sessions together, I introduced Avery to the Mindset Wheel I shared with you in chapter 1 to help him understand his current belief system and how it was yielding a reality he didn't want. Avery absorbed the work initially. But as we moved deeper into the process, he did less homework and more complaining, blaming/judging, and justifying around what he didn't have versus what others did. When I'd ask about his assignments, he'd say, "Oh, I was so busy that I didn't get to them." And then he'd complain about the same three things we'd committed to working on: his lack of a book deal, his boring but cushy "day job," and his desire for a serious relationship. He wanted the strategies, tactics, and tips for how to manipulate a situation in his favor, so he could "stand out," but no matter how much counsel he received, he'd still insist that "it's not working." Avery was not struggling for connections, so his lack of action had to do with something much deeper.

Not every client relationship is a love affair, and I'm the first to admit if I'm not meshing. But that was not the issue here. I adored Avery enough to challenge him. But Avery was beholden to his identity as a complainer and not ready to let go. Remember how I said that pain, even though it doesn't feel good, is familiar enough to keep around? Avery lived this concept and not only kept it around, he also refused to move past it. He'd spend our time venting about his colleagues and seeking validation for what a talented author he was, all the while hoping I would justify his anger rather than work with him to let go of it. What Avery couldn't see was how entrenched he was in his limiting beliefs and what they cost him. First, he was losing an enormous amount of time talking to me, other advisors, colleagues, and friends about the same three issues (book, boring job, boyfriend). He was also wasting money working with me, his therapist, taking courses, and going on retreats—literally tens of thousands of dollars blown on "intellectual entertainment" without making any move to improve his life. Worst of all, the time and energy he spent being frustrated and upset cost him his quality of life and experience. For Avery, complaining turned out to be an expensive habit that was in the way of his happiness and fulfillment. Avery's Greatest Hits got tons of airtime but also served as a perfect distraction from doing the work that could have transformed the very problems he complained about.

Accepting responsibility for your core limiting beliefs and the way they color your perception and experiences is absolutely essential to staying true to who you are and pursuing your calling. We are far more capable than we know. And the universe is far more willing to support you in co-creating the reality you desire than you think it is. But co-creating implies there's a partnership, so you've got to do your part to provoke change so that your wants and desires can be manifest in return. Taking responsibility insists that you acknowledge and embrace the fact that you are creative and have both the power and capacity to make choices and decisions that reflect who you want to be and what you want to have. This does not negate the fact that you will face tough challenges in life.

But it does mean that you'll have an opportunity to determine how those challenges will be used to strengthen you in the pursuit of your dreams.

Your Call

Are you ready to take responsibility for what you believe? Implement these two practices and two exercises over the next two weeks; they will help you recognize and own the impact of your Greatest Hits and give you a powerful opportunity to practice freeing yourself from the behaviors that hold you back.

PRACTICE 1

"I am responsible for my own thoughts, feelings, and perceptions."

Work with this mantra over the next two weeks as you track your Greatest Hit(s) in action. Every time you experience a strong emotion like fear, anger, hurt, frustration, anxiety, sadness, or disappointment, log it as directed in the following exercise, take three deep breaths, and speak the mantra.

PRACTICE 2

For the next two weeks, do one activity a day that makes you feel really good about yourself. It can be taking the time to do something you enjoy, eating in a way that enlivens you, or sharing your gifts in a way that makes you feel happy.

EXERCISE 1

Let's track your Greatest Hits in real time. If you don't know where to begin, take a look at your Belief Inventory exercise responses in chapter 1. Pay attention to the answers that point to what you believe about yourself. Are there any limiting "I am" statements that feel like a natural part of your everyday conversation?

Pick just one. Then for the next two weeks, before moving on to the next chapter, carry a small notebook with you and note all the factors that trigger this belief in you. Be sure to:

- Describe the situation: Give a quick overview of what is happening; get really specific.
- Describe your reaction: What did you say or do as the events were unfolding?
- Describe your feelings: What did you feel as you experienced this interaction? Why did you feel that way?
- What did you specifically say to yourself about what was going on? What was your inner dialogue? Try to capture the words exactly how you said them to yourself.
- How did you feel about your reaction? Were you proud, angry, frustrated? Why?

Every night take 10 minutes to review your log and jot down any insights from the day. This exercise can be very revealing, because it gives you an opportunity to see yourself in action, play by play. Try not to judge yourself—just highlight those parts of your internal dialogue that feel most difficult. Notice the words you are saying to yourself and how those words make you feel. This is where you have the greatest opportunity to actually see what your limiting conversations look like on the court of your life. For an example of a Greatest Hits log go to www .movethecrowd.me/TheCalling/resources.

Finally, give yourself credit for taking the time to recognize what's going on. You're taking responsibility for your beliefs, and that's not an easy task! Don't worry, we'll talk about how to transform these beliefs in the coming chapters. For now, just enter them into the log.

EXERCISE 2: WHAT'S YOUR FAVORITE BINDING BEHAVIOR?

Now that you know The Four Binding Behaviors, which one is your go-to? You already know mine! Over the next seven days, I'd like you to detox from this behavior by refraining from it as much as you can. Use your Greatest Hits log to help you identify when this behavior is happening. Try to catch yourself before you indulge, and remember, no judgment—especially as this is likely ingrained in you. If you slip up, it's okay. Simply recommit, and start over. Use the log to track your progress with your seven-day detox as well. You can download this worksheet at www.movethecrowd.me/TheCalling/resources.

3

Step #3: Forgiving Your Self and Societally Imposed Limitations

Now that you understand how powerful your beliefs are when determining how you see yourself and the world, it's time to eliminate any internal conversations that don't allow you to embrace your truest self and highest calling. As you face all you have inherited and see the impact it's had on your life, the next courageous step is to forgive—to let go of those perceptions that no longer serve you. You are amazing. Even with all the obstacles you've faced, you have still managed to achieve great things. You've educated yourself, cared for your siblings, helped to better your community, healed a physical challenge, repaired a relationship, etc. However, staying true now requires that you examine the thoughts and emotions that drive your actions so you can determine which traits you'd like to hang on to versus what you're ready to let go.

When you give up your limitations, you invite the potential of an entirely new reality. One where you get to say what's possible versus being at the mercy of anyone else's biased opinions. Forgiveness begins with first seeing all the ways these limitations have doubled as gifts—whether they've helped you appreciate your rich heritage and culture, allowed you to channel strength in hard times, or made you appreciate how far you've come no matter where you've come from—they've made a difference. All your bumps, bruises, and scars have contributed to the power of who you are and what you have to give.

As you prepare to let go, take a moment to thank those limitations for how they've helped you. Notice where your hardest moments have turned into lessons that have ultimately become blessings. Let yourself *feel the* feelings without complaining, blaming/judging, justifying, or avoiding. The good, bad, and unspeakable have all played a role in what's brought you to the here and now. It's important to honor that.

In this chapter, you'll come face-to-face with all the ways you've settled for less than what you deserve and are capable of. And you'll have a chance to forgive everything that's ever held you back, from your own limiting conversations to those that come from the people around you. You'll have an opportunity to make peace with the past in a way that'll clean the slate, make room, and create fertile ground for your true self to emerge. In this process, you won't just confront the self-imposed limits you've inherited from family, community, and other influences in your immediate environment. You'll also have a chance to let go of those societally imposed limitations that have been cultivated around every aspect of your identity—i.e., race, class, gender, orientation, physical appearance and ability, language, religion, geography, you name it.

I believe that we are living in a time when all of us are waking up to what's happening in the world. And as we awaken, each of us is being called to reconsider our views on what success and citizenship really mean. We're being challenged to look at who has been entitled to achieve versus who hasn't. We are being invited to revisit what we thought was "true" about things we've taken for granted—from the quality of our leadership to the potential of our children. But nowhere are we more challenged, or more called, than in how we're being forced to look at ourselves—who we are versus who we want to be and how the gap is causing each of us to examine what we are really capable of. We're being asked to defy the odds and push against the status quo in honor of a more authentic and powerful existence. It's time to make room, to identify and give voice to your own passions and values. By forgiving your self and societally imposed limitations, you'll free up more time, space, and energy to express your greatness and live your calling with a new level of integrity.

Where Does Forgiveness Come From?

The concept of forgiveness, as we understand it, has been around since the early days of the Roman and Grecian empires, and many religious and philosophical texts drawn from ancient times such as the Bible, Koran, and Torah refer to similar themes like "reconciliation" or "pardoning." Similar notions of divine and secular forgiveness date back even earlier to ancient African and Asian civilizations and can be found in Buddhism, Hinduism, and Islam. In fact, the word's etymology comes from the Latin term *perdonare*. When you break up the word to determine its literal translation, "per" means "completely" when translated from Old English and "donare" (similar to "donor" and "donate") means "to give." The definition of forgiveness, then, is "to give completely without reservation." This is where the modern translation of letting go comes from— forgiveness has come to mean the pardoning or "releasing" of an offense or "giving up" the desire to punish.

Implied in this definition is liberation from any "hold" that a belief, thought, or action may have on you. Forgiveness is a way to not only consciously break free from entanglements with past or lingering circumstances but also cleanse your heart, mind, and spirit from the energetic residue caused by those incidents. It's an opportunity to release mental, spiritual, and emotional bondage, baggage, or trauma, without reservation. It's also an opportunity to embark on a new path—one that holds the promise of greater joy, happiness, and fulfillment.

When it comes to the ancient topic of forgiveness, my mind immediately thinks of the story of Jesus's crucifixion (yes, I'm going there). His is one of the most compelling tales of forgiveness ever told. Whether or not you believe in his religious significance as the son of God, historically we know he lived from the approximate years of 6–4 BC to AD 33. What we also know is that during the last two to three years of his life Jesus became an avid evangelist and around the time of AD 33 he was crucified, as his teachings were said to pose a threat to the religious and political leaders of his time.

In Jesus, we learn about a man who endured great pain and suffering in the name of cleansing and purifying humanity's transgressions. During the six hours that Jesus hung on the cross, he made seven statements. The first came when he was encouraged by some of his followers to strike out and use his divine power and influence to exact revenge on those who put him there, but instead he simply said, "Forgive them." This story is part of our cultural narrative because it's one of the greatest examples of generosity in the face of abuse and brutality and demonstrates how to have love and compassion toward those who wrong you. Though this story is known in every corner of the globe, we, as global citizens, often find it hard to forgive—even when our circumstances are less severe than being beaten, ridiculed, and nailed to a cross.

Now, I want to be clear. Forgiveness does not mean that you tolerate abuse or become anybody's doormat. What it does mean, however, is that you refuse to allow anyone or anything to stand in the way of your good—that is, the joy, love, happiness, and fulfillment that's your birthright. You have a right as a human being to embrace your true self and your highest calling. And you have a right to live free from any limitation that compromises your ability to experience genuine peace and harmony within yourself.

Whether your hurt has been self- or societally imposed, your capacity to let go is a source of power. The truth is, forgiving is as much for you as it is for those you choose to forgive. You may never need to say another word to those individuals or entities, but you can be healed by the power of your own intention and liberated by the way you choose to show up once you let go.

Dealing with Self-Limiting Beliefs

When you take stock of your Greatest Hits and their impact, strong emotions are bound to come up, and it can be easy to get down on yourself. However, you must recognize that everything that you've gone through to this point has served a purpose. And whether it has influenced you consciously or unconsciously, every belief, for better or worse, has contributed to who you are. The process of forgiveness invites you to see this truth without giving in to the desire to retaliate against others or yourself. Being angry at the past will not "fix it" and being angry at others or yourself will only create more resistance and distance between you and your calling. In forgiving, you don't push the feelings or experiences aside, but you learn to honor and move through them in a way that lets you gain greater clarity, strength, and wisdom as you emerge on the other side.

When I help my clients work through difficult experiences in their lives, feeling their feelings is one of the most important yet challenging aspects of forgiveness. Over the years, I've developed a four-step ritual to address each aspect of forgiveness to release self-imposed limits. As part of your homework, you will have an opportunity to move through all four steps for each person or moment you wish to forgive. This ritual can move quickly or it can take time. Give yourself whatever you need to move through each stage, and know that with each step you are returning to your own magnificence.

Forgiveness ➔ as an Act of
Sacred Re-membering

Part of forgiveness is about "re-membering," which is the act of becoming whole again. When situations cause us to doubt and even abandon ourselves, we create and wear a mask that separates us from the truth of who we are in an attempt to protect ourselves from the world. Here I want you to simply acknowledge what happened. Tell the truth about what occurred for you and the impact it had on you. Acknowledge and take responsibility for your participation in this experience (if appropriate). Commit to embrace and care for that part of you that has been separated, hurt, or alienated by what occurred. Then, remember who you are by reclaiming your power and agency over your heart, life, and circumstances. You are whole.

Forgiveness → as an Act of Completion

One of the toughest parts of forgiveness is moving on. When we internalize limiting perceptions, we often replay those same messages and events in our minds, bodies, and spirits over and over again. We re-create the injury by reliving the offense. In this part of the ritual, you commit to look forward and not back. You express, feel, and release any lingering feelings associated with what occurred. You acknowledge that you do not need to relive that lesson. You express gratitude for the wisdom and strength you've gained from that experience and declare that it is *done*! You are complete.

Forgiveness → as an Act of Liberation

Here you embrace your freedom—you choose what honors you and release what doesn't. No more forcing or fixing or contorting to please others. Now that you are whole and complete, there is nothing left to do except be you! The slate is clean, and you can declare your freedom from that event and all its related limiting conversations and behaviors. As you embrace genuine completion, you now have room in your life for more of what you want, need, desire. You are free.

Forgiveness → as an Act of Self-Love

In this final step, you see yourself fully for the incredible person you are. You love, honor, and appreciate yourself for your courage and your commitment to return to love. You recognize that your true nature is divine. You embrace that you are a loving and compassionate being. You commit to setting healthy boundaries and stop beating up on yourself. You express that you are ready to receive the best that life has to offer. You are love.

FORGIVENESS IN ACTION

When I met Jasmine, she was already a brilliant wellness author, teacher, and coach with a deep passion for making a difference in the lives of others. She believed in and saw the best in others and went the extra mile to help them achieve success. When we began working together, Jasmine was looking to up-level her existing client base and bring in more revenue. But there was a problem. . . . The first red flag was that when we tried to put our coaching sessions in the calendar, Jasmine kept calling to shift the schedule or cancel at the last minute. When I raised the issue Jasmine was adamant about needing flexibility since she never knew when a client might need her and had to be available because they depended so heavily on her. I'll never forget the moment I had to stop the madness. We were on a videoconference call, and I actually asked her to lean in and look me in the eye. "This is insanity, my love. As much as I appreciate your dedication to customer service, you are not an EMT, or a doctor, or a crisis hotline worker. Coaching requires a lot of energy, so you have to create boundaries." As she shared how tired and overextended she was, I became even more concerned—perhaps because Jasmine wasn't just coaching her clients. "You don't understand," she said. "My clients need me, they have a lot going on, and I have to be available. Sometimes they need me to make introductions; shoot, sometimes my clients need me to help them find a babysitter, and sometimes when things are crazy and they are having a meltdown I've got to be there to talk them off the ledge." Because Jasmine played all these roles, she became simultaneously frustrated when they were not working as hard as she was on their wellness regimens. And in some cases, when they complained about her program in some way, she'd go off on them. When I asked her what was going on, she said, "People don't get it! They never appreciate how hard I work to help them be successful. And when they don't reach their goals, that reflects on me and I look bad, so I work double time to avoid that." "Listen," I explained. "I think it's awesome that you want to be there for your clients, but I think you need to find a more sustainable and fulfilling way to support them—mentally, spiritually, emotionally, *and* financially."

Jasmine sat back, crossed her arms, and her face was flushed with defiance, "Okay. . . ." *Okay my ass.* Jasmine had a lot of anger, toward her clients and toward herself, and she needed to understand the origin of this behavior and those feelings. "Before you go looking for new clients," I said, "you need to address why you are killing yourself to support people who may not be ready for what you have to offer." As we dug into her inner dialogue, Jasmine realized that she believed that if someone did business with her, it was her responsibility to make sure that they achieved success—even if they didn't meet her halfway. What's more, Jasmine had the same challenge in her love life, where she did all the giving and her partner didn't carry their weight. The more we explored this feeling, the more Jasmine realized, "Wow. I keep taking on other people's problems like they're my own, and then when they don't see how much I'm supporting them I get pissed!" This made her feel anger, resentment, frustration, anguish, hurt, abandonment, and much more. When we explored the source of this behavior Jasmine realized she'd been operating out of an unhealthy dynamic that she'd learned from her mother.

To be able to serve her community in the way she wanted, Jasmine had to go big on the forgiveness work. "You gotta let go, my love," I stated. She needed to forgive her mom for modeling this dynamic, her clients for not cultivating a mindset that helped them be good partners in coaching relationships. Most important, Jasmine had to forgive herself, which was the hardest. "I want you to make a list of everyone you're upset with right now, everyone who you think doesn't appreciate you, everyone who's recently let you down, everyone you think owes you something—let's start there." Over the next few weeks, she released years of pent-up hurt, anger, and frustration in order to move forward. Jasmine came to recognize that her mother, her clients, and even she were doing the best they could under the circumstances. "I've been holding on to so much negativity," she said, "and it's just not working for me—I'm miserable. I'm ready to let it go." Once she moved through the four-step forgiveness ritual, when she was finally able to let go she felt so much better. Next, we worked together for six weeks to revamp her business, including how her programs worked and what the criteria should be for new clients. We also rebuilt her coaching structure to have healthier boundaries and a higher price point to reflect the true value of her contribution. With this new protocol in place Jasmine was well on her way to making six figures by selling five-figure coaching programs to clients who truly appreciated her and worked hard to incorporate her wisdom and whom she loved supporting. Her business was growing, and instead of being exhausted and overextended, she was joyful and engaged.

Confronting Society's Limiting Beliefs

In the last chapter, we explored the impact of inherited belief systems, with a focus on family and community. Now I'd like to turn to what you may have internalized from society's beliefs and examine how that too may hold you back from embracing your true self and calling.

Society as a whole has a long legacy of inequity—one that's, frankly, been violent, bloody, and traumatic for many regions all over the globe. Even as you read these words, we, as a human family, are still grappling with war, hunger, poverty, slavery, human trafficking, political corruption, and upheaval. Historically, many individuals and cultural groups have had to fight for the right to pursue their full potential. And many groups are still fighting for that right today. Whether based on race, gender, class, sexual orientation, physical ability, tribe, geography, or religious affiliation, disparities in opportunity and dignified treatment have placed limitations on many hopes and dreams. When we confront all the ways that systemic inequities have played out, it can be overwhelming. It's easy to believe that nothing can be done or that progress will be slow coming. But every day, there is a glimmer of hope, as we watch trailblazers defy the odds and cross these boundaries, one inspiring journey after another.

Take my client Eren, for instance. I first met Eren at an annual gathering of spiritual teachers. She'd attended to spend quality time with her daughter, who is a bright, enthusiastic woman with a tremendous passion to bring yoga and mindfulness practices to kids everywhere. Though I was flooded with audience members hoping to connect after my talk, Eren slid right up beside me and said, "You're gonna want to talk to me." I laughed, because her courage and conviction were palpable. Her words may have sounded cocky to someone else, but I knew she was trembling with determination. And I knew it wasn't about me, but rather a calling that was moving through her and wanted to be answered.

As we moved to a quiet space down the hall, Eren told me she was the owner and president of a multi-billion-dollar aerospace company, with a unique story in the industry. "I've been avoiding the spotlight," she said, "but when I listen to you, I feel inspired. It's like something is telling me that it's time to raise my voice." One week later, Eren and I were on the phone as she shared her incredible story about how, at the age of 22, she sold everything she owned for a one-way ticket and immigrated to the United States from Turkey for an education—believing there'd be greater opportunities here for her as a woman. But when she arrived in the United States for graduate school, people were not as welcoming as she had hoped. They made fun of her accent, left her out of group assignments because they thought she'd hold them back, and didn't invite her to social gatherings either. Sadness and isolation set in.

But Eren pressed on, reminding herself that she couldn't let others get her down, she was a survivor, and she'd come to the United States for a reason. She worked and studied hard and soon met the love of her life. She didn't know it then, but their special connection would soon reveal itself. They were both recent immigrants from the same area and helped each other learn English. They got a job at the same company and, when the company was on the verge of bankruptcy, figured out a way to buy it, because they saw an amazing growth opportunity and didn't want to be out of a job! Not only did this dynamic duo turn the company around, but over the course of thirty years they've grown it to one of the top companies in the world in the field of technological innovation, aerospace, and defense. "We didn't have a plan," she told me, "other than to wake up every day and do our very best to deliver the best quality to our customers and care for our staff. We worked really hard, pouring our souls into making the company a success. I was good at running the business, and he was good at inventing new technologies. That is how we came together to make the company work."

I was moved as Eren shared her story. Because even though her peers alienated and ostracized her, she refused to let their limiting perceptions of who she was hold her back. It wasn't easy, and even to this day she's had to continue to let go of the negative and limiting perceptions about being a "foreigner" that are perpetuated by our society. After Eren and I began working together, I encouraged her to face this challenge head on: "You are a badass, and your heritage and story are part of what makes you so amazing. It's time to own all of who you are. You didn't succeed in spite of Eren; you've succeeded because of!"

"You're right" she said. "I've just never thought of it that way."

With those words, she started to face this challenge head on. Like Jasmine, Eren had a long list of people to forgive: "Oh my God, this is gonna be a lot of people!" From college students to coworkers, and beyond. Through the forgiveness work, she could now see how others' lingering perceptions created roadblocks to her own self-realization.

"I wanted to deal with what's been holding me back, and now I can see what's going on, I'm gonna fix this!"

What I love about Eren is that she possesses a rare combination of quiet humility, fierce determination, and a grounded sense of ownership of all she's been through and achieved. As she moves forward, toward her calling, she is letting go of those societally imposed roadblocks to inspire more women around the world to become leaders in her industry and beyond. "It's time, Eren," I said. "Give yourself permission to shine. The world needs your courage and your voice—now more than ever." If you want to know more about Eren, check her out on the *Forbes* list of the Top 20 Richest Self-Made Women in the United States—go, Eren!

No matter what a society dictates, you don't need to accept or internalize those limits. Those like Eren who defy the odds are fueled by an internal fire that adamantly refuses to allow their potential to be diminished in any way. They go to great lengths to pursue a better life, so long as it aligns with their values. Powerful rulebreakers not only beat the odds but also contribute to the freedom and growth of others. When you consider what you've taken on from society, where might you challenge the boundaries that seek to limit your true potential?

Forgiving Individual and Collective Trauma

There are many ways to rise above externally imposed restrictions (and in part 3, "Doing Good," I'll share more about how you can address systemic inequity and make a difference for others). But in this moment of personal evaluation, I want you to know that you have the capacity to overcome and heal anything that has happened to you—regardless of whether your trauma is personal or collective, whether you were born into it or experienced it later in life. You can heal and transform that blight and mentally, spiritually, and psychologically free yourself with dedication and support. I believe this because I have experienced it personally and I've seen people rise up from some of the worst experiences.

In 2009, I had the honor of being a Cultural Envoy to Rwanda. My role was to help inspire, train, and develop a new generation of creative entrepreneurs who were looking to leverage their artistic talents to economically sustain themselves and help build a creative industry for their nation. I arrived just two days shy of the ceremonies marking the fifteenth anniversary of the genocide, which recognized the 1994 uprising led by members of the Hutu majority government against the Tutsi and Pygmy Batwa tribes. For over one hundred days, nearly one million people, men, women, and children, were slaughtered—many of whom were tortured and murdered by their own family.

Before arriving, I was told by staff at the embassy to never bring up the genocide. However, I wasn't in town for more than two hours before reporters asked me in a press conference, "So, what do you think of this country? Were you scared to come because of the genocide?" As the days went on, I realized that many were deeply concerned about the way that the world perceived their beloved homeland. They wanted me and the other envoys I traveled with to know that even with this seemingly unspeakable past, they were more than what I'd read about or heard in the media. They wanted me to know their intelligence, insightfulness, creativity, tenacity, and courage. Through their beautiful dances, deep and thought-provoking questions, and their laughter and fierce business acumen, they wanted me to know they were amazing and worthy of so much more than global pity. And they didn't just want to show me; they charged me with going back and telling the world that there is another Rwanda here, one that is full of vision, promise, and opportunity. That their hopes and dreams were alive and that they had emerged out of the genocide as older, wiser, grateful, and now dedicated to rebuilding a country where all Rwandans could thrive and prosper. I fell in love with this country and its gorgeous people who taught me so much about what it means to have dignity and treat others with respect while not turning away from the truth. They were so generous with their living example of forgiveness, grace, and resilience. For me, they epitomized what it means to give up all forms of limitation in honor of who they were destined to be and all they would achieve as a result.

Forgiving the Biggest Limiting Belief of All

Being a conscious creator is not easy; it takes dedication and practice. Even if you have not experienced societal trauma, you still get limiting messages all the time from the external world. And nowhere is it more apparent than when it comes to the messages you receive about success.

This is where self- and societally imposed limitations often collide, because the very definition of our own self-worth is often tied to external expectations and standards set by those who don't understand or appreciate the full spectrum of the human family. Yet these standards permeate our culture and can easily take over our lives and become the central drivers for how we see ourselves and evaluate our own potential. They become the primary motivators for conformity, which is often the antithesis of liberation. Originality, authenticity, and courage: These are the qualities it takes to Stay True and pursue your true calling.

Though definitions may vary, what comes with success, in any society, is a kind of reverence and respect that is only afforded to a chosen few. We all want to be That Guy or Girl—not because we like or even necessarily agree with the anointing. We want to be them because we like the way they are treated, which is as inherently special and better than the rest of us. Yet no matter how many boxes we check on the success to-do list, most of us still walk around feeling that we're unsuccessful. It's not enough in our society to be a productive citizen. We compare ourselves to titans and movie stars who've acquired world dominance, and feel like losers, not realizing that we've usually been sold someone else's marketing plan instead of the reality of their life. When we consider that some of the world's most iconic people melt down at some point, perhaps we should question how valid this model really is.

The American Dream is one of the most dominant and misleading narratives ever written. The romanticized notion that it can belong to anyone so long as they're willing to work hard has inspired people from all over the globe to seek our shores. We've been given countless examples of those who came from nothing to achieve great things. When we hear these stories, we are motivated to turn our gaze to the horizon as if success is "out there" in the distance and it's our charge to "go out and get it." It's as if we must all do whatever it takes to turn ourselves inside out to reach this success. The world becomes broken into winners and losers, and you're charged with risking it all to win big. As with Eren, there are instances where this narrative *has* created profound inspiration and helped individuals to rise in the face of extreme challenges. But one of the major problems with this theory is that we've also simultaneously managed to define success as a scarce commodity—one that requires a special pedigree, a certain degree of genius, a certain set of connections, special gifts, a special personality type, and a special level of access. It's as if some of us are destined to do great things, while others aren't. Collectively it's a mixed and damaging message. On the one hand, success is yours for the taking, but not too fast, because you may not be allowed into the club. Or worse, you may achieve that "success" but find that happiness and fulfillment don't follow.

Time after time, the True. Paid. Good. formula has proven that little about this notion of success is true. *Every single one of us* is poised for greatness, and there is plenty of money, recognition, love, and fulfillment to go around. And the fact that so many of us believe that there is not enough when it comes to *our* success is the biggest limiting perception of all.

To forgive this, two things must happen. The first is that we must have the right relationship with ourselves by healing and transforming these internalized limits. The second is that we must be willing to consider a new definition of success, one where we get to be all of who we are, as well as pursue and acquire the things that matter most to us. Redefining your notion of success requires forgiving and letting go of personal and inherited notions that do not empower you—ones that keep you second-guessing your own ideas or tolerating an abusive boss because the job pays the bills. When you give up your claim to any form of limitation, you get to define success for yourself. You can then determine how you'd like to achieve it.

Whether you look at your finances, relationships, or desired contribution to society, you have an opportunity to decide right now what you'd like success to mean for you. Not what familial or societally imposed notions have said it should be, but what you believe it should be about. In fact, transforming these internal and societal limitations may become a part of your calling. If you embrace this opportunity, from this moment forward you are truly living *your* life.

Staying true insists that genuine success *only* comes from within— knowing who you are and how you want to use your gifts in the world. It comes from understanding what's really important to you and why. With this in mind, success then comes from the belief that your genuine happiness and fulfillment matter more than keeping up with the Joneses.

Now imagine that you are standing at a beautiful tree-lined juncture out in the wilderness and you are standing in front of two roads that represent the potential for true success. The road to the left represents a continuation of where you've already been. It's very familiar and pretty flat, so it won't require more of you then what you've already given. If you go down this road, you can bring everything you've carried with you thus far—your beliefs, perceptions, relationships, situations, knowledge, and skills—and simply allow your life to unfold as it has been. To your right, however, is a new road, a road that you can't fully see. That road has far more twists and turns. However, you've been told that the views on this road are amazing. You've also been told that on this road you have the potential to find your truest self and live your greatest calling. It's clear that the road is still under construction, and you know you'll need to roll up your sleeves to turn it into a path you can travel—you'll have to consciously create this path. You may need to clear shrubs, pull weeds, and remove broken tree limbs to navigate this terrain. And because this road is unpredictable, you'll need to reevaluate what you take with you on this journey—consider what's really important to move forward because you'll have to travel light.

After all that's been said, you're now ready to choose your road. Depending on your choice, you'll need to examine what's in your backpack and make decisions about what you believe is worth holding on to and what, you may find, is necessary to forgive, completely and without reservation.

From this moment forward, will it be the path to the left, which represents what you've always known? Or will it be the one to the right, which invites you to consciously create your own road into the wilderness of your truest self and greatest calling? The choice is yours.

Your Call

Are you ready to forgive all the false limitations that have been imposed on you? These practices and exercises, to be completed over the next seven days, will help you determine what you want to keep and let go of as you make room for more of what you want, need, and deserve.

PRACTICE 1

> "I release and let go; I forgive what no longer serves me."
> "I am ready to embrace all of who I am and all of who I'm meant
>   to be."
> "I release and let go as I make room to embrace all of who I'm meant
>   to be."

Work with this series of mantras over the next week as you complete the following forgiveness exercise. Set aside five minutes in the morning and five more in the evening to speak this to yourself while looking in the mirror. Keep the mantra on hand during the day and whip it out any time you feel burdened by your own assumptions or other people's assumptions of you. Remember to breathe with each declaration—continue to repeat the mantra until you feel your energy shift.

PRACTICE 2

Choose one person, situation, or circumstance every day for the next seven days that you're willing to forgive—let go without reservation. If you're anything like Jasmine, that person might even be you. As a matter of fact, if *you* are the hardest person to forgive, I suggest devoting the next seven days to seven things you're willing to forgive yourself for. Use the Forgiveness Conversations log to keep track of your progress. You can download it from www.movethecrowd.me/TheCalling/resources.

EXERCISE 1

Over the next seven days, look at all the areas of your life where you've experienced any limit. Make a list of the personal and societal challenges you are now ready to release. They can be people, situations, circumstances, experiences, messages—it's up to you. They can be personal, professional, or both. Write each one down with as much detail as you need, so you can see the areas you'd like to address. Choose *one* item on your list and use the four-step forgiveness ritual and protocol to work through this area over the next seven days.

Forgiveness Ritual—Four-Step Protocol

FORGIVENESS → ACT OF SACRED RE-MEMBERING

I acknowledge that this happened. I tell the truth about what occurred for me. I acknowledge and take responsibility for my participation in this experience (if appropriate). Now I re-member who I am—I reclaim my power and my agency. *I Am* Whole.

FORGIVENESS → ACT OF COMPLETION

I look forward not back. I express and release any lingering feelings associated with what occurred. I do not need to relive that lesson. I am grateful for the experience and it is *done*! *I Am* and We Are Complete.

FORGIVENESS → ACT OF LIBERATION

I Am Whole and Complete—lacking nothing. *I Am* Free. Free from choices and behaviors that keep me from being my true self. I *Am* Free. Free to create room in my life for more of what I need, want, and desire.

FORGIVENESS → ACT OF SELF-LOVE

I love, honor, and appreciate myself for all that I Am. My true nature is divine. I Am a Loving and Compassionate Being. I am ready to receive the best that life has to offer.

EXERCISE 2

As you consider the stories in this chapter of others who have courageously defied the odds:

What do you notice about their journeys?
Where are you being called to rise above your societally imposed limitations?
Who's inspiring you right now to break out of the mold?

Whether these are people you know personally or those you admire from afar, find their images and use them to create an Inspiration Board. You can see samples at www.movethecrowd.me/TheCalling/resources. Put up the board in a place where you can see it often. Use these individuals and their courageous journeys to inspire you, especially when you feel like you need some additional strength.

4

Step #4: Visualizing and Redefining a New Self-Narrative

Now that you've cleared the deck of core limiting beliefs and taken the lid off what you believe is possible, regardless of what society says, it's time to explore four important questions:

Who are you?
What brings you to this moment?
What is important to you?
What do you want your life to be about?

In this chapter, I'm going to help you look at your life and calling through fresh eyes by exploring the very essence of who you are and all that has led you to this moment. Together, we'll examine how your unique expression operates in service to your higher calling. As you become more connected to your true self, you'll give voice to the unique qualities and attributes that make you unlike anyone else. You'll also begin to discover all the ways you've actually been prepared through your life experiences for the contribution you are now being called to make in the world. It's time to pay attention to those ideas and dreams you've been putting off. It's time to take those urges and longings seriously. If you've allowed yourself

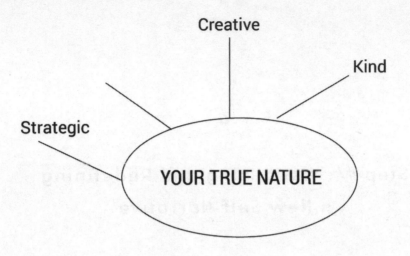

to become comfortable and complacent, it's time to wake things up and shake things up, because your calling shows up as all of the above. It's time to chart the new path toward your True. Paid. Good.

Your True Nature: Who Are You?

What do you think about, when you think about your identity? Beyond your gender, race, ethnicity, and orientation lies your spirit—this is the purest form of your expression, because it's not dictated by any of the social constructs around you. When everything is stripped away and set aside, like your age, job title, where you grew up, and who you know, and when you are not trying to fix, force, prove, or impress yourself or others, who *are* you?

There is a you that exists beyond your thoughts. A you that craves genuine love and connection. A you that is always curious and looking to learn and grow. A you that is always coming from a place of love. This is your true self. And this true self has a calling, a purpose, and a reason why you are here. Your work is to find that true self and begin to give voice and expression to that true calling.

In chapter 1, I talked about moving from having a victim-based mindset to having a vision for yourself. And though an awareness of your beliefs is a big part of creating the necessary freedom to move toward that desired vision, by itself it isn't enough.

When I began examining my own Greatest Hits, I was working as an artist and organizer and the very idea that I could choose to change what I believed both fascinated and motivated me. *I can actually change this struggling artist/activist thing?* I thought. *Awesome!* But you have to be ready. You have to activate your sense of adventure as you step onto new terrain. You've got to be willing to explore an identity that may no longer be defined by all the things you have been but, rather, a world where you have limitless potential. The moment I touched the concept of true self, I inherently understood it, because in all my years of working in social change that was exactly what I believed about those I served. No matter what their circumstances were, there was someone else inside who was amazing and dying to be set free. And this belief guided my approach. But I had to meet them where they were before I could invite them to go anywhere with me. And wherever I was inviting them to go needed to hold the promise of something better. All of us on some level know that there is more inside of us that wants to be expressed, and all of us aspire to reach our untapped potential.

This brings us to your *dharma*.

Now the word "dharma" comes from the Hindu, Buddhist, and Sikh traditions and is loosely translated to mean sacred duty or vocation, or path of orderly living. Often, when the term is used, these are the most common definitions attributed to finding one's purpose. However, in my work with clients, I explore an aspect of dharma that is unique—I define it as your true nature *expressed* as your highest contribution and calling.

Acting from this place is the most sacred, well-intentioned, and productive way to be of service, because it's the purest part of who you are. The work you've done in the first three chapters has begun to clear the way for this true nature, but here you will explore it with a more focused intent and you'll learn how your dharma is the foundation for your personal commitment to Stay True.

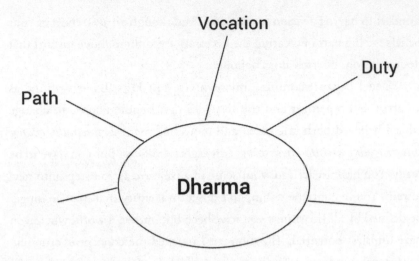

I believe the process of becoming True is actually an act of surrender, where we give up far more than we "put on" so that we can feel powerful. Just as you've been encouraged to forgive your limitations, when you become true you peel back the false concepts of who you are (i.e., how much you have, what you look like, where you work) so that you can explore the real you that has always been there, hiding underneath.

In your purest state, there are things you feel passionately about simply because you do and things you feel drawn to simply because you are. There are also ideas that flow to you all the time simply because they are supposed to. They flow to you because they are yours to create and manifest in the world; they are a part of your calling. They arrive on their own and compel you with very little energy or effort on their part. These are the natural impulses that guide you toward the opportunities and challenges you most want to engage in the world. These are all clues that point the way to your dharma, i.e., your true nature *expressed* as your highest contribution and calling.

When my client Dante came to me, he was working as a wellness coach in the corporate space, providing workshops and consultations on diet and exercise for busy executives. Before he started his venture, he worked among the executive elite as a marketing and branding expert. I met Dante in this posh building in downtown Brooklyn; I felt like I'd stepped into a Puffy video. ☺ We sat down in a gorgeous library, and after a brief grounding meditation he jumped right into it.

"I was a top performer," he said, "until I developed a rare illness called Hashimoto's thyroiditis; it basically attacked my immune system." He paused. "As a result, I had to make some serious changes; I had to cut back on sugar, increase my vitamins, exercise more, and, most importantly, work less." He sighed and I watched his shoulders slump. "The work less part was the hardest. I was raised to always bring my A game and I feared that cutting back would cause me to be overlooked for promotions and other opportunities to get ahead." He sat back and adjusted his posture. "That extra energy had to go somewhere!" He laughed. "I started researching about Hashimoto's like crazy, trying to understand the causes, searching for more natural remedies, and as a result I became super-interested in holistic health. I started to apply what I was learning and began to see great results almost right away." He shook his head. "Before long, I was able to completely heal myself of the symptoms—it's amazing when I think about it." He leaned in. "After that, I became less interested in my job, and more interested in using what I'd learned to heal myself to help other people."

"Wow," I replied, "that makes total sense."

He continued, "I started offering wellness workshops to my coworkers and pretty soon began offering those same workshops to my friends, who invited me to lead more workshops for their coworkers and friends; as the demand began to build, I put up a website and started taking on private clients." He sighed again. "I honestly thought this was it, I was having so much fun in the beginning."

"But . . ." I gently interjected.

"But, after a while, it just slowed down, and soon after that the opportunities began to dry up. Which forced me to ask myself, Is this really what I'm meant to be doing? Which leads me to why I'm here today and wanting to work with you."

"Dante, what do you want to achieve from our work?"

"I want to offer something that feels more authentic to who I really am," he replied. "There are tons of wellness coaches out there, and as I look at what I'm doing, I just don't believe this is me. Before I go investing in a rebrand and a new website, I want to get clear."

"Um-hmmm," I replied. "Good call." I moved to my easel. "Have you ever heard of the word 'dharma'?" I asked.

"You mean, like, my path?"

"Yes, exactly, but your path that's guided by your true nature. There is a bigger journey that has brought you here, one that begins long before you got Hashimoto's. I want us to explore some of the other events in your life that have shaped you. I want you to consider this present moment and look back on your life from the perspective of your desire to make a difference and see which events really stick out for you."

We dug in, and as Dante identified the most pivotal moments in his life from this perspective, it all began to click. When I moved into the brainstorm of his true nature, he was able to see the essence of who he was in the qualities and attributes he was able to identify. He realized that his innate goodness, curiosity, kindness, and intuition fed a passion to want to help people not only physically feel better but be happier overall.

"Yes!" he said. "I've always felt like true health has been about more than just the physical; I see all of these other aspects like the mental, emotional, the spiritual, and a real sense of purpose and meaning—they're like the ingredients to a really great recipe."

"Now we're talking," I replied. "So your homework is to actually write down all of the components you think are necessary to create optimal health and well-being—as *you* see it."

Once we zeroed in on this more specifically, Dante decided to create a new curriculum dedicated to a more holistic approach to nourishing his clients not just physically, but mentally, spiritually, and emotionally as well. He is currently on fire, piloting his new offering to great reviews.

"My passion is back!" he said. "There is so much I want to teach in each of these areas. I feel like there's a lot more that I can give here—that's drawn from my whole life, not just my past illness."

Not only did Dante map his curriculum, but he began to think about his ideal client, the platforms he wanted to engage them through, and, most important, the ultimate difference he wanted to make. When I say on fire, I mean on fire! Dante finally connected to his dharma.

In nearly every conversation I've ever had with a client about their true calling, it's never been a matter of the person "not knowing." Even when your fear masquerades as confusion, what you are being called to do is always there, nagging in the background, waiting for the right moment to take its place as the focus of your life. You must be willing to courageously come out and indulge your true nature, even if it runs contrary to popular opinion or belief. Don't allow yourself to be distracted by all the noise rooted in societal conditioning that would happily drown out these impulses. Your true nature and calling live in the silence, and the stillness, between breaths that you rarely allow yourself to take amid the daily hustle and bustle. That is your life force speaking, and it wants your attention more often than you may allow.

Your Unique Journey: What Brings You to This Moment?

Just as the question "Who are you?" begins to unearth your true nature, the question "What brings you to this moment?" asks you to trace the journey you've taken to arrive here. Remember that fork in the road at the end of chapter 3? Well, now's the time to really explore how you got there. Your story is the key to helping you recognize where you've always been true and how you've already begun on some level to put your true essence to good use.

To do this, you'll need to consider the most pivotal moments in your life, plus the interactions and events that come to mind when you think of how you've arrived at where you are today. Your calling is not something you should have to go outside of yourself to find. It emerges from the depths of your inner journey—you just need to see how these key moments have shaped you and paved the way to now. Revisiting these formative experiences can give great insight into the way your path is always unfolding in perfect alignment with the highest contribution you are here to make.

As you examine pivotal moments in your journey, you will find that there are lessons, affirmations, and insights that emerge through every experience. The life-changing challenges and opportunities you face every single day offer important clues to who you really are. When you no longer see your experiences through the eyes of your limitations, or through the eyes of someone else's expectations, you have the opportunity to perhaps tell a different story altogether. Your pivotal moments can reach as far back as your childhood, or they can be as recent as the last 24 hours. As a conscious creator and visionary, you get to tell the story of who you are on your terms. And you get to explore how it influences what you are here to bring to the world right now through your calling.

One of the most common complaints I hear when I consult with potential clients is that they struggle to stand out. There is often resistance to answer a vision or calling because "someone else is already doing the same thing." Or "my story isn't special or different. I don't have a lot of tragedy." Or "I'm not some big expert on *Oprah*—why would anyone care?" Among all your traits, however, your story is one of your most valuable assets because it is the one thing that is both personal *and* universal. Your challenges and triumphs are precisely what allow you to stand out and, at the same time, allow others to feel connected to you. It's human nature to see ourselves through others' experiences and get to know them in a way that invites greater trust, intimacy, and credibility.

Even if you've told your story often, there may be another story and a different aspect of your purpose that wants to be expressed now. If you've become comfortable with your existing narrative, I definitely want you to look. You get to decide right now if it's time to evolve or change that story.

Case in point, I met Ashley at a live event during a Q&A after my talk at a gathering for courageous entrepreneurs. She stood up in the audience and identified herself as the survivor of an eating disorder. The room hushed in reverence. She went on to say, "At first when I was sharing this as a wellness coach and spiritual teacher, it made me feel proud to show my students and social media followers that you can survive anything. But now, this is really hard to say, but I feel like I am beyond that and don't want to be the eating disorder girl anymore." When I asked her why she continued claiming this identity if it didn't reflect her truest nature, Ashley's answer didn't surprise me. "This is the way that people have always known me," she said, "and if I'm not that . . . then who am I?"

"Isn't that an awesome question?" I asked as we sat quietly together. When I asked her who she wanted to be, she laughed. "I'm a badass. I'm someone who knows how to move through obstacles, and who's smart, and loyal, and hardworking. But that doesn't sound exciting when I try to brand it."

I laughed. "Suppose we let go of your brand for a moment, and think about your life, what's calling you?" Silence. "Your truest message is more than whatever obstacle you're facing in any given moment." She stood there, wiping away the tears. I paused to let her take in the question. "Do you have a right, like your students, to evolve?" I asked her.

"Oh my God, there is so much more I want to teach them, so much more that I am discovering about myself that feels exciting to me," she said. I suggested we take a moment for her to reintroduce herself to the audience, with all the love and support that the room had to offer. With gratitude for the journey that led her to that moment.

"Ashley, I want you to invite your triumph over this eating disorder to become just one part of your personal narrative—it's not the whole story. Who are you? And what would that introduction sound like if you brought your whole self to the party?"

"Wait, I gotta write this down," she said, and we all laughed.

She took about thirty seconds, then popped back up and wiped her free hand on her jeans before turning to her journal and starting to speak.

"Put the journal down, mama . . . and just give it to us from your heart," I said.

She put her journal down, closed her eyes, and took a couple of deep cleansing breaths. You could feel the room lean forward; all of us were rooting for her.

"Hi, my name is Ashley," she started. "I'm a healer. I am a teacher. I am a spiritual guide." Deep breath. "I work in the Ayurvedic tradition. I incorporate yoga, breathwork, and many ancient modalities to help people transform obstacles. I know a lot about obstacles, because I've had so many." Her voice began to crack, but she held firm, took a deep breath, and continued, "I know a lot about obstacles. I've used these methods in my own life to transform a severe eating disorder. And now, I want to share everything I've learned with you!" Not surprisingly, the room erupted with shouts and applause. Talk about a badass . . . I blew her a kiss.

Taking the time and energy to connect to your journey is an act of self-love and honor. When you consider the whole road you've traveled, you'll get a bird's-eye view of your strength, creativity, vulnerability, and hard-earned wisdom. Learning to value your journey and discover aspects of your story that you may not have valued before helps you create a new narrative, for yourself and your life.

Your Unique Orientation: What Is Important to You?

So now, tell me: What is important to you? As you really think about the pivotal moments of your journey, notice if there are overarching themes and lessons that have guided your experiences. How have those experiences shaped and defined you? And how might those themes and lessons point the way toward your highest contribution and calling?

When I began working with Rhonda, she was already a powerhouse in her field as a financial literacy coach and advisor working for a big consulting agency. Clients looked up to her, solicited her advice and expertise, and always wanted to know how to be successful just like her. Little did they know, Rhonda was looking to get out of her field. There were some aspects of her job that she still enjoyed, but most of it was arduous for her and her heart just wasn't in it anymore. Rhonda came to me through a dear friend in the financial industry. I'd been working with a network that was full of investors, so I knew a little bit about this world. Initially, I was taken aback because her demeanor was, well, a bit stiff and actually kind of harsh. *You sure you want coaching?* I thought. But once I got through her serious vetting process, I began to understand why.

"I did what I needed to do to be successful," she told me when we finally sat down in her fabulous minimansion. What Rhonda wasn't sharing publicly was that she had a secret passion. "I love to write and speak and I actually believe I have something to say. Especially to all these other women who are trying to rise up in this industry."

In our first working session, I asked Rhonda, "What's brought you here? Can you identify four to five pivotal moments in your life that you think have contributed to this passion to write and speak?" I continued, "I'm not looking for your corporate résumé here; I'd love to hear about what motivates you to want to do this every day."

In no time, Rhonda realized that many of her milestones were underscored by a need to feel perfect. "Up until about two years ago, that's what my life was about: kicking ass at work and being perfect everywhere else," she noted. "A few years ago, I had a nervous breakdown. It was horrible; I felt like I was going to die. I had to totally rebuild myself from the inside out; mentally, spiritually, emotionally, everything became about overcoming this need for perfection."

"Where did this need start?" I asked.

"Oh, definitely from my childhood," she said. "There was a need for perfection from the very start." She paused. "As the oldest sibling my parents expected me to set an example and there was a lot of pressure to succeed. When I broke down, I discovered that I'd been carrying all of this pressure around with me for years, simply out of habit." One day, the pressure became too much. "I got on a plane to attend a last-minute meeting with a major client and literally had to disembark because I had a panic attack. That was when I realized I was killing myself in order to be 'successful'—whatever that meant."

As we deeply explored each of Rhonda's milestones, pre- and post-breakdown many, important themes surfaced. For instance, "Before my breakdown, I always strove for a standard of excellence; to be twice as good as my peers, that was the name of the game. I equated reliability with credibility." She paused. "But after I panicked on that plane, everything fell apart and I realized I had to make self-care my number one priority." I could tell she'd gone back to that moment. "I can't take on the weight of the world anymore without paying for it."

"Hmph." I looked her in the eye and said, "I'm not sure you ever could." I leaned forward. "Your breakdown was the result of an unbelievable amount of pressure that had just been building over time—it was clearly just a matter of time before you would blow up or self-destruct."

"Well," she said, "I guess I did both!" She laughed. "Always the overachiever."

As we reviewed these themes of perfection, success, and being the lonely top performer, Rhonda could see the stark shift in her philosophy, after the breakdown.

"Before it happened, I was like balls to the wall, make it happen—failure was never an option.

"But after, I was at a loss to even define what success was anymore. But now as I look at where I am, I can recognize how all of these experiences are giving me a unique perspective on a different kind of success."

"Say more," I said.

"Now, success for me is about having peace. I'm always going to be dedicated to excellence, but I've got to do it in a way that feels more loving and less brutal to my own nervous system. When I look back now at what I was killing myself for, I can see it was impossible to achieve. The person I was looking for to validate me has been dead for fifteen years. So I'm not gonna get that pat on the back."

"Do you think your breakdown is the reason why you want to teach and speak?"

She shifted in her chair and looked up. "No, I think this desire has always been here. In college, I wanted to major in the creative arts and journalism, but my parents refused to pay for school unless I majored in something they felt was more useful, like law, medicine, or accounting."

It wasn't until Rhonda did this exercise that she could see all the ways her life had led her to this moment. She could also see that she could leverage all the knowledge, skills, and insight she gained through her experience when building a new venture. When I asked Rhonda to sum up her highest contribution and calling in one sentence, here's what she said: "I'm here to help high-strung people, like me, see that they can achieve success in their professions without killing themselves and sacrificing their health and well-being."

This was definitely Rhonda's dharma.

Ready to give it a try? Ask yourself the question "What is important to me?," which will encourage you to reflect on your life's journey, which often provides the answers. All you need to do is consider where you've been and ask yourself, "Given where I've been and what I've learned, how do I want to go forward? Given my unique gifts and the current state of our . . . [industry, community, society, nation, or world], what do I want to offer as a contribution?"

The answers may not come right away, and that's okay. Just keep creating time and space to listen to yourself. Allow this exploration of where you've been to inspire the vision for where you want to go now—even if the path takes you in a totally different direction.

Being True: What Do You Want Your Life to Be About?

So, now that we've tapped into your true nature, honored your journey thus far, and invited you to trade out some old beliefs for new ones, I want to know: What do you want your life to be about?

When I consider real success, I take into consideration not just who the person is but also what they seek to embody and create throughout their life—from their work, to family, to friends, to community, and to society at large. There is a genuine congruency between what they say they are about and how they act. They live the answers to these four questions (Who are you?, What brings you to this moment?, What is important to you?, and What do you want your life to be about?) very actively.

When I think of what it looks like to rid yourself of limiting beliefs, forgive your past, and embrace your calling, I think of my client Daphne. As a VP of finance for a large corporate real estate development firm, she kept a close eye on the bottom line while skillfully managing the wants, needs, and desires of various departments. She was a stickler for protocol, plus a very clear and direct communicator. Daphne was paid very well for her expertise. As a phenomenal asset to the company, she cared about her work, the people, and her company's success. Yet one day, on her way to work, Daphne was in a major car accident. Luckily, she survived, but she suffered severe trauma to her head, neck, shoulders, and back. The pain was debilitating and required medical treatment and extensive forms of therapy just to sit up and learn to walk again.

Daphne's road to recovery was very long, and her doctors weren't sure she'd ever live without some form of long-term physical therapy. As Daphne began to heal her body, she continued to simultaneously explore her soul—including the limiting beliefs that were keeping her from her calling. Those same questions began to emerge within her: *Who am I? What brought me to this moment? What is important to me? What is my life about?* When she was referred to me by a dear friend and colleague, I immediately saw that she had the kind of brilliance that comes from being very observant and deeply reflective. Daphne didn't need my wisdom, but she did need someone to create space for her own. I became a safe space for her to explore the deep recesses of her own understanding.

"I returned to painting as a way to bring greater calm and peace into my day-to-day. And as I painted I would receive these messages during my creative process. Sometimes they'd be about what to add to the painting, and sometimes they'd be about what to do with my life."

Sometimes she would have questions during our sessions, and sometimes I would offer bits of information to help guide her on her path. She was vigilant about using this time of deep contemplation, self-reflection, and listening.

During our time together, Daphne examined all of the ways she'd participated on teams and in cultures where the energy was toxic: "I notice how these goals will come down from corporate, and the various teams responsible would just freak out. Running around, snapping at each other, trying to do the impossible with little to no guidance or resources." She took note of her own daily interactions—those times when she didn't raise her voice or when she allowed things to go down on her watch that she knew weren't right.

"Why did you remain silent?" I asked her.

"I don't know, I think in the beginning I'd drunk the Kool-Aid. I thought management was right and sometimes they were, but when I take the time to reflect on it, I can see they were pushing way too hard." In looking back, Daphne confronted the pain of what it cost her—mentally, spiritually, and emotionally.

"As you consider everything you've been through, what would you do differently?" I asked one day. "Or even better, how might all of what you've learned inform how you move forward?"

"I know I've got to forgive and let go, me, them, the situation, but I also know that another kind of culture is possible. One where people are honored and supported and encouraged to do their best, while being set up for success instead of failure." Even with all of those challenges, as we delved deeper into her journey a different story began to emerge, and so did a different Daphne. This version had fortitude and resilience, deep conviction, and preferred genuine truth telling over lip service—especially to those in power. "I respect these leaders, and everything they've built, which is why I have to give them the tough feedback when they ask me what I think. They aren't alone either; so many companies operate this way."

Through this new commitment to truth, Daphne's calling began to take shape and form as a painter. Her art was phenomenal and mirrored her soul—exotic, abstract, yet very precise—beautiful, brilliant, bright, and dark. People were immensely drawn to her work. What Daphne also began to discover was that her process of painting was just as soothing to others as it was to her, and the idea emerged to integrate her creative process with deep and profound dialogue and reflection. Her exploration took her to a place of wanting to pilot these immersive transformative experiences. We set the date for her first experience and she was on her way. When I recently checked in with Daphne, she was spending lots of time in the Caribbean while painting and piloting. She also opened herself up again to love and was dating a very cute guy. Daphne was not the same person she was three years prior; she shed her false self and, in the process, found a sacred and profound connection to the person she was always meant to be.

We've all had the experience of being seduced by charismatic people with beautiful language and inspiring messages only to get to know them up close and experience something else. This is why the mandate to actively live the four questions is so important.

When I ask clients what they want their lives to be about, their natural tendency is to think outside of themselves—meaning, their desire is to create a life where they really matter. Thus, not just to the people around them, but to have influence on the state of our world.

Some want to be famous, but many don't. What they *do* want is to make a difference. They want to know that all their hard work is contributing to something that is bigger than what they can see. They want to have influence where it really counts. They want to have a voice that others will listen to, consider, acknowledge, and respect. They want others to follow their lead. They want to be *seen and known* for their contributions. And finally, in these contributions they want to work in a way that creates a deep sense of meaning and satisfaction—in other words, they want to work with those they love, appreciate, admire, and respect on every level.

Over the years, I've noticed that there's a big difference between those who "have things" or are "good at things" from those I believe are living their truth. In my experience, the most fulfilled operate from a moral compass for every decision they make. And it influences where they say yes and no. Some develop this level of clarity at a young age, and for others it evolves, strengthens, and crystallizes over time. Either way, coming into yourself can be challenging and scary. But when you finally do come face-to-face with who you are, you set the stage to embrace your own definitions of what it means to be happy, loved, fulfilled, and *you*.

Your Call

Are you ready to embrace a new self-narrative and redefine your life on your own terms?

Do this practice and these exercises to recognize and honor your true nature and give voice to your own new vision for staying true.

PRACTICE 1

I am who I am and who I am is . . . (Fill in three true nature attributes here.)

Visualization: Every day for the next two weeks, take five minutes to visualize introducing your true self to the world using the phrase above. See yourself on the 360-degree stage and hear those voices of affirmation flowing to you from your loving audience. Jot down the phrases you hear each day and carry them with you throughout the day. Any time you feel your confidence waver or get the urge to look at those phrases, soak them up. Let them inspire you to keep moving in a positive new direction.

EXERCISE 1: MILESTONES

Whether you know it or not, every experience you've had up to now has prepared you to make your highest contribution. As you reflect on everything you've been through and learned, consider the moments that really stand out for you. In your journal, answer the following: What are the top three most pivotal experiences that have gotten me here? In what way have they contributed to what I'm passionate about? How have they helped foster my gifts? How have they made me the person I am? There are no coincidences; your journey has meaning and is part of the value you bring to every interaction you have with others. Following these clues can enable you to identify the true you and the elements of your true calling.

EXERCISE 2: YOUR NEW DEFINITION OF TRUE

Now it's time for you to answer those four questions:

Who are you?
What brought you to this moment?
What is important?
What are you really about?

Write down your responses in your journal. Spend the next two weeks just observing how you show up in your day-to-day. Are you giving voice to this new true you? Just notice.

5

Step #5: Aligning Your Actions with a New Vision for Success (Your L3)

Now that I've talked about who *you* are and begun to explore the roots of your calling, it's time to look at how you will define success in this new stage of awareness. In chapter 3, you had an opportunity to let go of any of the limiting notions that either held you back or caused you to pursue a version of success that did not honor what mattered to you. Now that we've let those old notions go and you've started to reclaim those aspects of yourself that ring true, it's time to lay the foundation for a new success definition, one that enables you to honor and strengthen your new commitment to staying true. It takes courage and rigor to find the center of your truth and dedicate yourself to living from that place. But once you discover it, it starts to flow effortlessly from you. And the more you feel yourself consciously choose this commitment, the more confident you become in pursuing what's important to you.

What you must also know is that your dharma, through the expression of your true nature, invites you into this more aligned reality every single day. When you look at the things that make you happy, pique your curiosity, or ignite your passion, your dharma is right there.

In this chapter, I'm going introduce you to the True. Paid. Good. formula for success and walk you through each aspect of the equation so that you can start to align your beliefs, thoughts, and actions with this new commitment. This is where your new context for Staying True, Getting Paid, and Doing Good come together in a powerful set of declarations that will serve as the moral compass and foundation for your life. When you hear me use the term "context," I am referring to the set of beliefs and principles that will now guide the decisions you make and the actions you take. Often when we feel victimized, it is because we're operating by someone else's rules and perceptions about what matters and is important. However, once you explicitly lay your own mental, spiritual, and emotional foundation, you now take that with you, no matter where you go. It becomes your "home base" or "true north." This is what I mean when I use the word "context"—it's your moral background, foreground, and foundation. It's the place you stand no matter what's going on or who is leading. Having this foundation takes you out of being a victim (i.e., someone who is always reacting to life) and puts you into the role of having a vision (i.e., someone who is consciously creating their life). And once you have a vision, you can now make informed choices about how you want to live, move, and be in the world. The formula I'm going to introduce you to will bring together your most deeply held values and convictions, your unique combination of talents and gifts, and your most desired contribution and impact. We'll also talk about the importance of embodying this new foundation as a vital part of expressing and achieving your calling. The declarations you create put you on the path and the corresponding actions you take enable you to bring your purpose and calling to life. Through this process, success will now sincerely be defined on your terms.

Introducing Your L3

In my final words to you in chapter 3, I declared that real success is an inside job. In my experience it's also a function of alignment—meaning that it comes as an outgrowth of being profoundly connected to your most genuine self and expressing that self in ways that are consistent with your heightened awareness and connection. Every truly successful person I've ever met or studied has operated from an aligned context, one that served as the moral compass and foundation from which they chose to create and live their life. In my experience, that foundation is built on three principles: (1) their most deeply held values, (2) their unique combination of talents, gifts, and abilities, and (3) the passionate impulse that guides them toward the opportunities or challenges they most want to engage in the world. This is the new formula for success or, as I like to call it, your L3. And it stands for how you Live, how you Love, and how you Lead. In our work at Move The Crowd, we have a saying: "More powerful than what you say is what you do, and more powerful than what you do is who you *BE*." Your L3 represents the articulation of your most authentic self in service to your highest contribution, aka your calling.

How You Live

How you live should be an expression of your life's highest vision. It's all about what you value—that is, the principles and convictions that guide you day to day. It is a reflection of your highest ideals for the kind of life you want to live, relationships you want to have, world you want to create and inhabit. For some, defining your values may be challenging because you've never had an opportunity to really think about them. For others, you know exactly what's important to you; the greater challenge may be acting in ways that make you feel like you are honoring those values. And for others still, you may be grappling with ingrained beliefs that may have once been values but now feel more like limitations. No matter where you are, how you Live poses the question "What do you value?" You'll notice that when we explored your dharma in chapter 4, I posed these questions in a slightly different way—though they are aimed at the same truth. What is important to you? And how do you live in a way that is truly aligned with your values and convictions?

How You Love

Your next priority is to determine how you Love. How you love should be an expression of your life's truest mission. It's about that unique combination of talents, gifts, and abilities that you have been called to share. It's about the knowledge, wisdom, and skills you've inherited or cultivated over time; it's those unique experiences and those special blessings that come naturally to you. They are the gifts that you've been given to share with the world. And what you are called to put into the world are your highest offerings, which is why I call this your Love. How you Love answers the question "What are you here to bring?"

I'm amazed at how many of my clients initially feel stumped when I ask them about their gifts, because they don't always see the value they provide in every corner of their lives. Some may see their value at work but come up short with family and friends; others win BFF of all time but can't describe how they benefit their major clients. To quote the great poet and philosopher Kahlil Gibran, "Love is work made visible." It is our purest, most authentic and unique way of showing up in the world and sharing from the depths of our souls. When we bring what is ours to bring, there is no competition. There is only a sense of goodness and contentment that naturally flows because we are responding to the natural urges of our calling.

How You Lead

Finally, how you Lead should be an expression of your life's greatest purpose. This is where your calling really comes to life. It is the place where your (1) deepest passion meets your (2) purest talents to (3) achieve your biggest impact. It's where you leverage your unique abilities to make a difference in the world and in the lives of others. It does not matter what the focus or scale is; what's most important is that you are operating from a place where you feel you can make your greatest and most desired contribution. It answers the question "What are you here to affect?" Just as every one of us yearns to be seen, heard, and understood, we also have a deep desire to matter. And whether we matter to our family or to millions of strangers, we have to know that our existence means something and that we're at the helm of guiding that existence that is driven by our purpose.

When these elements are clearly articulated and expressed through your declarations and corresponding actions, success becomes inevitable because each aspect of your L3 is designed to help you become more of who you really are. And as you become more of who you really are, you naturally start to speak and act in accordance with your higher calling.

A Three-Part Guided Reflection

Getting to the core of How You Live, Love, and Lead isn't always easy. Sometimes it requires real time and space for contemplation and self-reflection. To help my clients answer these questions, I take them through the following three-part guided reflection. Each series of questions will help you dig deep and uncover what lives at the seat of your soul. Your responses to these questions become the raw materials for crafting your declarations—don't worry, you'll get to work on these for homework.

For now, I recommend that you walk through the guided reflections with three sheets of drawing paper—one for each reflection. You can use markers, crayons, or pens. Begin this process by finding a comfortable posture. Sit in a chair or on a couch or on the floor, whatever is most comfortable for you. Bring your attention to your breathing and just invite yourself to relax. Then, take each reflection one at a time. At the end of each guided segment, take time to write, draw, or use words, pictures, or symbols that best represent your responses to these questions on the blank sheets of drawing paper. You'll use one sheet per reflection.

So let's get started.

REFLECTING ON HOW YOU LIVE

How you Live is all about what you value. As you think about your-self in your highest aspiration (i.e., your ideal scenario), think about the life you wish to live and the kind of world you wish to inhabit. What are the values that are most important to you? What are the principles and convictions that govern how you operate? What qualities make up those convictions—joy, love, peace, or freedom? How are they expressed in where you live or the kind of food you consume? In your relationship to the earth? In your relationships with others? What values govern those interactions, whether they're business or personal? How do you use your resources in a way that supports what matters to you?

How you live should be an expression of your highest vision for your life and it should answer the question: **When it's all said and done, what are you really about?**

REFLECTING ON HOW YOU LOVE

As you think about yourself again, in your highest aspiration (i.e., your ideal scenario) and as you think about what you are here to bring into the world, what are the unique talents, gifts, and abilities you were born to share? Is it deep listening, laughter, compassionate speaking, or creative storytelling? Think about the offerings that come easily to you, like cooking, or painting, or organizing. Think about the activities you have to sometimes force yourself not to do. Think about what others often look to you to provide. Consider what gifts and talents energize you and bring you true joy, when you are able to share them. Think about the gifts you'd like to share in a bigger way. What is your unique set of offerings to the planet?

How you Love should be an expression of the truest mission of your life. And it should answer the question: **What are you here to bring?**

REFLECTING ON HOW YOU LEAD

As you think about yourself in your highest aspiration, think about the difference you wish to make in every situation. What do you feel most called to change, create, reimagine, discover, enhance, shift, and/ or transform in the world? What issue(s) are you most passionate about? What are the challenges and/or opportunities facing humanity that you most want to engage in the world?

Are you most passionate about eradicating poverty? Is it about providing quality education? Is it about helping people find their greatness? How will you leverage your talents and gifts to make that contribution, and what will be different in the world as a result? You want to think big here—if you could create or change one thing, what would it be? What are you here to affect, and what is the ultimate impact you want to have on the world?

How you Lead speaks to your highest calling and should be an expression of the greatest purpose of your life. It answers the question: **What do you want to affect?**

When all three reflections are complete, put all three sheets out in front of you. Look at what you've drawn. Make any necessary refinements or modifications—you can even set a separate date to really take this to a whole new level with paint, sketches, or collage. Once these images are complete, post them in a place where you can see them every day. This is the visual representation of your True. Paid. Good.

Your L3 = Your Personal Formula for Success

When you can envision yourself as a person who's already successful, as you've done using the guided exercises above, it challenges any idea in your mind that you will be anything but. When you hold success as inevitable for yourself, you experience the vision for your life as something that already exists rather than something you're striving for. Your purpose is no longer about having something to "get to." You are already there, and it already exists. The only work left is to become more aware of it and act in alignment with this truth. Once you're clear on your L3, you've essentially built your True. Paid. Good. formula for success.

The success factor in this formula comes from the alignment of your vision, mission, and purpose—all of which define your calling. Once you know what you value, what you're here to bring by sharing your talents and gifts, and understand what you'd like to affect in the world, the only thing that remains is engaging in the world in a way that honors and celebrates your commitment to all of the above.

One of my most inspiring experiences helping to bring an L3 to life was with my beloved collaborator and, ultimately, client Chelsea. I'd met Chelsea at a spiritual retreat I facilitated about 10 years before we started working together. She was a total badass who was notorious for helping to lift everyone else's leadership but her own. From the fields of entertainment to social impact, from the environment to technology, she'd help launch and build initiatives that touched millions of lives. She sat at the table with lots of movers and shakers, and when the chips were down she was the glue that helped hold many of them (and their organizations) together.

Chelsea reached out to me because finally, after all these years, she was ready to take her life back. This meant, focusing on *her* vision and *her* leadership, her wants and her aspirations. And this time, there was a real fire burning within her that led me to believe it was going to happen. We started with a half-day retreat and we began by looking at what brought her to this moment. In our exploration of all the pivotal events that unearthed this desire in her, we saw along the way all of the dreams and desires Chelsea had abandoned in the name of coming to the aid of others. What became so clear was that she needed to give voice to a new commitment for her life, one that would allow her to reclaim those lost passions and create the time and space necessary to bring them into fruition. This was a perfect opportunity to create an L3. After I walked her through the guided reflections, Chelsea sat for a long time—just reviewing her journal responses to each aspect.

When she was ready to share, I jumped up and began pasting large sheets of chart paper to the wall (this is how we do it when I'm in personal retreat with my clients). As we looked at Chelsea's Live reflections, values like integrity, transparency, and community emerged. For her Love reflections, it was all about helping others give language and voice to what really mattered for them. Here we talked a lot about her incredible talent as a storyteller; helping people give voice to their stories in a way that honored their journeys and contributions was one of the greatest expressions of her love. In her Lead reflections, Chelsea was super-clear that her life's work was about fostering greater healing and compassion among diverse leaders and their communities—using the power of story. This brought together all of the previously siloed aspects of her expression. All those years developing brilliant stories as an artist and all of those years of supporting leaders from all backgrounds and perspectives gave her the passion, skills, and insight to create something incredible. It was all right there; all she needed to do was name it, claim it, and act on it. As we reached the end of the guided reflection and stood in the center of the room reviewing everything she'd put up on the wall she said, "This is me; this is what I'm here to do."

As we reached the end of our first half-day session, we'd really set the stage to move Chelsea back into alignment with her truest self and greatest aspirations. However, when I asked her what she thought could get in the way of embracing this new commitment, she got really serious. As she looked at the pages before her, she recognized that she was creating a whole new life. And this vision was going to call for a total shake-up of her current reality. "We have to begin at the very beginning," I told her. Why? Because her life was currently designed to be 100 percent responsive to someone else's whims, someone else's clock, someone else's needs—leaving little to no space for her own needs, wants, and desires. It was clear to me that we had to revamp: her current structure for self-care; the setup of her physical space; where and how she was blocking time to spend with her beloved husband and the lack of time to nurture her inner artist. Chelsea needed to make room for her own life. And for her own voice to be heard, as she was mustering up the courage to speak her truth in a new way.

Not so easy. Because Chelsea spent so many years supporting others while neglecting her own dreams, she'd built up a lot of emotions inside her. There was deep fear, anxiety, anger, and frustration; there was sadness and some resignation. What we both discovered was that Chelsea's voice was the central driver for taking her life back. It was actually in finally speaking up on her own behalf that she got to express what she really wanted and set crucial boundaries around things that infringed on her time and energy. These are two priorities she'd not made before now.

As we continued to unearth Chelsea's desires, she had a lot to express about feeling underappreciated and under-acknowledged for all her hard work and the support she'd given others. This was exactly what was playing out at her current company. She was working as the Number Two in a prominent tech start-up, and as often is the case, she was wearing a number of different hats. From COO to head of HR to head of Marketing, as the company rapidly grew she would fill in with whatever was needed. Each of these roles was challenging unto itself, but add a temperamental CEO into the mix and things got even more chaotic. Even so, Chelsea had a fierce commitment and responsibility—not just to the CEO but also to the vision for the company, because she helped create it.

And therein lay the rub, because for all of the titles she had been given thus far, Co-Founder wasn't one of them. And yet, when we evaluated all of what she brought, the title was definitely warranted, in addition to all of the other important acknowledgments that came with it (i.e., compensation, board and staff recognition, company stock, you name it). This prompted us to lay the groundwork for a conversation with the CEO that would be a true reconciliation and recognition of their partnership—and of her time, energy, and contribution. This was huge for her. In order to prepare, we spent three months taking a long, hard look at all Chelsea's various roles, her work structure, and the places where she herself was devaluing her contribution.

With every session, Chelsea's true voice got louder and clearer, and less apologetic. Her courageous speaking led to courageous acting, and through this proces, she began making a number of adjustments—but the big conversation was yet to happen. Finally, the date was set, and in our last-minute prep session I asked her, "How do you feel?"

She said, "At this point, I'm just ready to have the conversation, I know what I want and it's time I made it happen for myself. It amazes me that it took this long."

At that point, I had to remind her, "Listen, you've done incredible work. You've put yourself last for years and are turning that around. And the transformation took under three months!"

Two days later, I received a text from her: "Say hello to the new Co-Founder and Chief Story Officer!"

I texted back: "Damn Right! Congratulations, Chelsea! Well earned, my Sister."

Now that you have a strong foothold in your L3, you hold something very powerful in your possession. This is the foundation for your impending success; these declarations represent commitments you've now made to yourself—they are created by you, for you. Not only do you get to decide what's important, but now you also get to live from that place. By taking on this exercise, you'll emerge with a clarity that will enable you to assess what's happening in every aspect of your life. Your L3 (Live, Love, Lead) will become the baseline and the cornerstone for how you want to show up and be expressed in the world.

CREATING AND EMBODYING L3 DECLARATIONS

Now let's get to your declarations. Why should you create them? Because it's important to have a set of statements that genuinely reflect the essence of who you are. And because they play such an important role in facilitating your True. Paid. Good. reality, you're going to want to choose your words carefully. These declarations serve as a constant reminder of the commitment you've made to pursue your own brand of success. When creating these declarations, I take clients through a meticulous synthesizing process to arrive at the truest expression of themselves. Language matters.

Every one of us has a unique lexicon that we've developed over time to support our fullest expression. So when drafting your declarations, every word has meaning. You want to bring the same level of precision and care to crafting these as an artist would to creating a fine work of art. Your L3 is like a thumbprint after all; there are no two alike in the world, because there is no one else in the world just like you. As you speak your declarations, you want to feel as if you're coming alive for the first time—or finally coming home to your true self. They should move and excite you, instantly reminding you of who you are and what you're all about. Your L3 is your guiding light.

Here are a few examples of what these declarations sound like. (Shout-out to Josh and Dana for their awesome work here!)

Josh

I, Josh, live with audacity, devotion, and enthusiasm. I serve to create joy, connection, and love. In my presence, people do together what they could not do alone.

I, Josh, bring compassion, wisdom, deep listening, and fierce love. I am an orchestrator and a holder of sacred space. With my skills as a coach and a leader, I create a context of possibility and growth in which people do their best work and thrive.

I, Josh, lead to create a world in which everyone is supported 100 percent. I lead so that each person has the opportunity to follow what uniquely tugs at their heart, to savor the journey, and to know that their life has made a difference.

Dana

I, Dana, am committed to living a beautiful life by cultivating powerful and authentic relationships and catalyzing change with my passion, my integrity, and my voice.

I, Dana, love with a fierce compassion. I honor and use my gifts as a guide to lovingly support my own and other's clarity, courage, and transformation.

I, Dana, lead to move us all closer to peaceful coexistence, to see that we, above all, belong to each other. I am a midwife for the personal and collective graceful evolution into our magnificent and just future.

Once you've arrived at your unique set of declarations, your next step is to actually give voice to them on a regular basis. Declarations have the most impact when you engage them in real time. Speaking them in the morning and evening, adding them to your phone or recording them as a mantra or meditation, incorporating them into your workout, and incorporating them into how you introduce yourself are all ways of embodying your L3 and bringing it to life.

As you become more comfortable and connected to this way of expressing yourself, you'll also feel a new level of clarity emerge. You'll be able to tell pretty quickly what things feel aligned and right for you and what doesn't. Every interaction you have and decision you make is born from this new ethos. It takes time and practice to come into full alignment and a courageous commitment to continue to stay there. But the benefits of being in tune with yourself are absolutely worth it. The practice of staying true is to give voice to who you really are and what really matters to you. It's a choice you make in every moment of every day.

In all of the years that I've worked with clients on this process, it's never ceased to amaze me how profound the shift is when you take your L3 to heart. One of the most moving L3 embodiment experiences for me was watching my client Roni come to life. When Roni and I began working together, she was the executive director of a healthy childbirth advocacy and education organization in New York. She was overwhelmed and drastically underfunded, and she felt like she was not receiving the support she needed from her board to help the organization stay afloat. As we began to explore her own vision, she discovered that this organization, though doing incredible work, was not where she wanted to be. Roni wanted to work in a larger organization that was well resourced, so she could do really innovative work in the areas of fundraising and development. She felt a tremendous sense of excitement about being able to bring fresh ideas to a well-established entity, while learning all she could from a more seasoned executive leader.

To align her intentions with her vision, I took Roni through a visioning and calling-in process that allowed her to get clear about her ideal opportunity—and within six weeks, she'd landed her dream position with a salary that was $20K above her compensation goal. Her compensation goal was $30k above her current salary, so we almost doubled her income! In this new role, we felt it was imperative that Roni create her L3 to boost her ability to excel. After two months of revisions, we arrived at the final draft. When she read it out loud to me, she broke down crying.

Here's an abbreviated version of her L3: "I, Roni, live to bring joy, peace, and love to life, I love through my gifts of creating synergies that connect people, vision, and resources, I lead to inspire a world where people feel honored, cared for, and encouraged to live with dignity and respect.

"Wow. This is who I am," she said. "This is who I really am."

Roni used her L3 to introduce herself to her new boss, coworkers, and direct reports. She also used this foundation to think about how she would leverage her unique gifts to forward the mission of the organization. I gave her the assignment to consider how her purpose—"to inspire a world where people feel honored, cared for, and encouraged to live with dignity and respect"—would come to fruition and feed her new role as development director.

As we continued to talk about what this phrase meant to her, Roni was charged with raising funds for a new housing initiative for their elder constituents; she decided this would be the perfect testing ground! Rather than taking the usual POV of putting government agencies, funders, contractors, and management companies on different sides of the table with conflicting agendas, Roni led a series of in-depth dialogues designed to build greater trust and personal connection among the stakeholders first. Then she used the same strategy to foster a deeper connection for them to the stories and struggles of future residents. Rather than simply try to rush the process to get things done, Roni ensured that everyone involved in the project was invested in the possibility that this could be a model facility of which everyone could feel proud. All of the stakeholders (i.e., developers, city agency representatives, et al.) bought into her vision for dignity and care and, as a result, built a world-class facility that was featured in various media outlets and won the organization and its stakeholders numerous awards, not to mention a two-year waiting list for new resident applications. As we celebrated her accomplishments the day after the organization's annual gala, we reflected back to our original intention-setting work.

"There's no going back for me," Roni insisted. "As a leader, I know what I'm capable of now, and I see that we have the potential not only to thrive as an organization but to disrupt this entire industry." Now that's the power of an embodied L3 in action.

Your Call

Guess what your homework is? Yep! It's time to craft and refine your L3 declarations. Here we're going to do your exercise first and then your practices, since each follows the other. You'll want to get to the exercises and craft the first draft over the next two days and then spend the remainder of the next two weeks implementing the practices.

EXERCISE 1: CRAFTING YOUR L3 DECLARATIONS

Revisit the three-part guided meditation from pages 95–97; using words, pictures, and symbols, respond to the questions in each reflection that you are most drawn to. Then use these L3 Declaration Worksheets to create your L3 declarations. Next, use these Embodiment Tips to learn how to put your L3 declarations to work. Finally, use your Embodiment Practices Worksheet to choose the practices that inspire you most. Choose one to work with for the next two weeks. You can download this worksheet at www.movethecrowd.me/TheCalling /resources.

L1 – LIVE DECLARATION WORKSHEET

WHAT DO YOU VALUE?

As you think about yourself fully realized and as you think about the life you wish to live what are the VALUES that are most important to you? What are the principles and convictions that govern your ideal life? Are they . . . joy, love, peace, freedom, . . . etc? And how are they expressed?

How you LIVE should answer the question: What do you VALUE?

Ex: I, Jermaine, live a life that is filled with joy, love, passion, freedom, and ease; a life where all my actions and endeavors serve to uplift the health and well being of the planet and those who inhabit it.

HOW YOU LIVE:

_____

_____

_____

_____

_____

_____

_____

_____

The activities contained in this document are designed exclusively for Move The Crowd, LLC. Copying, duplicating, or otherwise reproducing in any form is prohibited. © 2012 All rights reserved.

L2 — LOVE DECLARATION WORKSHEET

WHAT ARE YOU HERE TO BRING?

As you think about yourself being fully realized and as you think about what you are here to BRING to the world-what are the unique talents, gifts, and abilities that you have been given to share? Is it deep listening, laughter, compassionate speaking, creative storytelling? etc. What can you recognize and own as your unique set of offerings to the planet?

How you LOVE should answer the question: What are you here to BRING?

Ex: I, Jermaine, love by respecting and keeping it real with everybody. I use my unique talents and gifts of lyrical storytelling and cross cultural bridge-building to celebrate, educate, and inspire.

HOW YOU LOVE:

_____

_____

_____

_____

_____

_____

_____

_____

The activities contained in this document are designed exclusively for Move The Crowd, LLC. Copying, duplicating, or otherwise reproducing in any form is prohibited. © 2012 All rights reserved.

 **MOVE**THE**CROWD**

L3 – LEAD DECLARATION WORKSHEET

WHAT ARE YOU HERE TO IMPACT?

As you think about yourself fully realized—think about the difference you wish to make. What do you feel most called to change, create, re-imagine, discover, expand, enhance, shift, and/or transform in the world? What issue(s) are you are most passionate about? Is it about eradicating poverty? Is it providing quality education? Is it about helping people find their greatness? How will you leverage your talents and gifts to make that contribution?

How you LEAD answers the question: What are you here to IMPACT?

Ex: I, Jermaine lead with power, passion and clarity. I lead to educate, challenge and uplift. I lead by igniting the human spirit and enrolling every day people in the vision of a just and sustainable world.

HOW YOU LEAD:

_____

_____

_____

_____

_____

_____

_____

_____

The activities contained in this document are designed exclusively for Move The Crowd, LLC. Copying, duplicating, or otherwise reproducing in any form is prohibited. © 2012 All rights reserved.

L3 EMBODIMENT TIPS

1.   Speak L3 Declarations aloud in the mirror daily in the AM, at 12 noon, and in the PM.

2.   Transform your L3 Declarations into a meditation, walking mantra, or chant— use daily.

3.   Develop a kinesthetic movement connected to your L3 Declarations—speak your Declarations and incorporate that movement.

4.   Create a screensaver of your L3 Declarations or carry them in your phone—refer to them often.

5.   Incorporate language from your L3 Declaration into your bio and personal branding.

6.   Create an awesome display in your work or alter area of your L3 Declarations.

7.   Share your L3 Declarations with your most supportive loved ones and friends.

8.   Integrate your L3 Declarations into your personal introduction at meetings, speeches, etc.

9.   Share your L3 Declarations with key collaborators for your project, venture, or initiative.

10.   Consult your L3 Declarations when making important personal and professional decisions.

The activities contained in this document are designed exclusively for Move The Crowd, LLC. Copying, duplicating, or otherwise reproducing in any form is prohibited. © 2012 All rights reserved.

MOVETHECROWD

PRACTICE I

Description:_____

Duration:_____

Frequency:_____

Desired Impact:_____

PRACTICE II

Description:_____

Duration:_____

Frequency:_____

Desired Impact:_____

PRACTICE III

Description:_____

Duration:_____

Frequency:_____

Desired Impact:_____

The activities contained in this document are designed exclusively for Move The Crowd, LLC. Copying, duplicating, or otherwise reproducing in any form is prohibited. © 2012 All rights reserved.

PRACTICE 1

Your L3 declarations double as ideal mantras. Once you create your first-draft declarations in Exercise 1, practice speaking them aloud throughout the day as part of your refinement process. Begin with saying them in the mirror first thing in the A.M. and then practice speaking them before going into any important meeting or before an important phone call. As you speak them aloud, pay attention to every word. Feel free to make any edits that make the declaration even more powerful and concise. Doing these in the mirror creates an even greater connection between you and your most authentic self.

PRACTICE 2

Once you've refined your L3 declarations, practice taking them with you. Incorporate them into how you introduce yourself and notice what people respond to. When you're introducing yourself, you don't need to say the declaration verbatim, but draw on the key elements to ensure that what you say feels totally aligned with who you really are. Aim to practice this L3-inspired introduction at least three times a day. Even if you aren't meeting new people, this is a great opportunity to reintroduce yourself to those who already know you but now know you in a new way.

6

Step #6: Celebrating Your
New True Reality

I've devoted the last five chapters to how you get true first by recognizing the fact that you are creative, next by understanding the powerful role your beliefs play in creating your desired or undesired reality, then by making clear choices about what beliefs you want to keep and what you want to let go of, and finally by reclaiming the purest form of your expression in honor of a new vision for success, one that represents what you're being called to do in this world. Your True. Paid. Good. now sets the tone for everything that will come in the subsequent chapters of this book. The goal is to get you to dig in with the same passion and gusto you felt when you first sat down to draft your intentions, particularly as we move on to the next part of this book—where I give you a primer on how to maintain your truth while simultaneously making sure you Get Paid for everything your truest self is worth. (Don't worry, Do Good will be right behind it. I got you!)

People ask me all the time, How do you get to your truth and stay there? The major key? Practice, practice, practice. Now that you've created a new foundation for your life and success, you must practice taking it with you everywhere. This is the highest form of honoring and celebrating your new commitment to True. Paid. Good. Your L3 is a whole-self proposition, which means you bring your whole self to the party. No more leaving your values at the door, no more conscious participation in things that do not work, no more handing over your better judgment in exchange for flimsy excuses, no more suppressing your voice in painful ways. No matter what scenario you're standing in, if you want to feel empowered in any situation you take *your* context with you. You must commit to this. If an environment feels hostile to the real you, then that ought to tell you something. If a relationship is threatened by your honesty, then you get to decide if it's one you are willing to work to transform. If an opportunity you're presented with *feels* wrong no matter how good it sounds, you get to choose if it's a fit or not.

What's more, now that you have a new baseline worthy of celebration, you get to experience the world differently. You'll clearly choose which environments support your most authentic self and which do not. Now that you're closer to knowing your calling, you can determine the quality of any other situation you find yourself in. You get to evaluate in every interaction: (1) what is valued, (2) what's being offered as an experience, and (3) what kind of impact it's having on you, those around you, and in the world.

You get to ask yourself, Do you feel honored here? Do you observe others being respected? Is this relationship, company, organization, or community making things better?

As you embrace your L3 and celebrate what it means to Stay True, Get Paid, and Do Good you may find it challenging to keep from slipping back into old patterns, especially when it comes to intimate relationships. After all, you've developed ways of relating to each other over time, so when it comes to communicating, you may choose and accept certain behaviors because you are on autopilot. To avoid this, you'll need to stay awake at the wheel. Remember, in a life of conscious creation awareness is essential. As you pay attention to where you feel alignment and where you don't, you get to choose where and how you'd like to engage. Sometimes it requires removing yourself from the environment, while other times it requires reorienting yourself to the current situation. With every choice you make, you'll invite in the opportunity to practice saying yes to what feels most authentic and true to you. I emphasize practice here because making this shift takes conscious, diligent, patient, loving, compassionate effort before it feels like second nature.

As you move deeper into this new True. Paid. Good. commitment, you'll find there's a lot to forgive and let go of, like the people pleasing and the false pretense that everything is "fine" when you don't feel that way. You'll have to turn away from hiding, running, and avoiding. This can cause you to feel incredibly vulnerable, but it can feel freeing, too—which is what answering the call is all about.

When you align with your true self, there's a lot to celebrate, too. You become a magnet for the things you desire. And by that I mean that you begin to attract people, resources, and experiences that are consistent with what you want. I've seen it time and again with clients and in my own life: Self-love and affirmation attract your greatest desires—as do clarity of vision, mission, and purpose for anything you want to achieve; plus acknowledgment and appreciation of what you have. These are powerfully magnetizing forces. And as you begin to develop practices that support your most authentic expression, you will begin to achieve in a way that feels natural, organic, and effortless. You feel good, opportunities move toward you, phenomenal people start coming out of the woodwork, and things that seem like they might take forever get done in record time. Success becomes a natural outgrowth of your expression. The more you share who you are and what you're about, the better you feel and the more successful you become. You look forward to each new day as an opportunity to practice being you and creating a life you love.

Your passionate impulses and deep-seated aspirations are part of your higher wisdom, and the art of staying true is about giving voice to who you really are and to the things that want to happen to and through you.

In this chapter, I want to add some rocket fuel to your conscious creating skills by teaching you a technique for calling in anything that you desire. You'll learn that the steps to calling it in are very straightforward. But in order to be successful, you must exercise the mental, spiritual, and emotional muscles necessary to make sure that the universe hears your call. Our world is skeptical, and we've all developed habits that make us very proficient at creating the things we *don't* want. You've been taught to shield yourself from disappointment to make sure you don't wind up defeated. In fact, your fear of not having what you want is the most common obstacle to actually having what you want! Here we'll raise your awareness of the challenges and opportunities that could arise when trying to call it in and you'll learn how to integrate supportive actions and practices into your daily life so you can experience more of the magic and less of the "grinding effort" associated with manifesting.

The exciting truth is, the universe is ready, willing, and able to guide you toward your greatest desires, but you've got to do your part to have it all come together. Here are some of the things I've encountered when helping clients consciously create on the road to their calling: (1) getting clear; (2) building trust; (3) aligning right actions; (4) making room to receive; and (5) aligning practice with commitment.

Getting Clear

Creating what you want requires that you first get clear on an idea or goal that's aligned with your dharma and your True. Paid. Good. vision for success. What do you want to have, do, be? So many of us just react to whatever circumstances show up, so unless you've been thinking about your desires for a long time, you may not even realize what you want to create. Sometimes you have an idea—it could even occur to you as a feeling—but it's hard to describe more concretely. So you talk around it, but it may require real focus, time, and effort to find the right words. Sometimes you're afraid to say what you think because it might sound silly, you doubt it's possible, or you worry others might not get it. This challenge can often masquerade as confusion. You see it, but you immediately dismiss the possibility and back away in search of something else. Speaking your idea aloud is actually a very important part of taking those initial steps toward manifesting that idea, because what you say has to align with what you want to call in. This has to do with your word choice and the state of your heart when you are speaking.

When I want to call something in, I ask myself three questions:

1. *What do I want?* I get as explicit as I can and I remember to align my ask in some way with my purpose: I might want to make $250K a quarter, get the perfect parking spot in front of my yoga studio, or weigh 120 pounds and double my level of energy. Yes, it can be that big or small. And when you're working with these questions, you want to take them one request at a time.

2. *What do I want to experience?* This speaks to how I want to *feel* as I am inviting in the very thing I desire. Many of us have been conditioned to believe that we have to struggle to accomplish something, that our calling somehow requires massive amounts of suffering. That we have to sacrifice in ways that are painful in order to "deserve" the thing we're trying to achieve. When you ask this question, also think about the role you'd like fun, joy, and ease to play in your process. Consider not just the goal, but the quality of the experience along the way.

3. *Who will I become as a result?* You're meant to grow in this lifetime, and your deep-seated aspirations, wants, and desires (i.e., your calling) are intended to serve your expansion process. When you consider who you will become as a result of achieving your idea or desire, think about the ways in which you also want to grow as a human being, leader, parent, and professional. Connect your aspiration to something deeper than the material acquisition. For example, if I want the perfect parking space in front of my yoga studio, who I want to become is someone who develops a mastery in conscious creation, and my ability to manifest my desired parking spot becomes the first step. Asking this final question also gives me the motivation to keep the original goal or desire in front of me, which is to grow in ways that im-

prove my quality of life and that enable me to live in my highest contribution.

My favorite calling-it-in story comes from when I was teaching a 10-week course on empowerment to a group of women who were transitioning out of a battered women's shelter and back into society. This work was definitely part of my calling and I felt humbled and honored to serve them, not to mention a little daunted by the task! I arrived at my first session and was thrilled to find 15 women waiting for me. I began by leading them in a guided meditation, which would soon become a practice that helped align their goals and actions. As I moved around the room, many were fidgeting, and I could tell they had never done anything like this before. Peace and quiet was not something they knew a whole lot about. When I got to a woman named Delores, she was so still and looked so regal that she took my breath away.

"Perfect, Delores. You got this," I told her. "You look like a *queen*."

She smiled and returned to her breathing. When we came out of the meditation, the women introduced themselves and shared their stories. Delores told me, "I've been here awhile, and I'm so happy to be leaving. Oh, and I really liked the breathing."

Over the next 10 weeks, these women did a lot of work on themselves and came to look forward to sitting in stillness. Delores embraced the practice wholeheartedly, and her demeanor even shifted. She smiled more, did her homework religiously, and continued to expand her time in meditation. About halfway through the program, incredible things began happening for her. She applied for a data entry job, which paid significantly more than the standard list of jobs made available to the women at the shelter. She wanted to leverage her organizational skills and her interest in computers in a way that enabled her to make 40 percent more money than what most jobs were going for. I suggested that in her meditation Delores see herself receiving the job she wanted. The next week during our group time together, she leaned over to me and whispered, "Got the job. Looking at getting a great new apartment next."

I said, "You know what to do. Write down the description of your ideal apartment and take it into meditation with you."

She adjusted her posture and returned to her breathing.

At the end of 10 weeks, Delores talked about all of the incredible things she'd been able to accomplish—from her awesome new job, to specialized computer training, to a great new apartment with an increased monthly benefit.

Delores was ready to start fresh, with a new and useful practice in her tool belt. As she announced to the group at graduation, "My name is Delores and I meditate now. It brings me peace of mind and helps me get clear about what I want to have in my life, so I can go out and get it. I am so thankful for this practice." Amen, Delores, Amen!

Building Trust

When you aim to consciously create an idea or pursue an aspiration it requires a lot of trust—specifically in your own creative abilities and in your collaborative partnership with the universe. When it comes to achieving and receiving the things that matter most, we each bring a particular history to this process. Whether it's due to childhood experiences or bad bosses, we all have something going on around trust. Even when you've had awesome experiences, it can be hard to stay focused on them, since so many of the messages you get from society encourage you to be distrustful. Yet nothing blocks your creative flow quicker than a lack of trust. The symptoms show up as fear, anger, worry, doubt, sadness, and anxiety. Even the root cause of stress is a lack of trust. And all this stems from a deep need or desire to control things that are beyond your obvious scope. Beyond any tangible work you may be doing, you are also mentally working to try to predict and manage and protect yourself from the things that "might happen"—and it's exhausting.

Trust comes from what you believe is true, not only about any specific situation but also from examining what is at the core of your belief system. This ultimately influences your ability to create and receive what you want especially when it comes to your calling. You've already heard me talk about affirmations. Saying words you don't believe is not going to get you there. Speaking is a very important part of it, but what you say has to align *energetically* with what you want to call in. This is why I'll ask you to revisit what you believe here and expand on it. Do you believe the world is a friendly place or an unfriendly place? Do you believe that you have a mission and purpose that is uniquely designed for you? Do you believe that you and the universe are in a co-creating collaboration? The answer is going to influence how much trust you can access in any given moment.

Aligning Right Actions

After you've called in your idea, you must align it with the right actions. You want to put in the work, but it has to be the right work—work that serves your dharma and intentions. Too many people are killing themselves trying to get back at their hyper-critical fathers by being "a success" or convincing their bosses to find them worthy by working late every night. There is a delicate balance between trusting and efforting, forcing and allowing. When you make a commitment to becoming a master of conscious creation, you aren't just paying attention to the things you want but giving clear instructions to the universe around your desired quality of experience. How you move into action is just as important as the actions you take. Is the work joyful? Even if it's boring but necessary, you have to create an inspiring context around it so that you feel motivated to move forward. Aligned, right action brings velocity to any desire, so if you're killing yourself, you might want to hit pause and ask, *Why am I doing this? In what way does this action forward my vision? In what way is this action bringing me closer to my calling?* There may not be anything wrong with what you're wanting, but you may be battling with yourself by trying to force something to happen that's not ready to happen or that's not in alignment at all. Conscious creation ought to feel joyful and exciting, even in the challenging moments, because you're working in concert with the forces of nature.

Making Room to Receive

Finally, you must do what I call "making room" to receive guidance, support, and direction from the universe. As my mother used to say, "There's your business and then there is God's business." Even if you don't ascribe to any spiritual principle, the Natural Law of Reciprocity is all about giving and receiving, doing and allowing. Most of you have been conditioned to be masterful doers, but when it comes to allowing, not so much. Scarcity in any form usually stems from challenges with receiving from others. You may not realize how to put in your best effort and then allow that effort to be rewarded. Creating room to receive means believing good things are coming, and even embracing how vulnerable you feel. This form of receiving is rooted in surrender, as well—tapping into that part of you that genuinely believes you're taken care of by a higher power and always working toward your highest good in honor of your highest calling.

One of my most joyful calling-in experiences came from working with Mita. At the time, Mita was transitioning out of a role in corporate to lead a nonprofit she co-founded to create more opportunities for underserved young people in the fields of finance and technology. Mita had huge goals for the coming year—including quadrupling her existing budget and tripling her staff. We spent quite a bit of time architecting the right strategy, looking at the best team, articulating the top goals, you name it.

At the end of one really challenging working session she confided, "Yes, I want all of this, but what I want more than anything this year is to get pregnant."

Mita and her husband had been trying for some time but had not been successful and were in the midst of seeking additional support so that she could conceive.

I asked Mita, "I know that you want this baby, but have you created room to receive them?" As a leader Mita's daily reality was demanding, her days were long, and her responsibilities extensive. Having space to receive anything that wasn't part of her professional calling was a new one. "Let's create a practice that supports both calling in and making room to receive this baby."

I took her through a guided meditation that enabled her to relax and imagine herself receiving this baby. Welcoming the baby into her body, creating room for them in Mita's home, and most important making space for them in her life. When she emerged from the meditation, there was a beautiful sense of peace that came over her.

"This is the practice." I said. "Keep seeing this baby in your arms and in your life." Four weeks later I got the call.

"I'm pregnant. This time it feels different," she said.

"Just keep making room," I replied.

Nine months later her beautiful baby girl was born. This on the heels of a record year of success in her organization. Sometimes we are called in many different ways and in different areas of our lives; we are whole people who have a vision for whole success. This is what the commitment to True. Paid. Good. is all about.

Aligning Practice with Commitment

There are two types of practices in the realm of staying true that feel important to name. The first kinds of practices strengthen and align your energy. They support your State of Being—i.e., your clarity, your joy, your focus, your level of motivation. The other set of practices relates to areas of growth—the places where you are being invited to develop new habits, skills, and disciplines that align with your commitment. These practices guide the development of new habits that govern how you interact with people, situations, and circumstances you find yourself in. These practices are just as vital to ensuring that your new context becomes ingrained. For example, learning to raise your voice in places where you've been traditionally silent might be a new practice for you, or staying out of the middle of things that don't concern you might be a new practice. Devoting the majority of your time and energy to the things you say are most important is a crucial new practice in support of your new True. Paid. Good. foundation. These practices stretch us in ways that send the message to ourselves and others that we are ready to embrace something new. Finally, there are three central practices that I want to encourage you to take on in honor of your calling:

1. *Stillness:* Even if you start with just three minutes a day, finding time to be in total quiet and solitude with your inner world is important. This is the place where you get to connect with your source and listen for the wisdom, ideas, and inspiration that want to flow to you in any given moment.

2. *Subtle body observation:* Observe your feelings and the subtle energies of joy, love, and peace that move through you all the time. Your feelings hold tons of wisdom and insight about what is happening with you—they are the pathway to supporting your creation abilities, and the more you bring your attention to those feelings of well-being inside of you, the more those feelings start to grow and the quicker those things that you desire begin to move toward you.

3. *Conscious, courageous choosing:* This embodies everything we've been talking about, choosing from a heightened state of awareness so that your energy can align with your intentions and deliver your most beneficial outcome. And choosing from a place of devotion to what really matters. Goal achievement is simply a series of choices you make about when and how to act in any circumstance. The more awake and aware you can be, the better and more aligned your choices are.

Practice as Discipline

As you pursue your own definition of success, discipline also requires a new understanding. When you're engaged in your calling, this isn't something you have or don't have. It's something you cultivate through the experience of your supportive practices. It's a muscle that you strengthen over time—one that enables you to show up powerfully and consistently for the things you feel are most important to you. It's the capacity you build to be able to see when you are misaligned. And it's the skill you develop to move back into alignment quickly.

I am a passionate advocate for practicing as a way of life. I believe it's the quickest path to achieving anything you desire, especially when that practice aligns with your calling. Once you align the (1) right practice with the (2) right commitment and develop (3) a true sense of devotion to that practice, you become unstoppable. Commitment inspires us to practice, practice enables us to form new habits, and discipline helps us maintain our original commitment when we face obstacles. In my experience it takes about 90 days of consistent (vital) practice to develop the devotion and discipline you need to achieve whatever you desire. When you apply this to the things that matter most, your devotion to that commitment deepens as you achieve greater benefits over time—this is the kind of dedication you want to bring to your calling.

Conscious creation is a dance—a partnership between you and the all-providing universe. You do your part and then step back and leave room for a higher power to do its work. Allowing is as much a part of the work as the actions and practices you take on every day to achieve what you desire. Learning to work this way makes sure that not only do you manifest what you desire, but also the journey to manifestation is as sweet as can be.

Your Call

Are you ready to test drive your True. Paid. Good. commitment and call in what you really want and receive it? These two practices and two exercises will help you get on the court, move through any current creation blocks, and take your manifestation game to a whole new level.

PRACTICE 1

Choose one mantra to work with over the next two weeks. Use it to get you into creation mode. Speak it before you do the three-step process for calling it in. Speak it before you walk into any major meeting or event, before you give a speech or make a presentation; use this mantra to evoke your creative powers as you navigate your day-to-day. As always, take two or three deep breaths before you begin, then speak the mantra at least three times as you deepen your connection to these words:

"I am ready to create and receive everything I want, need, and desire."
"All that I desire is manifesting right here and right now."

PRACTICE 2

For the next two weeks, just practice *receiving*. Pay attention to every interaction, from the dry cleaner returning your change to your new client giving you a hug. Any time someone goes to hand you something (literally—whether live or over the internet) take a moment and give it your full presence and attention, pause, and then say, "Thank you!" Show the universe you are ready to receive all of the wonderful things you're calling into your life right now.

EXERCISE 1: CALL IT IN

Identify at least one thing related to your purpose and calling that you're ready to call in. Use the three questions from the "Getting Clear" section of this chapter to give voice to what you want to have, experience, and become. Spend time in stillness every day, connecting to what you've created. Don't worry about the duration of the practice right now. We are aiming to implement consistency. Even if you do it for just two minutes a day, the goal is to get you on the court. You can expand the time as you gain more confidence in the effectiveness of practice. Finally, as opportunities begin to move toward you, show up with the knowledge that what you've called in *is* manifesting. Work with this practice over the next 90 days. Focus on one desire at a time.

EXERCISE 2: ALIGN YOUR ACTIONS

Over the next two weeks, follow your natural impulses and take one action each day that aligns with your true calling. For example, you may be moved to send an email or make a phone call, or attend an event, or take a walk outside at 2:00 P.M., the aim is to learn how to listen for guidance and then take the step. Notice how you are feeling as you are taking this action, even if it's a stretch for you—you should feel joyful excitement and a deep connection to your own creative energy. Also note, the assignment is *one* action, not twenty and not zero. Just one. ☺ Use this assignment to learn how to dance in co-creation with the universe.

Part II

GET PAID

7

Step #1: Recognizing Your Relationship with Money

Now that you understand what it is to Stay True, let's look at what it means to Get Paid inside of this new reality. You don't need me to tell you we live in a capitalistic society, and just like we've inherited notions around success in general, we've also inherited notions around money— boy, have we—making it, spending it, saving it, investing it, and giving it away. Whether we have money or don't, these inherited notions deeply affect the way we operate when it comes to handling our business. Just as you examined what you believe in your quest to Stay True, if you want to cultivate freedom and authenticity around the earnings from your call- ing, then you need to evaluate what you believe about money and what it means to do business.

First, we'll examine how you define capitalism. As much as you might refer to capitalism as an economic system, you must also recognize that capitalism operates as a culture—and as such, it's had far-reaching im- plications for your finances. Just as capitalism as a system has given you the concepts of the free market, and supply and demand, as a culture it has also given you the categories and constructs of winners and losers, haves and have-nots, entitleds and unentitleds, of hardworking and lazy, and many more. Depending on what your experiences have been, you've probably found yourself on the right or wrong side of these descriptions and that has determined whether you feel empowered or disempowered when it comes to your finances.

In this chapter, we'll explore your current belief system as it relates to money and doing business. We'll help you unearth the top five conversations shaping your current financial reality, and you'll learn the five root causes for why so many of us experience a lack of power during our money and business transactions. Finally, we'll begin to explore how your primary beliefs have influenced your past relationship with money, current state of affairs, and financial future.

As you are a conscious creator who is serious about your calling, it is imperative to cultivate a new relationship with money and a new vision for how you'd like to do business. But before you can give rise to that new vision, you must understand what has colored this impression so that you can determine what you'd like to let go of and what you'd like to keep in your commitment to True. Paid. Good.

How Do You Define Capitalism?

Similar to how you've traditionally viewed success, you've likely held the economy as something that lives outside of you, too. When you think about how you've been conditioned to think about money, this shouldn't come as a surprise. The term "economy" is defined as the wealth and resources of a nation or region, based on the production and consumption of goods and services. When I share this definition, I typically get the (not sarcastic) response, "Oh, is that all?" When it is broken down to its barest bones, you can see the economy doesn't have to be the complex financial system thought to operate over our heads, according to the media. It doesn't have to intimidate or even scare you, despite the fact that it seems the economy is always in trouble! We hear pundits, newscasters, and our nation's leaders tossing around terms like "deficit" and "struggling," with proposals to cut spending and incentives to boost recovery.

Everyone in a tie and jacket these days seems to have an opinion on how to stimulate the economy, so that it can grow. I don't know about you, but if the economy were a person, I'd think they were on life support with very little chance of ever regaining their health!

This doesn't, of course, stop us from simultaneously feeling bombarded in the media by profiles related to the megarich; old institutional money and twentysomething billionaires—typically college kids with cool ideas that take off overnight. You hear about the 99 percent and the 1 percent but not a whole lot in between. The big takeaway, then, is that unless you were born rich with a team of savvy financial advisors or dreamed up an algorithm for the next Facebook, you shouldn't quit your day job, or worse still, you might want to add another one.

Bottom line, you've been conditioned to be at the mercy of our economic system, not to mention the way the economy dictates your emotional and financial relationship with the world. It tells you who to be, and what to buy, and where to work so that you can conform to its standards. The issue here is that these mandates are designed to serve the current economy's interests, which only benefits a tiny portion of our population. The traditional system of capitalism has fostered a culture of greed and exploitation for that tiny portion in power, and a culture of scarcity and separation for the rest of us. If you buy into this, you not only experience feelings of scarcity around money, but those feelings also bleed into other facets of your life—you feel a scarcity around love, acknowledgment, opportunity, time, health, and well-being.

This scarcity mentality breeds various forms of stress and anxiety, which typically comes to define how you live. This context drives your desire to buy and consume as much as you can and creates an ambitious state of desperation and unhappiness, along with the impulse-cum-habit of always needing to reach for more. Nothing is ever enough. Such a "never enough" mindset can be so deeply embedded that it's part of your subconscious. Sure, you might be more aware of it when you get your credit card bill every month or pull clothes out of your closet with the tags still on, but even so, you might shrug your shoulders and assume that this is normal, which is exactly what scarcity-based conditioning tells you.

My beloved friend and money mentor, Lynne Twist, co-founder of Pachamama Alliance and founder of the Soul of Money Institute, said in her groundbreaking book, *The Soul of Money,* there are "3 Big Lies" around our economy that we need to get past: (1) There is not enough, (2) more is better, and (3) that's just the way it is.

Think about it: Do you believe that the economy is something you have the ability to affect on any level? If you believe that you *can* affect it—i.e., that it's inside your realm of influence—do you only see that potential when you have a robust bank account? Or do you trust in the power of your own effort to affect it? If you believe the economy is out-side of you, then you probably don't feel empowered to change it. But that couldn't be further from the truth.

In order to Get Paid in your new reality, you absolutely must believe that the economy is something you *can* impact. This starts by becoming aware of what you believe and then understanding how that affects the way you engage with it. Just imagine if instead of defining economy as the wealth and resources *of a nation or region,* based on the production and consumption of goods and services, you thought about it as the wealth and resources of a community or person—that person is you! You control the acquisition and allocation of your own wealth and resources and therefore have the power to make decisions about how *your* economy will operate within itself and as part of a larger economic system.

Plenty of people have contributed to our global economy but have come by their wealth in the most maverick ways. This has always been the case. Some are well known, like Richard Branson, who dropped out of school at 16 to live in a commune for musicians, or George Soros, who narrowly escaped the Nazis' invasion of Budapest in the early 1940s after helping his father create fake passports billed on a sliding scale to keep many Jews from being shipped off to Auschwitz. Some of these pioneers are lesser known, like your neighbor's "hippie" sister, who shares a beautiful Victorian home in Columbus, Ohio, with four other women with gorgeous furniture and cultural artifacts and travels around the globe eight months out of the year, with temporary residences in local communities, in Thailand, Indonesia, and Ecuador as she works to support herself three days a week teaching English or giving painting lessons to local elites who seek to soak up American culture by day and waiting tables while hanging out with the locals by night. She has no credit card debt and can manage just fine on $50k/year.

Neither Richard, nor George, nor this awesome hippie sister lives in reaction to mainstream messages. These are people who live by their own set of rules and values. I'm not talking about those who are out to cheat or exploit the system, but those who have created a powerful vision for how they want to live and be in the world. They live unconventionally, yet have agency over how they deal with money. They have already figured out how to Stay True, so they feel confident being adventurous in how they Get Paid.

When I work with clients around money, they may have certain views about capitalism as a concept, but they're rarely aware of how prior messages inform their personal financial state. Or they *are* aware of this on a personal level but have no idea how the larger, systemic cultural conditioning impacts their values and perceptions of what is and isn't possible for them. Very rarely do they see and work through both layers of conditioning at the same time, but that is what's necessary when you embrace the vision for your own economy. In other words, you have to look at those self- *and* societally imposed beliefs all over again.

What's Your Personal Relationship to Capitalism?

To understand your relationship to the process of making and having money, I want you to examine the top five "conversations" you have with yourself about it. As you do this, pay close attention to the language you use here—I'm after your inner dialogue. When it comes to our finances, we usually don't pay attention to what we tell ourselves, yet we are talking all the time in our minds (or sometimes aloud!). If you can become aware of what you say to yourself, you'll be able to transform what isn't serving you. If for some reason, you're finding it hard to locate your inner dialogue, go back to your Belief Inventory homework from chapter 1. In that assignment, you identified six types of beliefs: beliefs about yourself, others, your current situations/circumstances, the world, success, and Source. Did any beliefs about money or doing business factor into these answers? If so, how? Personally, when I did this exercise, I was shocked to discover all the limiting conversations that were alive and kicking in my inner dialogue. I had a ton! I believed that making money was hard and that society did not value the work I was doing and therefore most people wouldn't value it either. I believed that in this life you had to make a trade: Either you did work that made a difference in the lives of other people or you sold your soul to make money, but that the two could never coexist. I believed that those who wanted to work with me couldn't afford my services, so that meant that I couldn't charge much for my work. Not only was I immersed in these beliefs, but I held them with conviction! I believed them to be the truth—no ifs, ands, or buts about it. Yet I couldn't have been more wrong!

When I unearthed my conversations verbatim here's what I found:

- *They want to work with me, but they don't have a lot of money. So, I'm going to have to figure out what else I need to do to make up the difference* (sigh).
- *We just got a donation, which is great, but it's not going to be enough to pay for this program. I'll just cut my fee to help make up the difference.*
- *I really believe in these folks and think what they're doing is important . . . so I guess I've just gotta make it work.*

I'm sharing these examples because the last thing I want is for you to judge yourself around money. Judgment, especially self-judgment, gets in the way of self-exploration; as soon as you go there, you will fall into the

Binding Behaviors I talked about in chapter 2; there's no complaining, blaming/judging, justifying, or avoiding allowed here, just courageous looking.

Where Did These "Conversations" Come From?

Ask any great investigative reporter what their "source" is and they'll clam up on you. A seasoned journalist never reveals their sources! But you have to not only investigate what your thoughts are about capitalism but also recognize where they come from. This is one of the toughest and most important inquiries, because it reveals where and how you've been influenced. For some of us, these messages come from our families and how we were raised; for others, they come from our massive consumption of media; and for others still, they come from our work environment, spiritual beliefs, or educational communities.

So, what's your source? Where have these messages come from and how did they manage to seep in? Try to narrow it down to even the exact person—living, dead, fictional, televised, you name it—and think about how you internalized them as your own. When you embrace someone else's beliefs, you play it in your mind over and over and, after a while, you forget where it even came from in the first place! Figuring out the origin of these messages allows you to examine the source in a new way. Does your belief about making money that you adopted from your super-freelance, shopaholic best friend in college, still make sense to you as a 40-something adult with two kids? Does it serve you to still admire your grandfather's tightfisted wealth, even after traveling the world and seeing firsthand how much poverty is out there? Finding the origin of a message allows you to examine it in a new light. Just consider: Does your older and wiser self still see these original messages as gospel? What are all the ways you've held them to be true? Are you willing to challenge this belief? Does this belief limit or empower you?

As you expose your sources, these messages may also be accompanied by lots of emotions. I'll talk later about what to do with those feelings, but for now use this as a chance to better understand the strength and influence these inherited conversations have had on you.

What's Your Vision for How You'd Like to Do Business?

If you had your way, what would you like your moneymaking and spending experiences to be like? What's your vision for how you'd like to do business as an entrepreneur or as a client or a customer?

When you've played the role of economic victim for so long, it may take some real convincing to believe you actually can do business in a way that feels in line with your values. But we see brands reposition themselves all the time to meet the changing demands of consumers who've given voice to how they want to spend money. These days, those changes are often based on their values. And this is exactly how you can influence the marketplace, too. Whether it's as a radical start-up jumping onto the scene to fill a void or as an influential consumer who's willing to put their money (and in some cases social media following) where their heart is, both factor into the nature of our economy and both of these people can, in fact, be you.

When you reimagine your relationship to the economy and reconsider your vision for how you'd like to do business, return to your newly defined L3 (Live.Love.Lead.) declarations from chapter 6 for guidance. Then ask yourself, What are the actions that are most consistent with your values? What practices would lead you to your notion of success? How would you like to actively participate in this new economy—as an entrepreneur? Executive leader in a corporation? Founder of a nonprofit? Or well-informed client or consumer? You have the ability to influence and redefine how you do business with others. And the more intentional you are, the more others will positively respond to you.

When I consider my most enjoyable spending experiences, I think about the love and care that's demonstrated by the business owner. It doesn't matter how big the business is; if I can feel the owner's best intentions through the beautiful attention they give to every detail of their business practices, it's a win for me. Whether this is related to the quality of the goods they offer, to how they're packaged, to how they're displayed, to the store clerk's smile or character, to the store's ambiance . . . so much integrity and heart goes a long way in translating to a terrific consumer experience. Think about your own buying experiences. You might not be consciously aware of why a business draws you in, but you can certainly *feel* it when there's a higher level of care brought to your experience. This is what builds recognition, trust, appreciation, and devotion.

What's Your Vision for Professional Success Now?

You've already created a new definition for life success, so where and how does your professional success fit into that? As you consider the potential to create your vision to Get Paid on your own terms, what's really important to you now? Consider everything: from the kind of work you want to do, to whom you most want to work with, to how much you want to make, to whom you most want to be working for as your client or customer, to how much time you even want to spend working—all of it is up for grabs. You get to create exactly what you'd like the recipe of your professional success to be.

So let me ask you: As you consider how you will begin to actually pursue your calling, what professional and/or entrepreneurial ideas will serve others in a way that feels true to you?

When we talk professional visions coming to life, my client Zahava (who goes by "Z") always comes to mind. Z is a brilliant dancer, coach, kink educator, and leadership trainer who had big aspirations for the work they wanted to do in the world (Z is gender transcendent and uses the pronouns "they"/"them"). When Z and I began working together, Z had been teaching workshops for years but still needed a full-time day job to meet their financial goals. Z was working on their soul work during lunch breaks and after dinners and often teaching weekend workshops on dance, sexuality, and spirituality. Z barely had time to perform and didn't see much possibility around financial success as a performer and teacher.

The first thing Z and I examined was their fear around charging people for their services. "Have you ever created a menu of offerings with pricing?" I asked.

"Oh my gosh," Z replied, "I'm afraid my community can't afford to pay very much."

Clearly, someone (the wonderful Z) needed a new vision for their success!

That's when I asked Z to examine their views on money. Z's mom grew up in the Appalachian Mountains of Kentucky and was the first one in their family to go to college. I asked Z to examine what "being Appalachian" meant to them. Z made a collage of images of white trash, beer bellies, and stereotypical rednecks as they examined their internalized shame. Z had a fear of losing connection with their lineage if they became financially successful and had an easier life than the people they came from. Z wanted to demonstrate a loyalty and connection to their roots and had fear about leaving behind people in struggle. I helped Z to see that there could be another way to connect and honor their lineage so it didn't have to manifest as a shared struggle. Z made a family tree and looked at each person's relationship to money in the family. Then Z asked their elders and ancestors if they would hold a vision of wealth with Z. Z was incredibly surprised and moved by receiving so much love and support from the family.

Up until that point Z was unconsciously attracting clients who also came from poverty or marginalized identities. Z had no problem creating healing offerings and workshops. But Z was nervous about charging rates that reflected the value of the work. Z's day job was enrolling people in a five-thousand-dollar online nutrition school. While Z was learning sales techniques it felt much more vulnerable to sell their own work than it was to enroll students in someone else's program.

We started to look more closely at how Z related to their own value. Using the L3 (Live.Love.Lead.) declaration process, I helped Z create a new foundation for how they would see their value, what they wanted to contribute, and how they would invite people to their offerings. So much of Z's awareness as a dancer, yogi, and bodyworker was a felt experience. Z needed to learn how to translate the power of the experience they were having with clients into words. Z learned how to partner with their existing clients to identify the benefits they were receiving so Z could share them with potential clients. Their L3 declarations guided Z's new biography, vision, mission, and purpose. I asked Z to read their L3 aloud every day as an anchor and to hear their own voice and experience their presence as they read it. This process gave Z a new way to see and speak about their role in the world.

It wasn't long before Z's sense of value transformed and they realized that the same kinds of people who purchased the five-thousand-dollar online nutrition school enrollment would absolutely be the kind of people who could afford to work privately with Z. We adjusted Z's pricing strategy to more accurately reflect their experience, including certifications in yoga, Pilates, massage, Tantra, health coaching, and thirty years of professional dance training. I asked Z to practice scripted conversations about pricing in front of a mirror until Z felt confident that they could share their value in a conversation.

It takes time to transform beliefs and learn new skill sets for visioning and enrollment, but after three years of devoted work Z got there. With this new passion, conviction, and clarity, Z took their calling to the next level. This past year Z has launched two leadership programs earning thirty and forty thousand dollars, respectively. I couldn't be prouder of Z!

The Five Root Causes for Your
Limiting Financial Beliefs

Just as there are legacies of wealth, there are also legacies of scarcity, anger, shame, and neglect. You may be the first in your family to go to college, enter the corporate world, or stay afloat without public assistance. Every one of us has something we carry—good or bad, obvious or more subtle, indifferent or limiting—when it comes to our history and past experiences with money.

Remember too that even the wealthiest can feel as if they're lacking in some way. Sure, they have more resources, but they can still maintain core feelings of fear, shame, guilt, anger, and anxiety, which influences how they earn, save, spend, and experience every transaction.

Over the years, I've discovered five primary roots that lend themselves to a scarcity mentality. And when I tested these insights at a recent conference, I felt like I'd landed in the evangelical pews of a Pentecostal church! Lots of Amens here! ☺

ROOT CAUSE #1: "THERE IS NOT ENOUGH"

When you feel you don't make enough money, whatever that number is and means to you, you may find yourself living from paycheck to paycheck—no matter how big that check is. Feeling that there's a lack of abundance is deeply ingrained in you, so it feels normal for you to operate as if your wallet is always emptier than it should be. Even when you get a raise or take on a side project for bonus cash, you automatically find ways to spend the money or increase your expenses or that a series of unexpected circumstances drag you back down to your "not enough" baseline. No matter what's happening to your actual money, you live and operate from a state of perpetual fear about when and where your next check is coming from.

ROOT CAUSE #2: "I AM NOT WORTHY"

When you consistently feel you're unworthy of respect, acknowledgment, or appreciation you will resist opportunities that would increase your revenue and/or your value or the value of what you have to offer. This feeling of unworthiness shows up as a belief that you don't deserve more of what you currently have or can earn. Sometimes this belief shows up in how you view yourself, and sometimes it shows up in how you think others view you. Either way, it makes you feel undervalued, and because that is your normal, you naturally appropriate this toward money, too. Put another way, if you don't think you are worthy of love or friendship or a nice home or even time off, you will not feel worthy of financially rewarding opportunities either. You will not be clear on what you want and how to earn it, what you have to offer, and you always compare yourself to others because you consistently devalue what you have to bring to the world.

ROOT CAUSE #3: "I MIGHT BE CHANGED"

It's not so surprising to hear that a lot of us aren't comfortable discussing capitalism or business acumen with any kind of self-possession or confidence, but there are others who simply struggle with the idea that money could be a good thing. In other words, you think it will cause you to compromise your values, corrupt you, or alter who you are or what you stand for somehow. You might suspect that money is the root of all evil and/or have been taught not to trust those who have it. This means that if you start to seriously think about making money in a real way, you worry that any forward motion will threaten the essence of who you are. This comes up a lot with clients who have a strong spiritual, poverty-based, or social justice activist history. There is a concern about "agendas" and constant worry about "selling out" and compromising integrity to get ahead. You might resist every good opportunity, then, that comes your way or, when moving forward, try to overcompensate in a very public or private way to "prove" that you are still you.

ROOT CAUSE #4: "I'M AFRAID OF WHAT IT'S GOING TO TAKE"

When this internal conversation plays in your head, you worry over the amount of work that's required to achieve a different financial reality. The concern here is around burnout, physical fatigue, abandoning friends and family, or another way that your quality of life may become compromised en route to greater financial gain. This is different from choosing to opt out of a more work-intense lifestyle for more quality time with yourself and your family. Similar to #3, this conversation suggests that a trade-off must happen and you're not willing, ready, or able to take that step. The belief, here, is that the cost of that trade-off may be too high. This is a common conversation when someone reaches a certain level of success and must then figure out how to "maintain it." It falls in line with the old saying "getting there is one thing, but staying there is something else."

ROOT CAUSE #5: "I'VE GOT ISSUES WITH CAPITALISM"

When this is your internal refrain, you might have multiple offshoot conversations going on in your head at the same time; all of these are fueled by the various aspects of capitalism that you most despise. This internal dialogue refuses to accept that you could ever participate in a moneymaking endeavor from a place of values-driven power, so therefore, you don't have to participate at all. In other words, it's financial self-defeat. You might (1) feel angry about the fact that everyday items cost so much, especially when premium price tags are linked to necessary items like fresh organic fruits and vegetables; (2) feel guilty or shameful for charging a certain amount of money for your offerings because the work is spiritual or traditionally considered to be charitable (here a sense of "wanting money" feels immoral or greedy or wrong in some way); or (3) feel frustrated because you want to serve a population that really needs what you have to offer but may not be able to afford it; this can be combined with a tension that comes from your own financial inability to offer it for free. In all these scenarios, capitalism becomes the villain because it's at odds with a set of values that underscore the notion that none of the former realities should exist at all.

If you dig into your own internal conversations, which root is most relatable to you? The clearer you are on what you believe, the greater your opportunity to make crucial choices that allow you to preserve your values and simultaneously make the money your calling deserves.

Your Call

Are you ready to put your conscious creation skills to work on transforming and/or expanding your financial reality? Let's start with two practices and two exercises to help you recognize what is ruling your current thoughts on money—and which ones may even be getting in the way.

PRACTICE 1: MONEY MANTRA

"I am taking my rightful place as a conscious creator of my own economy."

For the next two weeks, repeat this mantra at least five times a day, especially when you are in the middle of a money or business transaction. Notice how it shifts the quality of the exchange. Begin by speaking the mantra first thing in the A.M. as a way to ground yourself in your new commitment and then throughout the day as suggested earlier. Then finally, do it again in the evening after you prepare for bed, come back to the mirror, and look at yourself and repeat the mantra. Feel your own conscious creation powers at work every time you say these words.

PRACTICE 2: RECIPROCITY EXERCISE

All day long, our time is filled with financial interactions of every kind. For the next two weeks, when you're handling your business, no matter how big or small the task, practice conscious giving and conscious receiving. When you're giving money, give with your full presence and heart. Notice what it feels like to be totally aligned with your purchase and what it feels like when you are not fully aligned. When you are receiving, notice what it feels like to receive with your full presence and heart, plus the times when you have difficulty receiving. Keep a daily evening journal about your experience.

EXERCISE 1: UNDERSTAND YOUR RELATIONSHIP TO MONEY

To do this, answer the six questions found on the "Understanding Your Relationship with Money" worksheet (see next page). Use these responses to create a road map for helping to transform your current relationship to one that fully empowers you. If you already feel empowered, use this exercise as an affirmation for those visions, insights, and beliefs that you want to take with you. You can download this worksheet at www.movethecrowd.me/TheCalling/resources.

EXERCISE 2: TOP FIVE CONVERSATIONS

Review your top five conversations from Question 2 in the "Understanding Your Relationship to Money" worksheet. Refine them as needed to be sure you're capturing your inner dialogue verbatim. Hold on to these answers, because we'll revisit them in the next chapter.

MOVETHECROWD

INSIGHTS ON HOW YOU HANDLE YOUR BUSINESS

1. How do you define capitalism?

_____
_____
_____

2. What is your personal relationship to capitalism and what are the Top 5 conversations you
   have with yourself about your business and/or money transactions?

_____
_____
_____

3. What are the sources of these conversations? Where or how did you inherit them? (for example, media, messages you received growing up, etc.)

_____
_____
_____

4. If you had your way, what would you like to experience in your business and/or money transactions? What is your vision for the way you'd like to do business as an entrepreneur? As a
   client or customer?

_____
_____
_____

5. What would professional success look like for you at this stage in your life?

_____
_____
_____

6. How do the Top 5 conversations you identified in question 2 either support or hinder your
   success?

_____
_____
_____

The activities contained in this document are designed exclusively for Move The Crowd, LLC. Copying, duplicating, or otherwise
reproducing in any form is prohibited. © 2012 All rights reserved.

8

Step #2: Accepting Responsibility for Your Current Financial State

When you take a look at the conversations you've inherited around money, as I mentioned in the last chapter, you may be surprised and very emotional about what you find. It can be hard to face your inner dialogue and see all the ways you may have been negatively influenced by family, friends, and society—and it may be even more challenging to own all of the ways you've taken these messages to heart. When you do see the truth, it can be really hard not to blame others, beat up on yourself, or feel resigned to doing nothing because fixing it feels overwhelming.

Taking responsibility for your current financial state can be difficult, no matter how much money you're making. This sense of "lack" may have nothing to do with what's in your bank account. I've known people with incredible wealth panic about a shift in the market, and I've had people with no shoes welcome me into their shack as if it were the Taj Mahal. Digging beneath the psychological and emotional wounds that limiting perceptions around money can inflict is imperative to creating a new Get Paid reality. People love to skip this part, so bear with me as I lovingly hold your feet to the fire; if we don't go here, you could unwittingly create more of the same and never bring your true calling to fruition, much less to a financially rewarding fruition.

If you are financially struggling, this is an awesome opportunity to begin to take your power back from an inherited economy that may not be serving you. Accepting responsibility for the state of your finances, while staying away from a standpoint of victimhood, can be one of the toughest challenges you'll face—especially when you consider the state of our world and the fact that more than half the world lives on only two dollars a day. And did I mention that 1 percent of the world's population controls over 20 percent of the wealth? There is too much messaging out there that can create fear, anger, and uncertainty around your current and future financial states. Don't let it take up room in your psyche, in your heart, or in your potential to do your thing.

The true work here is to look at what you believe while resisting the urge to resort to the four Binding Behaviors we've discussed in the past—complaining, blaming/judging, justifying, and/or avoiding. Remember, this only keeps you stuck in your old reality. Acceptance is about becoming an observer of what's going on. That means you're facing it, embracing it, and telling the truth about everything that's working for you *and* owning your role in it once and for all.

Being powerfully and purposefully aligned with your money goals is the ultimate game changer when it comes to pursuing your calling. In fact, this is the number one reason that most of us compromise our visions—we don't believe we can do the work we feel most passionate about and feed our families doing it. This is also the lie that keeps so many of us from our truest selves and our highest contributions.

In this chapter, you'll have the chance to examine your Greatest Money Hits (drawn from your top five conversations) and the subsequent impact those hits have had on your current finances. We'll delve into the source of these messages so you can see your most prominent money influences up close and personal. For those who may feel confident about what you're earning, there may be other aspects of your financial reality that warrant examination. Beyond the discussion of what you have or don't have is the foundation of what governs how you feel about money and choose to view it. And just like what we believe about ourselves, what we believe about money is loaded. Telling the truth about it isn't easy. However, the more we become aware of what drives these decisions, the more options we have for transforming it.

Getting Clear About Your Current Financial State

In the last chapter, you identified the top five conversations you have with yourself about your money and business transactions as you began to explore your relationship with money. When it comes to "the almighty green," noting your inner dialogue can be tricky because your feelings are so deeply ingrained and move through your mind so instinctually! Let's do this as thoughtfully as we can.

Think back to the top five you identified in the last chapter, and pay particular attention to how you feel when you talk about each one, because these can be important clues about beliefs that need shifting. Remember, your current financial state is less about what you have or don't have and more about the underlying beliefs and perceptions that consume your inner dialogue and produce the kinds of experiences that leave you either empowered or feeling like a victim.

Let's try a quick exercise. Below are a series of questions related to most people's top five conversations that I'd love for you to mentally answer; just quickly observe how you respond. As you do, notice which are easy to answer and which give you pause. Notice which elicit a joyful response and which cause frustration. What top one or two conversations shape your current money reality? Remember, your Greatest Money Hits are topics that stay on heavy rotation, whether they're part of every sentence or whirring in the background; either way, they run the show.

Conversation #1: Earning money. Think about how and what you earn and how that makes you feel. For example, when it comes to earning money, what immediately comes to mind? And how is that reflected in your bank account? What do you tell yourself about what you have to do to earn money? And how is that reflected in how you make your money?

Conversation #2: How you spend your money. What do you tell yourself as you write out checks and throw down your credit card? And how does that reflect in your monthly expenses? Do you have a judgment about how much you should be spending? And how does that influence the way you approach future expenses and paying your bills?

Conversation #3: Saving money. This is always a touchy subject. When it comes to saving money, do you have an opinion about what you should or should not be doing? And how is that reflected in your savings account? What do you tell yourself when you stick, or don't stick, to your saving beliefs?

Consider your relationship to giving money, as well. What do you tell yourself about this practice, and how does it impact your actions? On average, how much do you donate every year? How do you feel when you give? What do you say to yourself when you don't give?

Conversation #4: Investing. What's your take on it—and is this even part of your inner dialogue? If so, what do you invest in, and how would you describe the state of your current investments?

Lending and borrowing money is also a very personal subject. Do you find yourself in a position to do either of these with any frequency? How do you relate to this topic? Do you have debt? Do others owe you money?

Conversation #5: Your feelings around contracts and formal agreements. What do you tell yourself about your formal business and/or money transactions? Do you deal with these often?

Real talk—we can all get a little funny about money, and my client Victoria was no exception. When Victoria and I began working together, one of her big goals was to double her income as a thought leader and convener in the women's leadership and empowerment space. She had already built a wonderful business coaching nonprofit leaders and hosting women's gatherings, and she was ready to envision the next level of her business—though she wasn't quite sure what this meant. She'd been approached by some well-known consumer brands about a number of opportunities that would allow her to grow, but she knew that what was missing was a clear, overarching vision that would (1) articulate all that she was already doing and (2) help her get clear about which direction she wanted to take. Victoria needed me to help her clarify her brand and develop her growth strategy, so we got right to work.

We met at a trendy work space in midtown Manhattan. As we dove into Victoria's professional milestones and true nature, I wanted to encourage her to speak her full vision: "I live to support powerful women leaders who want to make a difference in the world—this is our time!" And this was her calling. As we turned to the elements of her business model, I wanted to get a sense of how she felt about her current offerings: "I love bringing powerful women together, challenging their thinking, and advising them on how they can make an even greater difference through the missions of their respective organizations. Whether that's serving more people or introducing a new solution around their issue."

Victoria was a masterful networker and her events were always well attended. And because these aspects brought her so much joy, I knew they needed to continue being part of her Get Paid strategy.

"Imagine yourself five years from now, standing in a gorgeous venue, wearing a beautiful dress, and raising a big glass of champagne—what are you celebrating?"

As she gave voice to where she saw the business in five years, Victoria was bold, confident, and really clear about the size and magnitude of the impact she wanted to have: "I want to be touching millions of women leaders, I want branded collaborations that earn me tens of millions of dollars, and I want to be celebrating my second *New York Times* bestseller."

However, when Victoria talked about her current finances, she became a totally different person. She was tentative, doubtful, and full of criticism—about herself and others.

"Everything is so expensive," she said, "but, you have to spend if you want to do it right. I make good money, but I'm not really paying myself."

"Really?!" I asked. "Can you show me your profit and loss statement? I'd love to get a feel for where the money is currently going."

She sighed. "I don't have a clear way of tracking what's coming in and going out right now."

"Why not?" I asked.

She shrugged. "I've been so busy doing all of the other things to make the business work that I just haven't had time."

So I gave her a homework assignment: "Listen, I don't care if it's a simple spreadsheet—do your best to jot down what you've earned and spent this year to date and let's see where you are."

Two weeks later, she sent me a spreadsheet that didn't make any sense. This had nothing to do with Victoria not finding time to plug in a few numbers but everything to do with her internal dialogue and the way she generally viewed money and doing business. This was what was getting in the way of her financial liberation!

"I've looked at what you've sent me, and I can tell you, you're not going to be able to fully receive all of the success we've outlined in your five-year vision without adjusting your financial reality." I set up an extended working session, and we took it line by line—three sessions later, we finally finished one spreadsheet. Along the way, we tracked all the conversations that bubbled up—comments like, "I'm not good with money," and, "I have so much to do, I just can't get to all of this, too." Victoria and I had to confront and clean up her current financial state, and her views on finances foremost, as the first step toward her growth strategy.

Through lots of excuses and tears, we finally got to the bottom of why Victoria's finances were a hot mess. She did not feel worthy of being this rock-star go-to brand for women leaders (hello, Root Cause #2—"I am not worthy"): "It's easy for me to attract clients who are willing to pay me for my skills. This work is my passion and so it comes so easily to me, I feel guilty sometimes charging for it. But then, when I look at all of my expenses, I feel like I can justify it."

In fact, each time Victoria brought in a new client, she found a reason to immediately spend the money they paid her because just having it in her account made her uncomfortable! *Who am I to be coaching these incredible women?* she'd think. Doubting her own value kept her from being able to accept and hold on to the money. "We've gotta heal this, my love, before you grow the money, because if we don't you're just going to have more of the same. Bigger numbers, but messy finances with no profit."

As we worked on her feelings of unworthiness, she saw the root of her Greatest Money Hit: "I know where this feeling of unworthiness comes from," she said. "You know, growing up, my parents made lots of money, but my mother always complained about not having enough no matter how well her real estate business was doing." She paused. "My father would give me a particular monthly allowance and I remember one day in frustration she turned to me and said, 'Why should you get all that money? What do you do around here?'" Victoria literally gasped when she remembered this incident. Tears rolled down her cheeks and she shook her head. "Wow. This has nothing to do with me. I love my mom, but this is her struggle, not mine."

"Amen!" I replied.

After that realization, Victoria became open to paying herself more. We worked on her spreadsheet, and sure enough, as we challenged those limiting conversations about her worthiness and brought order to Victoria's finances, more money rolled in. The difference now is that when the money comes in, Victoria is ready to fully receive it—and make more conscious decisions about paying herself and saving up to start the next phase of her growth strategy, which we've determined is a more formalized sales process for her clients.

Fast-forward to three months later, Victoria was on track to *quadruple* her prior year's earnings. She was over the moon and crying like a baby—but this time, her tears were full of joy!

Often when I introduce the mindset work with clients around their finances, I can encounter skepticism, but it is, by far, the most game-changing aspect of working with money. Your money story is important, and it's as much about the narrative as the numbers.

What's Your Money Persona?

When it comes to our personal accounts and/or business transactions, each of us has a persona that we've developed over time. And our Greatest Money Hits serve as the soundtrack to our persona's starring role in our finances.

So when *you* examine your current finances and consider the choices that have gotten you here, who do you see? Is it a person who's empowered, capable, and engaging in ways that are aligned with their values? Or do you see someone barely treading water? Do you see a person who must know and control every single detail? Or do you find someone who hardly ever looks at their checkbook? Now, when you consider your new commitment to getting paid in a way that aligns with your true nature and highest calling, who do you *want* to be? Your relationship to your financial self is the next important frontier that needs to be explored in your quest for liberation.

As with the notion of success, there are many cultural messages out there about what you must do to make money—and it often comes with compromise. Think of all the times you or someone you know has said, "I don't want to do it, but, I need the money," or, "This person is a nightmare to deal with, but they pay good money, so . . ." The idea that earning money involves a trade or compromise of some kind is part of most financial conversations we have. And it's this trade that takes away our power. We feel we're trading time, convenience, and even our own dignity or self-respect for dollars. You could argue that we've created a world where money is more important than human life, and as much as we point to those in power and blame them for this state of affairs, we submit to this ideology, whether we're aware of it or not. And if we submit, that means we participate. Combine this with so little education around finances and you get a society willing to compromise itself at every turn to keep the lights on. Whether that person wears a standard-issue uniform or a Brooks Brothers suit, their inner dialogue is the same.

So are you conforming or resisting? In my experience, the answer is often a little of both. You may conform when it comes to earning—meaning, you are willing to "trade" to have a particular quality of life or amass a certain amount of wealth. But when it comes to spending money, you may opt to share your finances in a way that demonstrates real love and generosity to loved ones, your community, or organizations and institutions that matter to you. On the flip side, you may choose to resist higher earnings and not make a lot of money—opting for meaningful work over a fat paycheck. This means you're working with fewer financial resources but may also be working long hours or neglecting your self-care. There's still a trade-off, and this becomes part of your identity and how you see yourself in relationship to money. Making any aspect of your finances part of your identity also makes it feel harder to change.

When I began working with my client Steven, he was at the top of his game in the hospitality business. He worked for a chain of gorgeous boutique hotels that were considered *the* places to stay by A-list celebrities and hotshot CEOs. As a director of marketing, he was tasked with coming up with innovative campaigns that would keep the chain on the cutting edge of the industry and earn them awesome press in the travel and leisure pages. Though Steven was great at his job, he was over the politics and bored to death with the creative constraints that his parent company placed on the brand. Steven went to work every day but wasn't fully energized or engaged in his role. He spent so much time working through various levels of bureaucracy—asking for permission, getting approval, and smoothing ruffled feathers—that by the time an idea got the green light, either he'd missed a window of opportunity or the idea was a shell of its former self and not exciting anymore. At the same time, Steven was in the process of his own spiritual awakening and one of the big realizations he'd come to was that he was ready to step out and create his own thing. He envisioned a cutting-edge creative shop that would leverage the various aspects of culture to service the biggest brands on the planet. The problem is, he was plagued by tons of fear and doubt. Our work was to get to the heart of what was holding Steven back so that he could make some important decisions about his future.

As we began to unpack his limiting conversations, Steven and I naturally bumped up against his financial self. Steven had come from a modest working-class family and watched his father struggle to put food on the table. He worked in construction and would often drag himself into the house at the end of the day, dead tired. Steven loved his father but was starving for his approval and attention. When Steven got his job at the hotel, his father was proud. He told me that his dad said, "Good job! Now you won't have to get your hands filthy like me. With a gig like this you can really make something of yourself." Though now that Steven had decided to go out on his own, his first worry wasn't about his own money but how he'd break the news to his dad that he'd given up a cushy job to grapple with the uncertainty of starting a new venture, and all because he wanted to be more creative. "He's going to think I've lost my mind," he told me.

As we delved deeper into Steven's relationship with money, I learned that he made a great income but spent a lot. He felt the need to portray a certain image to maintain the perceived status he'd achieved when he hung out with his family and friends. This meant fancy watches, big vacations, a super-nice car, and cool clothes. And while he swore he didn't care about any of that stuff, so much pretending made a real dent in his finances and stood in the way of his ability to build the kind of nest egg that could sustain him through his new venture's start-up.

When I asked Steven, "Who's really spending all this money?" he was confused at first; then he said, "It's the little boy who always wanted his father's attention." Tears welled up in his eyes. "I feel like I'm spending all of this money just to say, 'Look at me! I'm finally somebody.'"

As he moved deeper into this realization, his Greatest Money Hits began to emerge. He felt like a nobody from Iowa, and having this cushy job in the big city had become an integral part of his coming-up story. But weeks later when we met again, Steven was ready to turn it around. He created a spreadsheet detailing how much he'd need to sustain himself for a year. "This is awesome!" I said. "Now let's map out the rest of the plan." We banged out all the details of a transition plan to help him create a high-integrity move, financially and professionally.

Before wrapping up, Steven said he'd talked to his brother about his father's potential impression of the move: "We don't ever talk about much, but this time I really poured my heart out about our dad. And I asked him if he had the same fear." Turns out, he was more insightful than Steven had imagined. "Bro," he said. "Dad loves you and he was miserable working that construction job. What he wants for you, more than anything, is for you to be happy."

"And who do you want to be?" I asked Steven.

He looked me in the eye and said, "I want to be *me*—courageously happy, free, and authentically me."

Confronting your financial self helps you determine if you still feel the need to succumb to social conditioning or if you're ready to forge a new path. When you reflect on your five root causes from chapter 7, know that each root conversation breeds a financial persona. And when more than one root conversation is operating, it's easy to fold these into an identity that can cause a ton of internal conflict and strife when it comes to how you handle your money. Whether it's about how you earn, spend, lend, or invest, each aspect deserves scrutiny. Every financial decision speaks to the heart of who you are when it comes to what you believe is possible.

Identifying Your Most Prominent
Money Influences

Just as your Greatest Money Hits unearth your most prominent money conversations, they also reveal your most prominent money influences. Whether it's your hardworking grandma or jet-setting neighbor, your money influences tell you a lot about what you value and believe is important when it comes to how you Get Paid.

Many years ago when the financial training industry exploded, there was a common belief that your finances reflected the top five people you spent most of your time with. This caused many people to look around and consider if the people in their life were inspiring them to grow— not only mentally, spiritually, and emotionally but financially, too. When this stat came out, I remember trying to sort out what it meant for me as the leader of a nonprofit organization at the time. If my finances weren't up to snuff, should I abandon my work? Get a whole new set of friends? Does wanting to be around more financially savvy people make me a snob? How do I feel about those who have money? How do I feel about those who are struggling to make ends meet? Is money the only thing that is important to me when it comes to the people in my life?

As you know by now, you have multiple influences on how you make money. But to this stat's point, when I consider my influences now, they are completely different from those I inherited while growing up. I am also aware of how deliberate I have been at changing those influences, not to mention how challenging it's been to keep those more empowering influences front and center, given all of the mainstream conditioning each of us is exposed to day in and day out.

I've seen this stat play out in real time, too. When I started working with my client Taylor around her Get Paid, I was so excited to dig in— this collaboration was a long time coming. I had known Taylor through my work in the creative activist community for many years, and I had a deep admiration and respect for her company's work. She was super-smart, compassionate, dedicated, and incredibly talented. Her work produced meaningful events and experiences for organizations and individuals that were passionate about social change, which I found truly inspiring.

The possibility of working together began at a reception for a mutual colleague. We were standing there, beverages in hand, catching up, when Taylor tilted her head to the side and said, "Things are going good, but I think I need to come work with you."

My face lit up with excitement: "I would love to work with you!" For me, Taylor was the epitome of the kind of leader I most wanted to serve. And I knew that if she could operate from a more abundant place, so many more people and organizations would thrive and prosper as a result.

Taylor and I talked on and off for two years, and in every conversation I could hear her challenge her own skepticism and ingrained beliefs about whether she could actually create a different financial reality for herself. "A lot of people pretend to be doing really well," she said, "but when you get down to it, not much has really changed around their finances. It makes me wonder if it's really possible." Taylor wanted to know more about my personal journey and how I was able to make the shift.

"I had to become adamant about it," I said. "I had to commit to myself that I was going to take responsibility for my life and challenge every limiting conversation I had about money and doing business." As we discussed my process, I could feel Taylor's simultaneous excitement and reluctance. "Why does the idea of getting paid really well to do this work feel so foreign to you?" I asked.

She said, "Because I don't personally know anyone who's really done it." I knew then that for Taylor to really buy in, she had to see it up close and personal. I also understood her need, because I knew she operated with a very high moral standard. And because I came from a similar history, I knew we'd been taught as activists that you had to trade, and many of us who had taken the road of resistance to capitalism did trade—our health, financial stability, free time, you name it.

So what excited me most was that I could totally relate to her journey. "Before we create the plan for your finances," I told her, "we've got to take a look at all of what's influencing your current state. I want you to see what's operating, so that you can make some choices about which conversations will support you in moving forward." We began with her parents, who immigrated to this country with her older brother before she was born.

"My parents worked really hard to make ends meet, and they made a lot of sacrifices along the way to ensure my siblings and I got a great education. I was good in school, and as a result, I won a number of scholarships to support my college education." I could see her reflecting back. "I was always aware of my parents' sacrifices, as well as the additional support I got from various organizations and foundations. This was one of the reasons why I was so passionate about giving back." She looked off for a moment. "When I first came out of school, I had offers to work in corporate, but I opted to go into the nonprofit sector where the expectation is to work hard and make lots of sacrifices to ensure others have access to the same opportunities I did." Taylor was very practical, and as a seasoned nonprofit professional, she understood the way the world of philanthropy worked. "There's always a negotiation between what foundations are interested in funding, and the work that actually needs to happen in the community—you come to expect it after a while. But . . ." she paused. "There comes a moment when you start looking at all of the compromising and begin to ask yourself, is it really worth it? There is so much scarcity in the nonprofit world."

"What's having you finally decide to explore another way?" I asked.

"I don't think I'm doing my best work. I know what that work is, but because of all of these experiences I know I'm not dreaming big enough. There's so much I want to do and I ain't getting any younger." She laughed, I laughed, too, because she is one of the most gorgeous women I know—inside and out. "The big question for me is, Can I get paid for this?"

When I asked Taylor to think back to herself as a child, she remembered herself as a very talented visual artist who had decided to give up her craft for something more "practical." And because of the nonprofit world she immersed herself in, she was surrounded by tons of people who had done the same thing. Just by virtue of being in her community, Taylor only knew those who either tried and financially failed or had been conditioned to play it safe.

"We've got to take the lid off," I told her. "You need to see more examples of amazing creatives just like you who are doing it! And when I say 'doing it,' I mean they're leveraging their creative talents through very profitable strategies." Taylor welcomed these examples like a breath of fresh air. She began to develop a bold new vision for the next chapter of her life, and one part of our financial strategy for her was to help her find new circles to engage in and to spend time with creatives who were more entrepreneurial in their strategies and their thinking.

"I want you to see these strategies operating in the day-to-day, so that you can be inspired by having greater insight about the inner workings of these models and allow that to start informing your own changes."

"Oooh," she said, "I would love that."

So I went to work, introducing her to a number of our amazing entrepreneurs, people who were definitely making it happen on their own terms; of course, Anna, Heather, and Z were among them. Finally, we set the goal to double her earned income. "I want to increase your capacity to earn and receive more," I explained. "I want you to see earning as an affirmation that having multiple forms of financing is a sign of fiscal strength."

We then reexamined all that she had inherited so that she could determine which influences would continue to serve her versus which would have to be retired.

"I can't do the hard-labor nonprofit model with little return anymore."

"I hear you loud and clear!" I said.

Taylor told me that what she most wanted to offer were creative and artistic experiences that helped women recover from physical and psychological abuse, but she was unsure if there was a market for it. Here meeting people with other success stories in the creative and social impact world proved helpful. In addition to introducing her to Heather and

Anna, I took her through a series of case studies, where she'd exclaim, "Wow! These folks are doing it!" Now, armed with new inspiration, her confidence grew, and Taylor set out to create her own model with no trade or swap necessary.

What's so great about the process of reviewing your influences is that you get to make a conscious choice about who and what will empower your calling and allow you to Get Paid for it. Remember, no matter what's going on in your finances, you always have the opportunity to move your money into greater alignment with your true self and with your true calling.

At the end of the day, the decisions we make every day in the name of the almighty dollar can be overwhelming and even traumatic when we face them. But when you can step inside of them and look around, you give yourself far more room to choose whether you want to continue with the current state or you'd like to take a different route to honor your calling. There is no need for fear or doubt, no reason to not accept responsibility for where you are and how you got there. The self-examination process will only lead you closer to where you're meant to be—serving others from your greatest gifts and vision and not feeling hamstrung by finances.

Your Call

Are you ready to take responsibility for your financial reality? Two practices and two exercises should be implemented over the next two weeks to help you recognize and own your Greatest Money Hits. You'll also have the powerful opportunity to practice freeing yourself from the beliefs that may be standing in the way of you and your money.

PRACTICE 1

"I am ready to take responsibility for my current financial state."
"My money is my responsibility."

Let's work with the following mantras for the next two weeks. Select the one that really speaks to you. Use it through all of your money and/or business-related transactions. Notice what happens when you speak the mantra before you finalize a financial decision, versus when you make a financial decision running on "automatic pilot." Even if the decision is the same, do you feel differently when you take a moment to consciously claim responsibility? Paying attention to how you feel and act when you speak your chosen mantra is super-important to observe, so you may want to write it down.

PRACTICE 2

Identify one new money influence that you'd like to bring into your awareness. Log on to www.movethecrowd.me/TheCalling/resources for my Money Mentors Top 10 Annotated Bibliography.

EXERCISE 1: EXAMINING YOUR MONEY PERSONA

As you reflect on this idea, what do you notice about yourself? When it comes to your money persona, where are you conforming, where are you resisting, and where are you creating and forging your own path? As you become aware of who you are ask yourself who you want to be. Write down the vision for that persona and take it with you into the next chapter.

EXERCISE 2: TAKING STOCK OF YOUR CURRENT MONEY INFLUENCES

Who are your most influential teachers when it comes to money? What are the specific messages coming from each source? Notice if those messages feel empowering to you (or not). Write these messages in your journal, verbatim, and evaluate whether you'd like to keep or let go of them based on whether they will serve and support your calling.

9

Step #3: Forgiving the Constraints of Your Financial Past

As you face your current financial reality, you might, on some level, feel like a failure because you know that you're not following your true dreams or living up to your full potential or even earning as much money as you would like. And odds are, you may be having a really tough time resisting the urge to engage in those blessed Binding Behaviors also known as the famous four—complaining, blaming/judging, justifying, and avoiding—for every one of your sufferings. But until you're fed up enough to stop playing small, hiding out, or making excuses for the fact that whatever you're doing is not working, you won't follow through on any potential solution, no matter how much help you receive; and as a result, money will continue to be a major obstacle to pursuing your calling.

The beautiful truth is that actually telling it like it is—especially to yourself—gives way to so much possibility. Once you are willing to own it, you can make peace with your soul and let it go. Which brings us back to the subject of forgiveness. Whatever you have done or not done, or whatever you've unjustly experienced in the name of money, now is the time to release those feelings around those incidents and make room to create something new. Whoever has hurt you in the domain of business and/or finances, now is the time to end their energetic grip on your happiness and put it behind you. You may need to take specific actions like ending the partnership or renegotiating an existing agreement or even potentially taking them to court—but the drain on your mind, body, and spirit ends now.

In this chapter, you'll discover all the ways you may have compromised your true self in the name of money. And you'll have a chance to forgive everything that stands in the way of realizing your full Get Paid potential. From your own limiting conversations to those you've inherited from family, friends, community, and our global culture, you'll confront any form of scarcity that is operating in your life and decide just how ready you are to show these limiting conversations the door. We'll also get underneath your Greatest Money Hit by identifying and transforming your corresponding root cause, whether it's (1) "There is not enough," (2) "I am not worthy," (3) "I might be changed," (4) "I'm afraid of what it's going to take," or (5) "I've got issues with capitalism." Finally, you'll make peace with yourself and your past to make room for more abundance—not only in your bank account but in your mind, heart, and soul, too.

Facing Your Financial History

So many of us feel fear, shame, anger, and even guilt when we confront our financial past and often don't seek the support we need in order to transform those emotions. We have demons that haunt us about what others have put us through and what we have believed about money, not to mention our potential judgments about our (in)ability to live abundantly—both financially and personally—in the world. But I want you to know, you have the capability to turn anything around. And the actions you may need to take to do so become so much easier once you've forgiven not just everyone else but yourself most of all. You would be amazed at the clarity and joy that returns when you are able to release all the drama and self-judgment around your finances. Can you believe that you did the best you could with what you had? Can you consider that same is true for others—say, your partner, your boss, your spouse—even if their actions had a negative impact on your financial reality? And if you genuinely believe you've been wronged in the money department, can you free yourself from the emotional bondage while still taking the necessary steps to address what happened?

To achieve the kind of financial empowerment that is in alignment with your true self and highest calling, you've got to forgive anything that may be holding you back from fully receiving all the good you desire and that naturally wants to move toward you. Fear, anger, anxiety, and doubt can all block your flow. Meanwhile courage, clarity, creativity, generosity, dedication, and integrity can move you toward your most authentic self and your highest contribution.

From Scarcity to Abundance

When you consider all the financial obstacles you may have faced over the course of your life and how they've influenced the limiting decisions you've made, I'd bet that some form of scarcity was the cause. Now when I talk scarcity, I'm not referring to the physical manifestation of less but the internal belief system that makes you feel a sense of desperation—whether it's around something you have or something you want. Every one of us has been conditioned to operate from a place of scarcity around something. It is baked into the DNA of how our global society is structured. The deeply ingrained belief of not having enough or being enough or deserving enough permeates every facet of our lives, from the way we structure our institutions (there is only a certain type of people who can get in) to how we organize leisure activities (there are only a certain number of people who can afford to do this). They mirror a capitalistic culture that insists there's a fundamental hierarchy, and thus disparity, when it comes to determining who "gets ahead" and who's entitled to experience the happiness and fulfillment that life has to offer. Even when you come from a place of financial wealth, depending upon how that wealth is acquired, you can also experience the same feelings of lack because you did not "earn" it, so therefore, you might resist it or even resent it—as you become present to how much the rest of the world struggles.

Feelings of scarcity can be painful, because it's often paired with tons of judgment, whether it's about having too little money or not enough friends. This is because, at a fundamental level, you believe the lie that says you're somehow lacking as a person and therefore must struggle, suffer, or prove yourself on all levels, including when it comes to money. The most damaging messages we receive can cause us to separate from ourselves and act out in ways that are hostile and violent. And whether those actions are directed inward or outward, they cause us to abandon our connection to our own humanity, which makes it very difficult to recognize the humanity in others. When our humanity is abandoned, we can become cruel and dispassionate or numb and checked out to what is happening in our lives and in the world around us. These kinds of behaviors actually pose the biggest threat to our greatest contribution.

However, identifying and transforming your own Greatest Money Hits and underlying root cause(s) will make room for a completely new reality. One where you are profoundly connected to who you are, why you are here, and what you are being called to do. This is the basis of your Get Paid ethos. You know there is enough, that you are enough, and that whatever you want to achieve that is in alignment with your highest good is available to you.

When you've been financially hurt, moving on isn't easy. But it is possible. In the hundreds of conversations we have every year with potential prospects for our True. Paid. Good. Academy, I can tell you that shame, vulnerability, guilt, and ultimately courage show up enormously when we talk finances. I'll never forget the opportunity I had to witness real courage with my client Giana. She came to me at the behest of a dear celebrity client. "You need Rha!" my client told her. Giana was a brilliant psychology professor with a private practice helping people with severe anxiety disorders. She was also in the midst of getting divorced from her husband of seven years. "I knew the marriage was over about three years in, but I was too afraid to end it," she said when we came together in my LA retreat space.

"Why did you hold on for so long?"

She looked at me and said, "Because he made most of the money and I believed I could not financially survive without him." Giana and her husband had three children, and when she calculated what it would cost to support a life without her spouse her finances came up short.

"You know, you are not alone. So many people, women in particular, come up against this challenge and it's often the reason why they stay in unhealthy relationships and ultimately don't pursue their purpose."

"Tell me about it," Giana replied. She went on to say that the fact that her husband was the major breadwinner was a very sore point in the marriage. "He constantly reminded me of that fact that he was the one making most of the money. And because of this, I became insecure about my ability to earn more," she said.

During our first meeting, Giana spent a lot of time and energy re-hashing how powerless she felt in the situation. And for as much anger as she held toward her husband, she was even more angry at herself because she'd allowed herself to become a prisoner to her circumstances. "I don't know why I let the things he said cause me to doubt myself. I should have left years ago," she told me.

"It's important for us to understand what's having you financially doubt," I said. "So let's get into it." When I took Giana through the exercise of understanding her relationship to money and the economy that I discussed in chapter 7, she was able to quickly identify her Greatest Money Hit: "I can't make enough to support me and the kids." (Root Cause #1—"There is not enough.")

As we dug deeper, she revised her hit more explicitly to become "I can't make enough to support me and the kids doing what I love." She continued, "Having to trade the only other thing that brought me joy beyond the kids, which was my work, in order to empower myself financially also felt debilitating." As it turned out, Giana had watched an aunt she deeply admired give up a career she loved working in a museum so that she could support her children after leaving her husband of 11 years. "She just wasn't the same after that," she recalled. "It was like she'd given up this huge part of herself and instead picked up this tough, no-nonsense persona. The thing that was supposed to make her happy—freeing herself from the marriage—ultimately wound up robbing her of the very joy she tried to seek."

"I hear you. But you are not your aunt," I reminded her. "Or at least, you don't have to be." I paused and she nodded, taking it in. "And recognizing the hurt, anger, and disappointment you felt around your aunt's choice can also help you recognize the hurt, anger, and disappointment you've felt toward yourself." I asked Giana, *just before I ducked!* (LOL), "Are you willing to let some of the anger toward your husband, aunt, and yourself go in exchange for a more joyful existence?" When it comes to the question of forgiveness, I always ask how much one is willing to let go on a scale of 1–10. There should be no judgment about the answer. Rating this simply helps us see how deep the wound is. At this point, Giana sat up and said, "I'm at an eight! Okay, I think I'm done crying and whining about this. I want my mojo back!" That's my girl.

Giana went to work using the four-step forgiveness process. As she became even more aware of her aunt's choices and circumstances, she began to notice similar patterns of behavior playing out in other women in her family, including her older sister. Seeing this as a "legacy" issue gave Giana even more courage and determination to break the cycle: "Wow. This is what the women in my family do!" She shook her head. "Well, I'm not trading my happiness for anything or anyone else anymore," she told me. "I know I'll be an even better mom if I'm fulfilled inside." At that point, we began to explore how Giana could forgive her past and see her choice to leave as an act of self-love and liberation. Then, it was all about the money, honey! So, we also looked at how she could bring in the kind of revenue that would make her smile, doing what she loved while still having plenty of time to be present for her beautiful children.

It wasn't long before Giana told me, "Creating a media brand that focuses on healing the causes of stress and emotional anxiety is what I want to put my attention on, not how much child support I'm going to get in the divorce settlement." She went on, "I know my husband loves our kids and will do the right thing. But even if that's not enough, I want to feel confident that I've got them." Once we created the plan, Giana was on fire; she redesigned her solo client offerings, launched a group offering, raised the prices on her more intensive therapies, and updated her gorgeous website to reflect all of the above. Within six months she was not only covering her expenses but also able to start contributing a little to a savings account. When I saw her three months after we completed our work, Giana looked amazing! She was vibrant, lighthearted, and laughing as we hugged on the street. "Thank you," she said.

"My honor," I replied.

Though we don't say it out loud, so many of us have resigned ourselves to the fact that life is a struggle, that pain/suffering/self-sacrifice, especially when it comes to money, is necessary and this is the ultimate form of scarcity. Facing and forgiving our financial past allows us to regain so much of our true strength and power—and for that reason, I'm adamant about helping you let go of any kind of limiting story that stands in the way of you and your calling.

Transforming Your Root Causes

When you do the courageous work of identifying your Greatest Money Hits and underlying root cause(s), you can transform and forgive any form of scarcity in your life. Remember, your root cause is the mother weed that holds your Greatest Money Hit in place—and when you yank that weed, you'll feel reborn around that issue. As I walk you through the forgiveness process this time, take a moment to feel the power you have to heal the constraints of your financial past in honor of a new Get Paid reality.

For the following four-step forgiveness ritual I'd like you to work with your #1 Greatest Money Hit and one underlying root cause.

Forgiveness ➞ as an Act of Sacred Re-membering

As you consider the origins of your Greatest Money Hit, I want you to select one incident that really stands out for you. What happened? What occurred for you in that incident and what was the impact it had on you? How did it make you feel? About yourself? About the world? About other people? How has it contributed to your underlying root cause? Is there an aspect of what happened that you need to take responsibility for? If so, what is it? What part of you needs to be cared for as a result of this experience? Are you ready to reclaim your power over this incident? Are you ready to remember who you are? You are whole.

Forgiveness ➞ as an Act of Completion

As you examine this incident and all of the ways that it has affected you, are you ready to identify the lesson and acknowledge and express the feelings associated with what happened? Whether you write about it, talk it out with a trusted friend, or sit in nature and bare your soul to the universe, this is your opportunity to energetically release any negative thoughts that have been holding you back from your greatest contribution and keeping you stuck in an emotional loop of anger, shame, guilt, sadness, or frustration. Also, are there any specific actions you need to take for yourself or with others to complete this? Get clear about what those are and make a list. Commit to yourself that over the next thirty days you'll take the actions you need to take to get this resolved. Finally, as you come face-to-face with your learning, you get to appreciate all of the ways that this challenge has strengthened and enlightened you. Stand in gratitude as you declare this incident as done! You're ready to look forward, not back. You are complete.

Forgiveness → as an Act of Liberation

Now that you've chosen to put this incident behind you, consider how you want to make money and handle your finances moving forward as your true self. The slate is clean now. You are free from the limitations of that incident. You now have the opportunity to create a whole new experience for yourself that is not linked to anything that's happened before. Feel your creative power in this moment—see your ability to choose a financial reality that is drawn from a sense of abundance rather than from your root cause. Celebrate your newfound freedom. You are free.

Forgiveness → as an Act of Self-Love

In this last step, I'd like you to simply become aware of just how awesome you are. From the courage you've just shown, to the commitment you've made, to recognizing the necessary steps you must take to move forward, I'd like you to appreciate all you've been through and all the ways that your wisdom, insight, and learning are now going to serve you. Recognize that your root cause is simply an illusion and dedicate yourself to living a more abundant truth—one day at a time, one choice at a time. You are love.

Forgiving Societal Limitations

As you release the grip of your root cause and awaken to the potential of creating a healthier, more empowering financial reality for yourself, you're going to come face-to-face with many of the roadblocks that may have slowed you down in the past, particularly those imposed on you by our larger society. Just remember that for every rule, there is a rule breaker. Someone who has always been willing to step outside the box, challenge the status quo, and achieve by their own Get Paid mandates. We are living in a time when the wealth gap is getting wider by the minute. But we are also living in a time when smart, talented everyday people—just like you—are putting their creativity and innovation to work and spawning awesome new industries and economies as a result.

When I think of the way a whole new generation of entrepreneurs have been able to break the mold and utilize the internet to build awesome new enterprises for good, I think of my beloved sister Paula. I met Paula at a three-day training event in New York when she followed me into the ladies' room after I got offstage!

"I want to bring you to Brazil," she said. "This is what I do in my country and I know that my people will love you."

There was something about her smile, her poise, and that little bit of mischief twinkling in her eye that made me smile. *She's a rock star,* I said to myself—I could just tell. She was laid back but, at the same time, very determined. She connected with one of my team members and a couple of months later we were on the phone. That's when Paula shared her story.

"I began my professional career as an attorney. I was working in the area of Civil Law. I felt very passionate about helping people and I put a lot of my energy into my cases and as a result I became very good at what I did."

"But . . ." I offered.

She laughed. "Yes, there is always a but, isn't there? In my case, it was the long hours and the demanding schedule. Add on top of that the tragic cases and office politics and I began to feel drained. After a while, it became too much and I started to get sick. I was tired all of the time and I just had no motivation to do anything. All I did was go to work, come home, and collapse."

"Wow. I can totally relate," I shared.

"Quietly, I started to wish for a new opportunity, something that would take me away from the relentless procession of difficult cases and heart-wrenching stories." She paused. "Then one day, I came to work and was told that the firm was merging with a larger firm, that they would be restructuring and as a result my position was eliminated because it was redundant. As I walked out of that office, I thought to myself, 'Now what are you going to do?' My son was very young at the time and it was just me and him. So I had to figure something out."

Around the same time, Paula began taking online personal growth courses at the urging of a dear friend. Paula started a blog sharing what she was learning and began attracting a number of followers online. Pretty soon they started asking her for advice.

"My friend was coaching people and was really happy, so I thought, Why not check it out? I started coaching people who reached out to me online. And I found out that I was really good at it."

"I bet you were."

"After some time, I took a coaching certification program. Soon after, I created my first online course because my clients were asking me how I was getting clients through the internet. So many people kept asking me; after a while I realized there is an opportunity here, so I launched a membership and charged fifty dollars.

"Then I met my mentor in 2013 who was based in the United States, and I began working almost exclusively with him, taking all of his on-line training courses, and going to his live events; after a while, I joined his mastermind and that's when I started to refine and scale my online programs."

Paula was being very modest.

"One day he challenged us to set a ninety-day goal and I challenged myself to launch an online coaching program, which was the first in Bra-zil. I became a top affiliate of his work, sharing his teachings with my community. And soon after that, I became the first woman in Brazil to have a seven-figure launch in seven days."

"Amazing," I declared, trying to wrap my mind around what it must feel like to earn $1 million in one week! "What do you think is happening right now in your country that is having so many people start to look for this information?" I asked.

"So many people have been afraid to leave their jobs or go against the wishes of their families. This is a big thing in my culture. People are very religious and are very close to their families. They don't want to do anything that will embarrass or disappoint them. But times are changing. People are no longer willing to settle for being unhappy. And they don't have to.

"There has been so much political upheaval in Brazil, and everyday hardworking people have been the hardest hit. Where they had trust in a system of government and its formal leaders to sustain the economy, they have come to realize that their own economic fate must be taken into their own hands. There is a new generation of workers who are questioning the status quo in ways they never have before. I want them to know that they can dream, that they can have a better life, and that they don't have to stay in positions that make them miserable. They can get free. I especially want the women in my community to know that."

The more Paula spoke, the more I could feel her conviction. There was no sales pitch or complex algorithm driving her success; it was just Paula, speaking from her heart and igniting a movement of self-realization on behalf of a country she loved.

"I want to bring you to Brazil, so that you can work with my community. I do a live three-day event in the fall and I would love for you to be there. Last year we had about two hundred and fifty people, but this year I think we're gonna double that." (Her event actually drew more than six hundred people!) "I know that they would be deeply inspired by anything you wanted to teach them."

"Paula, how many people are in your community?" I asked.

"With my various social media channels and my database I have about five hundred thousand people I engage with every day."

What?!

"How have you built this community?"

"With my heart and my hands. This has never been about trying to trick people. I do my best to consistently provide amazing content on so-cial media and really take the time to engage with my audience so that they know how dedicated I am to their success. Many of the people in my community may never buy anything from me. That's okay; they still get to take in the knowledge I offer for free and use it to transform their lives.

"When I left that law office, I was a single mother with no job. I wasn't sure how I was going to make it. But I knew that if I worked hard at something I didn't have a passion for and got really good at it I imagined what I could do with something that I was really passionate about. Starting this business was about forging a new future for myself and my son. I was saying, in effect, 'I've looked to everyone else, but now I'm going to bet on me.'"

I was blown away. Not just by the size of the numbers and the amount of wealth this thirtysomething rock star had generated. But rather, there was something deeply grounding, honest, and inspiring about her. How she moved, the way she thought about her community, and her passion and desire to make a difference in the lives of her students. It felt com-pletely authentic and genuine. I was sold—Brazil, here I come!

As your embrace your new Get Paid vision, you may feel tempted to go against your values and ideals, and it takes courage and discipline to stay the course. It's easy to admire our heroes who defy the odds, but we forget to notice all the years they spent working in obscurity and staying true when no one cheered them on. Just as the acorn does not become the tree overnight, your Get Paid vision comes to life through the conscious micro-decisions you make every single day when faced with the oppor-tunity to follow your heart or succumb to the false limitations imposed by society.

Healing Economic Trauma

Whether driven by natural disaster or man-made corruption, economic disenfranchisement is one of the biggest culprits in creating an insecure economy and culture. Remember the Great Recession of 2008? Communities were literally abandoned as people left their homes and neighborhoods in search of scarce economic opportunities. It was a painful time, and very few of us escaped untouched. When you are in economic survival mode, you can be forced to make choices you aren't proud of—decisions that are totally out of character and go completely against your sense of pride and integrity. Often, when you move to a better place those choices can haunt you. Forgiving this kind of trauma is especially difficult. Even after you are "out of the woods," there is a period of time when you may continue to look over your shoulder or find yourself immersed in an old memory that triggers all the feelings you felt back then. Your healing journey and Get Paid commitment must call for a new level of engagement—one where your finances are in your hands and you see yourself as a conscious, active shaper and participant in your own destiny. It needs to be an opportunity where you feel you have something valuable to offer the marketplace and something to gain, as well. When you can align how you share your gifts with your conscious participation in a more empowering economic system, you have all the ingredients to foster a new way to Get Paid. I met my beloved brother (from another mother) William while hiking a gorgeous trail outside Aspen; we were part of a small group of leaders who'd been invited to gather for a two-day laboratory on collaboration. The people in this room were literally working on some of the toughest social, political, and economic challenges of our time and I was honored to be among them. We gathered to explore the notion of collaboration and to push one another's thinking about our respective and potentially collective work. This was a room primed with the kind of urgency that called for big visions and bold actions—these were game changers—actively looking to move the needle on war, poverty, corruption, and the environment. It's one thing to think about how to heal your own personal economic trauma, but what does it take to heal a war-torn global region filled with hostile and conflicting ideologies? William was one of the co-facilitators of the event, and as we wandered along the steep and rocky ridges he shared his life story with me: "I'm an anthropologist by training. And a wonderer and wanderer by nature."

I was fascinated by all the places he'd been around the globe, from the ancient Mediterranean region of Mesopotamia (in the Middle East) to significant sacred sites like Chichen Itza (the Mayan ruins in Mexico), not to mention all the fascinating people he'd met. William is a global citizen working in some of most volatile conflict regions in the world. Given this, one would think he'd be dark, gloomy, and jaded, but he was just the opposite. He was funny, dynamic, and thoughtful, with one of the most radiant smiles I've ever seen. As we walked and talked, he told me about a set of hiking trails he'd helped create that were situated in the Middle East. They are a network of intersecting trails that actually trace the anthropological steps of the prophet Abraham. The trails begin in Urfa (a city in Turkey) and stretch down to Hebron, south of Jerusalem. They connect six countries and span hundreds of miles. As he began talking about the path, I got goose bumps all over my body.

"I will be hiking the main trail, the Masar Ibrahim al-Khalil, in early spring," William shared, "to celebrate the trail's tenth anniversary."

Before I knew what was happening, I blurted out, "I'm coming with you!" (LOL.) He looked at me and said, "Okay," and then we kept on talking. Meanwhile, I was freaking out inside, thinking, *What did you just get yourself into!?* Fast-forward six months and I am standing in the lobby of a small hotel in Jerusalem, meeting my fellow hikers.

That evening at the kickoff dinner, William talked about the promise and potential for peace in this region and about how the power of walking and talking side by side could be a transformative practice for those who were committed to building a bridge between the things that currently divide us as humanity.

"Economy is tied to this," he said, "because as people are able to care for themselves and their families, there is a sense of calm and well-being that gets restored to these regions and their respective communities.

Peace and economy are related." This really rang true to me because I know that even in our own country economic insecurity has become a breeding ground for violence and is its own form of trauma. To participate in a strategy aimed at leveraging economy and culture to heal collective trauma was right in the center of my mission and calling—being a part of this moment was a dream come true for me.

Over the following week, we covered more than 60 miles of ground on foot, walking through some of the most precarious regions of the West Bank, and I can tell you that I have never felt more welcomed or cared for than I did in these communities. I could feel the wonderful generosity and connection as well as see the promise of great economic potential. The residents of these communities were handling their business with love, excellence, and generosity. "Welcome. You are most welcome" was the mantra we heard over and over again. From budding technology labs to gorgeous quaint guesthouses run by women in a refugee center, tradition was woven seamlessly with modern strategy to drive entrepreneurship and ecotourism. I could feel the hope, determination, and dedication in every interaction and it just moved me. Beyond war and devastation, people can rebuild through partnerships and collaborations that hold out a new vision for a new reality. I'm proud to continue to support William's leadership and this amazing work—as he continues, in his words, "to heal our global wounds."

No matter what your financial history, just like the resilient (refugee) women owners of the Aqabat Jaber guesthouse in Jericho (where we stayed), you can forge a new Get Paid vision, one that embodies all the values, passion, and commitment that lives at the center of your true self and calling. Forgiving is central to this process, because new ideas deserve to be planted in fertile ground so they can be nurtured and cultivated into vibrant new realities.

Forgiving the Greatest Money Myth of All

Transforming the lie of scarcity is a game changer. Even so, the greatest myth we have to contend with in our global society is the disproportionate value we place on money—because this tradition holds the biggest potential for derailing your purpose and challenging your liberation perhaps more than any other.

Though we rarely tell the truth about it, we've created a society where money has shown itself to be even more important than human life. And as author Lynne Twist says, this is the cultural wound that all of us are in need of healing. Every time we watch our appointed leaders sell their integrity for financial favors, our faith in humanity is challenged. But it doesn't end there. As you reimagine the role money will play in your life, I urge you to consider one final act of letting go. I'd like you to confront and then forgive any place where you may be economically benefiting from someone else's misfortune. Whether it's the sneakers you wear, or the waitstaff you underpay, or the street artist you unnecessarily haggle with even though we already know he's underpriced, all of us participate in the quest to economically "come out on top." Even if you have not done so directly, you've (consciously or unconsciously) supported institutions that operate this way.

Guilt is powerfully debilitating when it comes to money, because it causes us to perpetually shrug our shoulders and say, "But what can I do about this?"—that is, if we talk about it as a problem at all. When it comes to money, much of our modern activism is spawned from guilt, and that in and of itself is a problem. I firmly believe that you cannot create anything new from a disempowered place. You've got to check your Binding Behaviors—complaining, blaming/judging, justifying, and/or avoiding—at the door. Step one of the forgiveness ritual requires us to look unflinchingly at, and tell the truth about, how we participate in this. What role do you play?

A false perception about money will convince us that if we cut these corners, no one will know or it won't really matter. But when it comes down to the integrity of your soul and the sanctity of your relationship with your finances, nothing goes unnoticed. All of these acts separate us from our true selves and ultimately dilute our capacity to answer our true calling.

Mind you, the guilt will not disappear overnight, and you are not guaranteed to catch every behavior. It will take time, patience, and consistent practice to overcome. What's most important is that you become conscious of your choices so that you can choose differently.

In the third part of this book, called "Do Good," I'll offer lots of options for how to work to transform this on a larger scale. But in this moment, as you create your own personal economy, I don't want to leave anything off the table that would impede your full healing. Money does have a role to play, but how does it move out of the place of overblown importance and toxic distortion to find its rightful place in our respective societies?

Just as you have redefined success on your own terms, I want to encourage you to bring the same dedication to how you will Get Paid. You may not know the intricacies of every interaction, but you can hold an intention that a central part of your financial participation will be to bring greater dignity and respect to all people, as you earn and spend, borrow and lend, in ways that foster greater love and compassion for us all.

Your Call

Are you ready to forgive and let go of any limiting beliefs and perceptions drawn from your financial past? Over the next two weeks, use these two practices and two exercises to arrive at a new level of freedom, creativity, and possibility as you reconsider your financial future.

PRACTICE 1

"I release and let go of any financial perception that does not serve me."
"I forgive myself for operating from any form of financial scarcity."
"I am ready to embrace a more loving, abundant, and compassionate financial reality."

Work with this series of mantras over the next two weeks as you transform your root cause through the forgiveness exercise. Set aside five minutes in the morning and five in the afternoon or evening to speak these three statements to yourself while looking in the mirror. Also, keep this mantra series on hand and use it before you make any major financial decision. Remember to take three deep breaths before speaking these words. Keep repeating the series until you feel your energy shift to a more expansive place.

PRACTICE 2

Every day for the next two weeks, choose one incident from your past that you're willing to forgive yourself for when it comes to how you have handled your finances. This includes how you've earned, spent, lent, saved, invested, and given your money. Rate yourself on a scale of 1 to 10 for each incident. How willing are you to let the situation and surrounding emotions go? Ask yourself, Why is forgiving myself around this situation important to me?

EXERCISE 1

Identify the root cause, i.e., your #1 Greatest Money Hit. Then, use the four-step forgiveness process to transform an incident related to this limiting conversation. Pay close attention to how you feel at each stage of forgiveness. Take stock of all the important insights you glean from your chosen incident. Notice where this lesson may apply to other areas of your life.

EXERCISE 2

As you consider your current financial state, is there any place where you've allowed a societal limitation to dictate what is possible or not possible for you financially? If so, where? If you could forgive that limitation, what would your new financial reality look like? Meaning, what could you achieve financially if that mental roadblock was removed?

10

Step #4: Visualizing and Redefining Your Role in Your Personal Economy

Now that you've challenged traditional definitions of capitalism and success, it's time to create a set of guiding principles that support how you plan to Get Paid and thrive in the marketplace. Just as you've brought your creative powers to bear on developing a new personal story, so too can you rewrite your role in your own personal economy.

Consider the following: When it comes to money and how you wish to receive and allocate your financial resources, who do you want to be? What do you want to create? What is important to you? And how will your economic priorities play out in your day-to-day?

Before I had my own eureka moment about what the concept of economy means to me, I used to scratch my head over complicated media reports about the Dow Jones and GDP—seemingly foreign terms from another land. I never, ever considered how a change in my *personal behavior* could influence how I felt about money and doing business. As I shared in chapter 7, our economy is just the culmination of how individuals and institutions choose to acquire and spend their resources. Hence, *your* economy is how you choose to acquire and spend *your* resources.

In this chapter, you'll reclaim your power to participate in ways that enliven and inspire you, as well as help create the kind of world you want to be part of. You'll learn about the three pivotal shifts I made to move from financial victim to financial visionary, so that they might inspire you to do the same. And finally, you'll explore a new vision for financial success by giving voice to your own true desires around money. You can make choices that have a positive impact not only on you but on your community, society, and world—and influence how the rest of the world does business too. Your goal is to ultimately reimagine your financial reality in a way that aligns with your Get Paid vision, values, and money aspirations. I want you to own your capacity to actively shape how your resources are both acquired and spent, and explore what it means to handle your business in a way that is totally aligned with your vision for getting paid and answering your calling.

Reclaiming Your Power to Participate

I want to tell you a story about myself, with the hope that it will inspire you to recognize just how much power you have when it comes to putting your money where your heart is.

When I look back at my own story, I can see that even though I was able to tap in to a sense of purpose and calling relatively early in life, it took me much (much) longer to find a true sense of financial success. This is one of the reasons I'm so excited about the work we do at Move The Crowd. I know how challenging it can be to align your money goals with your values, especially when you confront all the limiting societal messages that dance around you. When I was receiving my very unorthodox financial education by sitting at the feet of some very smart businessmen, taking in their teachings and soaking in their wisdom, I recognized pretty quickly that the prospect of making money by itself was just not going to be enough to motivate me. Maybe it was because of my parents and their strong give-back value system, or all the people I knew who acted like virtual prisoners working in jobs they hated, or my jaded view at the time of how wealth corrupted certain business leaders and politicians. All I knew was that I needed a bigger reason to want financial success—because I needed to transform my financial reality, like, pronto!

My inkling about needing more didn't come out of nowhere. It grew out of my frustration with the sales tactics used by some of the presenters in the trainings I attended to become more financially empowered. Despite their best efforts to dress it up, a lot of their language and references still felt like more of the same traditional capitalistic views that produced the same disparities I was trying to heal. For example, I noticed how much reverence certain presenters gave to participants in the room with money—in countless conversations they painted people who had money as winners and those who didn't as losers. And they actually used that language: "You're a loser if . . ." and "We all want to be winners, don't we? Not like those other people who . . ." Every time they made a comment about "lazy people with no money" and "people who didn't want to work," I thought about Louisa, one of the older women from my community who scrubbed toilets and mopped floors to put food on the table, for her grandchildren—she was busting her you know what yet, despite her best efforts, was still unable to make ends meet. *Louisa is a loser? Really? I don't think so!* As a matter of fact, when I thought about most of the people I knew every one of them worked super-hard. That wasn't the problem. I looked to my left and right and saw most of the room nodding in agreement. Moreover, many of the people who took this stage did not seem equipped to bring a more nuanced economic or cultural analysis to their examples. Moreover, their stories for the most part only referenced white men. They were the authorities, the experts, the best in the world. They applauded people who were making lots of money and patted people who wanted to make a difference on the head like puppies: "Good for you. Now, when are you going to get out there and make some money?" This led to a pronounced difference in how we were treated in the room. Here we were in an empowerment seminar and it was actually mirroring exactly what happens in society—and I'll be honest, it pissed me off!

Thanks to my frustration, I immediately recognized that capitalism wasn't just an economic system but a culture that created a pecking order, and rather than try to "get on top" as many other participants in the room attempted to do by touting their financial success, I was much more interested in shifting the culture of these trainings and the society that created this false pecking order in the first place. It took me a while to land on how to achieve this, but when it came to me, I was on *fire*!

My company Move The Crowd would set out to shift the culture of capitalism in a way that enabled more individuals to thrive and prosper. We would teach people how to Stay True, Get Paid, and Do Good through the passion of their own efforts and ideas. This became my bigger reason for being—this became the next chapter of my calling.

I want you to consider what your bigger reason is, too. Beyond money accumulation, what motivates you to want to participate in our global economy in a more conscious way? There is a famous belief that money doesn't change you but simply makes you more of who you already are. And as you begin to discover your true self, you have the chance to explore what it means to really *be you* while still managing to financially thrive and prosper—the best of all worlds. So, who do you want to be when it comes to money? What will be the primary principles and motivators for your wealth, however you define it? How will those principles and motivations actually drive your participation? And how can you operate in ways that make the pie bigger rather than smaller?

In chapter 7, I encouraged you to consider what your ideal vision was for doing business. What did you see when I posed this question? Taking our power back means that we consider all the facets of our participation, that we look at both sides of the equation as business owner and customer, and that we create a vibrant image of how we want to engage through each vantage point.

This is a very edgy conversation. Though lots of people are speaking about alternatives to traditional capitalism in concepts with economic strategies that range from bartering to blockchain, however, in my experience there are very few who have achieved true mental, spiritual, and emotional liberation from this ingrained reverence for the almighty dollar. But as more people are waking up to the notion of a values-aligned economy, it's becoming more of a *societal* aspiration.

This is one of the reasons why I am so in love with my dear friend Theresa, because of her commitment to always be in her highest calling, which right now is all about creating what she refers to as a Peace Economy.

Born into a poor rural family, Theresa knew from a very young age that she was a rebel. She is tall and beautiful, with a radiant spirit and very sassy tongue. ☺ She doesn't care who you are; if you are out of line, she's quick to put you back in your place. Theresa loves rock-and-roll music and hung out with hippies and artists growing up.

"As I became more aware of how the world worked," she said, "I saw the disparities that existed between people who had money and influence versus people who did not and I decided that somebody had to tell it like it is!" She laughed, then sobered. "And apparently, that somebody would be me."

In the years that followed, Theresa proved she was hardworking and a fast learner, paying close attention to local politics and local leaders, organizing rallies around issues of environmental safety or equal education, and helping an honest public servant get elected. She also read voraciously and absorbed information and ideas on alternative political systems and economies: "All these thought leaders and visionaries whose work I read began to form new ideas in my mind and spirit about how we could live individually, communally, and thrive as a society."

Theresa is big on challenging herself to live "outside the box." She sees herself as a global citizen and to this day spends about 250 days on the road a year, educating a new generation of change agents and building authentic communities all over the world. She is an international advocate for peace and has spent significant time in conflict regions working to support courageous activism on the part of everyday people. From the women in Iraq and Afghanistan, to the mothers of veterans in Crawford, Texas, to co-owning a number of farms that support a new generation of organic planters in being able to strengthen their craft of working with the earth. Her wealth and generosity come from a deep commitment to buck the status quo and always seek what is true for her. She recognizes and even seeks to understand the social and political constructs of any environment, but she does not allow herself to be manipulated by them. This requires a heightened level of awareness, tons of practice, and a lot of courage. And when she makes mistakes, even with the best of intentions, she gets up, dusts herself off, and tries again. There are many things I love about Theresa, but what I admire most is the freedom and generosity that ooze from her every pore. She is one of the most liberated people I know, and I actually believe that because of her clarity and true sense of agency, money seems to follow her. She's self-made and is consistently leveraging her wealth and the wealth of others to create a more just and sustainable world. In this way she has become an absolute role model for me as I've brought my own vision for my own economy to life.

Though Theresa has never worked directly with me as a client, she has called on me to support her leadership efforts in empowering other women to stand up for a world that works for all of us. We are kindred sisters in this commitment to help people find their true voice and calling and we both see reclaiming our right to create and participate in more empowering economies as being central to this effort.

Three Pivotal Shifts Toward a Get Paid Reality

When I realized I was far more interested in transforming what the idea of economy meant to me rather than just making a whole bunch of money, I experienced a shocking and ironic shift. I became incredibly motivated to make a lot of money! Why? Because I wanted to test whether I could put my money where my mouth is—that is, put my values to work and be financially successful. Not only did I prove I could, but I've also helped others joyfully earn millions of dollars with a similar approach. Everyone has the potential to experience three pivotal shifts in their financial reality. These shifts were game changers for me in my journey, which is what gave me my compelling reason to *want* to be in business, make money, and bring my L3 (Live.Love.Lead.) declarations to life.

My hope is that in pursuit of your calling, these pivotal shifts toward a new Get Paid vision will do the same for you.

The first shift I'd like you to embrace is one that moves you from being at the mercy of the current state of our economy (i.e., a victim) to being a conscious, active shaper of your own financial ecosystem (i.e., a visionary). Being a conscious active shaper means that you engage and actively participate in the practices associated with handling your business, with a clear intention for who you want to be and what you want to have, do, create, and experience. This encompasses everything from how you select a business partner to how you negotiate a contract and everything in between. You take full responsibility for your own experience, you let your values lead, you focus on what matters, and you believe in the power of your own capacity to say yes to scenarios that align with your L3 (i.e., mission and values) and no to scenarios that don't.

The second shift I'd like to you embrace is to go from resisting to creating. Too many entrepreneurs and creatives think that if they "shun" capitalism, it will just go away, or they'll no longer be affected by the choices they *aren't* making when it comes to their finances. But if you are going to participate in the economy—in other words, expect to be paid for what you do—then you need to come up with a viable alternative for how to get to your own vision for getting paid. Much of the prosperity coaching I've experienced in the past encourages you to shift your attitude toward how to treat your money, from the way you organize your wallet to your energy around paying bills, which is great. But most of my clients actually want to feel love and excitement around every facet of their money—whether they're making or spending it—so I encourage them to pay attention to *who's* receiving their cash and *who* they are receiving cash from. This means they pay attention to the relationships, visions, and dreams being fostered by their currency exchange. If you're going to participate in any economy, what do you want to experience when you spend your money? What do you want to experience when you receive money? Who do you want to do business with?

In a Get Paid world, start to see your transactions differently—from your dentist to your dry cleaner, from your clients to your collaborators. Choose individuals and businesses that inspire you. Align with visions and missions that reflect what you care most about. Cultivate financial practices rooted in building authentic, caring relationships. In my own life, even when I deal with very large organizations, my intention is to bring the same principles to the table. Doing business has gone from being something I dreaded to becoming very joyful for me. It is no longer about trying not to be taken advantage of but honoring a profitable exchange for all.

The third and final shift I hope you'll make involves moving away from limiting, inherited notions for doing business and starting to operate according to your own money truths. For instance, maybe you aren't looking to kill yourself in order to make a dollar. Or maybe you don't need a 20-bedroom house in order to be successful. In my own life, I never considered that I even *had* a truth when it came to money or could aspire to something different from what had been handed to me. As you consider the financial reality you desire, ask yourself: What values do I need to let go of? What do I want to keep? What role do I want money to play in my life? What do I want it to buy me? When I asked myself these questions, I discovered that I did not need a lot personally; I just wanted to be comfortable. Yet, when it came to my vision, I wanted access to a significant amount of resources, because it would allow me to touch more people. Therefore, my vision for financial success became driven by my vision for contribution.

Whether you are earning, saving, investing, or spending . . . you are choosing. Becoming a conscious, creative, and responsible shaper means you know what you're choosing and why. It also means that when you are aware, you make choices that align with your values more often than those that align with what everyone else thinks.

Finding *Your* Money Truth

Too many of us have assumed there's an amount of money we're supposed to want, which is a number that's dictated by society. But this is always in flux. I remember when the magic number was a million dollars—the benchmark for having "made it." Now everybody's chasing the b-word, because as a client recently told me, "a million dollars is chump change." Really? To whom? Remember, more than 50 percent of the world lives on less than two dollars a day. There's a lot of room between a billion and two dollars, and it's your job to listen to your own wisdom when it comes to the question of what is "enough" for you. Yet, again, I've got to point to Lynne Twist's wisdom in *The Soul of Money* as she calls out: "Sufficiency isn't two steps up from poverty or one step short of abundance. It isn't a measure of barely enough or more than enough. Sufficiency isn't an amount at all. It is an experience, a context we generate, a declaration, a knowing that there is enough, and that we are enough."

Your current notion of "enough" may be far less than you've been conditioned to want, or hey, it might be significantly more. It all comes back to your values and why you want money in the first place. What does money buy *you*? Is it freedom, time, space, ease, or mobility? How would you steward those resources to achieve all of the above? Are you looking to stockpile out of fear or to share it far and wide in honor of the things that enliven you? The key is to look at your life and ask yourself: How much do I need to in order to be content and do all of the things I desire, for myself and others? What allows me to be fully aligned with my values? What enables me to make my highest contribution? Your truth number is the amount of money that aligns with your true nature, your true calling, and the belief that you are enough and that whatever you are being drawn to contribute is enough, too.

Like most of my clients, your answers may depend on what stage of life and work you're in. And those answers may change over time. If you have a huge Get Paid vision for the kind of life you want to live and the kind of impact you want to have in the world and you suspect it will take lots of resources to deliver, then a multi-million- or -billion-dollar vision might be right for you. However, if you are nurturing a more local vision for your home, neighborhood, or immediate community and what you seek is enough to care for yourself in the work, enable you and your family to live comfortably, and put some away for future wants, needs, and desires, then your money truth may be more like five or six figures a year depending on your lifestyle. No matter what the number is, your money truth should represent a combination of what you think you need in order to be fulfilled and what you believe gives you the greatest amount of freedom to pursue your calling.

I'm always intrigued by the stories of people who've actually done this process of getting free, because it's never just one kind of path. I met Galina through a wonderful new friend who'd recently reached his goal for seven-figure success just two months shy of his thirtieth birthday. "Galina is the queen of financial freedom!" he told me. "She's got that part down and now she's ready to explore her purpose, so you two should definitely talk!" It just so happened that Galina and I were in LA at the same time, so we happily made plans for lunch. On a sunny Friday afternoon, I made my way into one of my favorite cafes and walked right into Galina's open arms!

"Ayyy, hello!" she said. "I have heard so much about you!"

"Me too, me too!" I replied.

After we settled in and placed our orders, we got right down to business. "So tell me all about yourself," she said, sitting up in her chair.

"Uh-uh," I said, "you first!" We laughed. The waiter came; we placed our orders and dove right back in.

"What brings you to LA?" I asked.

"Well, I've been traveling quite a bit the past few months, some *kizomba* dancing in Europe, visiting family in Russia, and business training in Texas. Looking forward now to settling in LA for a few months . . ."

Now, I have to say that one of the first things I noticed about Galina was her glow. She was dressed in a gorgeous sundress with flowing fabric and beautiful vibrant colors, and she just had this air of fun, joy, and mischief. At the same time, I could also tell that she was no-nonsense kind of girl. Spiritual with an edge—definitely my kinda people. ☺ "I'm so curious about your journey; how did you get to this wonderful place of financial liberation?"

Just then, the waiter delivered our food. After we took our first bites Galina continued to share: "Before creating my plan of exit from the business world, I was an IT consultant living in the US. I was born in Russia and lived there for most of my childhood; I came to Seattle right after graduating from a university and never left." We ate in silence for a moment and then she continued.

"My job was okay—I liked it well enough and was good at it—but I always knew that I wanted something more. Reading Tim Ferriss's *The 4-Hour Workweek* changed my life forever. He talked about a freedom lifestyle and how you can have income coming in without working too much, so you can travel the world and do what you want. That book inspired me, but it wasn't until ten years later that I realized I had a desire for a freedom lifestyle—because I made no progress to create it."

"Wow. What finally shifted for you?"

"I asked myself one question: How committed was I on the scale of one-to-ten to making it a reality? It was then that I realized I was never committed; I had it as a desire but not a goal, big difference. And so one day I was talking with a friend and he invited me to this seminar on investing." She grabbed a napkin and wiped her mouth. "I'm an avid learner, so I said, 'Sure.' The training wasn't just about investing; it was actually about cultivating a mindset for wealth. At one point in the training, the presenter asked, 'What is the life that you most desire?'

"This made me think," Galina said. "Even though most of the training didn't fully resonate with me, this question definitely hit home."

"I bet," I chimed in. "This is a question I ask my beloved clients all of the time."

"Growing up, I knew what I was 'supposed' to do—you know, study hard, get good grades, and get a job so that I could support myself." She smiled. "But the idea of desire—related to your career path—was completely new to me," she said. "I realized that I wanted to travel the world and not have any concern about money. I sat down and calculated what it would take for me to be financially free, and once I had my number I began to put together a plan."

At the time, Galina was working for a consulting firm that took 50 percent of her income as part of her agreement. Yet shortly after her eureka moment, she moved to a different agency that only took 5 percent, and essentially got a 45 percent increase on her income—and used that money to start investing.

"I dove into learning about investments and began to educate myself like crazy by reading everything I could get my hands on. I attended seminars to show me how to structure my vision for wealth." She paused. "It wasn't rocket science. It's surprisingly formulaic."

Galina got clear about how much she needed to earn to live comfortably. She also researched places where she could do the things she enjoyed most and where her dollar would stretch the furthest. She really took the time and effort to explore how to make her vision real while she continued to work and put away as much as she could to support her investments. Talk about creating a powerful vision!

"I set the goal to reach six-figure passive income and retire in two years. And within a year and ten months I reached that goal and gave notice to my boss."

"Wow! That is amazing." I paused. "What do you think your biggest learning up to this moment has been?"

She thought for a moment. "Realizing that I desired to be free and then committing to making it happen and taking the actions necessary to honor that desire. It has literally changed my life."

"And now you're ready to explore your purpose," I surmised.

"Yep. With everything I've learned about money and following my own truth, I believe that I can help people create financial freedom in two to five years so they can do what they love, have the lifestyle they want, and live their life on purpose. That's how my company Effective Freedom was born."

"I love that!" I said. "I believe that people get stuck on the belief that the idea of freedom is far more difficult to achieve than the reality of freedom." I leaned in. "I think if people could really sit down and ask the questions you asked and had real room to think about it, then crunch the numbers, it probably would be much closer than they imagined."

Now it was her turn to agree: "Absolutely! It's about a mindset and an openness to learning how, then committing to making it a reality." We raised our tea mugs and laughed.

"One final question," I said. "What has been the most rewarding thing of all?"

She beamed. "Recently, when I was back in Russia, my father wanted to find some viable investment options for his money where they don't have the risk of just disappearing one day (which is very common in Russia), and when I said, 'Sure, what would you want to invest in?' he said, 'Into whatever you believe is best.' I was shocked and humbled. He really trusts me," she said, adding, "This is the biggest reward—it feels amazing to be able to help my family in this way. And I hope with your support, I can do this for many more."

"Indeed," I replied. "Let's do this!"

When you arrive at your money truth, you may find that you do still want to keep working, and that with the exception of a few more pairs of great shoes and maybe an upgrade on the quality and frequency of your vacations, not much else changes in your daily life. But what you may surprisingly discover is that your perspectives on money and life come into greater harmony with each other. As you find your truth zone—i.e., that place where your money lines up with what's most important to you—you can release all of the external mandates and arrive at a place that feels more in line with who you are and what you want to have, be, and do in this world.

Your Get Paid Vision for Financial Success

As much as we are in a time of great challenge, we are also in a time of tremendous opportunity, and your capacity to give full voice to what you truly want—and then lean into the aligned right actions to fulfill that vision—will be the engine that drives you toward a new Get Paid reality.

In all the work I've done with clients over the years, their greatest financial challenges have been around moving beyond the internal skepticism driven by limiting beliefs, past experiences, and external perceptions. If you consult anyone around you, most will have an opinion about what is and is not possible for you. Yet when it comes to your truth, who will you listen to? Are you willing to give *yourself* a chance to experience the kind of fulfillment you may have only previously dreamed of? Are you willing to take the time to articulate that vision in as much detail as you can? It takes great courage to openly want what you want, and it takes even greater self-love, honor, and trust to move in the direction of your deepest longings.

Just as I am inviting you to shift, I also want to acknowledge that we have witnessed massive shifts in our global economy as well. Since the Great Recession, ventures like Airbnb, TaskRabbit, and Uber have changed the game, earned tens of billions of dollars, and created opportunities for millions of people, from all walks of life, to earn money in a way that aligns with their desired lifestyle—that is, they participate in what's come to be known as the Share Economy. Every time I take an Uber or Lyft, I am fascinated to hear these drivers' stories, whether it's about being an immigrant college student earning extra cash, a retired insurance broker looking to get outside the house and stay busy, or a part-time university scientist who runs environmental impact groups in the area and wants to use his Prius to interview people on their perceptions on the environment. What all these fascinating folks have in common is that they love the flexibility that their jobs and related choices afford them. Getting paid is joyful for them, and in every way it comes to align with and embody their money truths.

Your participation in the economy should also be a source of joy, inspiration, and motivation. So if that's not what you're experiencing, you owe it to yourself to examine what it would take to create that reality. There is an abundance of possibilities when you honor your truth, because you give yourself permission to go after what you desire. There is magic to honoring your most honest and deep aspirations and I promise I'm gonna talk more about that in the chapters to come. The more you are willing to speak and act in concert with your money truth, the more rapidly that truth will become your new Get Paid reality.

Your Call

Are you ready to create and participate in the economy, your way? Over the next two weeks, use these practices and exercises to create, acquire, and share your financial resources.

PRACTICE 1

"I am taking my rightful place as a conscious creator of my own economy."

Speak this mantra every day for the next two weeks. Say it just before you have any money or business transaction and notice how it increases your awareness about how you're currently acquiring and spending your resources and, ultimately, how it informs the choices you make. Share your biggest insights with those you love, trust, and admire.

PRACTICE 2

After you complete Exercise 2 choose one thing you've decided to *start* doing and implement it over the next two weeks. What do you notice? Has it made a difference in how you feel about your money and/or business transactions? In what way has this practice moved you closer to your desired Get Paid reality? As you become more aware of your money practices, you'll be able to make conscious choices about which support you. Dedicate yourself to those actions.

EXERCISE 1

I'd like you to take one hundred dollars out of your account and then spend it in a way that considers these questions: How would you like to participate in the current economy? What kinds of products, services, and ventures inspire you? What do you want for you and your family? How about our society and world? How can these desires begin to influence the way you earn and spend? Keep a log of your transactions and review them at the end. See if you can come up with a percent allocation for each category that represents how you chose to use the money. Could this be the beginning of a blueprint for how you think about allocating your financial resources?

EXERCISE 2

As you start to recognize what is true for you, how will that affect your vision and strategy for getting paid? I'd like you to calculate what I call your "freedom number." This is the amount of money you want to passively earn that joyfully exceeds your monthly expenses. For instance, if your monthly expenses are $8,000/month, your freedom number might be $12,000/month, taking into account the additional amount you may want to have available for vacations and other fun stuff you want to do. Examine both your active and passive income streams. How do you feel about the way you currently earn your money? If you could have it your way, how would you earn it? To move toward financial freedom, what do you need to do? Then, name three specific changes in the following categories: What will you *stop* doing? What will you *start* doing? And what will you *continue* to do? Remember, freedom doesn't just exist in the numbers; it exists in the feeling, too.

11

Step #5: Aligning Your Business Propositions with Your Values

Now that you have a clear sense of how much money you'd like to make and how you'd like to make the economy work for you, let's talk about how to actually be in business. As we discussed earlier, we are in an exciting moment in history, because we are redefining economy and culture in real time. We are moving out of what has traditionally been the Age of the Celebrity and into what I call the Age of the Citizen. Here a different set of values and priorities drives our market-based interactions and our lives. And at the top of the list is letting go of the iconic worship of what big companies and celebrities dictate and define as being important in what we consume and want to be like to instead focus on what our own personal brands want to express and contribute. The Age of the Citizen is all about you—who you are, what you want to bring to the world, who you want to serve, and the impact you want to have. These are what drive how you Get Paid and answer your calling.

In the last five years, we've seen an explosion of "normal people" who've made it big. These experts are not touting their degrees but using hard-earned experiences, proven results, and everyday perspectives to build massive followings; what's more, they share their wisdom via their own personal stories, which resonate with and attract a like-minded audience. From the whimsical to the meaningful, from the blog *The Buried Life* to the popular web series *#AskGaryVee,* a new generation of voices have emerged using social media outlets to promote their ideas and boost their audience. Technology has enabled us to create branded platforms with little investment. And since you can reach your audience with few barriers, you must be equally accessible on an emotional level, too. It's an online world hungry for authentic, meaningful interactions; relevance and connection are as paramount as your knowledge. There is also a greater emphasis on trying to make a difference—this goes a long way with audiences versus just being consumed with personal achievement.

In this chapter, I'll explain how the idea of being entrepreneurial is about more than just having a business. Being entrepreneurial is about cultivating the kind of *mindset* that lets you take full ownership of your ideas and aspirations. In this chapter, you'll decide what you want to offer the market and, whether you're working in an existing organization or running your own shop, learn the four core tenets of marketplace participation. From there, you'll create what I call a "value proposition" that aligns with your unique talents, gifts, and abilities to help you put your personal values to work and define the role you want to play in manifesting your Get Paid vision. How you participate is based on using your true talents to serve others while you answer your own calling. This is the vision of the Citizen-era economy. Finally, we'll look at the power of positioning and how your L3 can help your proposition stand out.

Thinking in an Entrepreneurial Way

True entrepreneurs believe in their power to create—but to be honest, just because someone owns a business does not mean that they are entrepreneurial. There are many business owners who run their shops by default, just as there are many leaders at corporations who intentionally run business units that soar. And much like the concept of sufficiency, entrepreneurship begins as a state of mind. How will your new perspective on money and economy inform your choices while doing business? Whether or not you consider yourself an entrepreneur, as a conscious creator you will find tremendous value in bringing a conscious entrepreneurial approach to your business interactions.

To that end, I've come up with 14 keys to thinking in an entrepreneurial way. Which of these resonate with you?

1. *You have a bold vision:* You have an idea or inspiration that won't go away. You can't stop thinking, dreaming, scheming, and sometimes, much to others' chagrin, talking about it. Basically, you're obsessed—and you won't be happy until you do something about it.

2. *You're goal/action oriented:* Your natural inclination is to go the extra mile and do more about things that are important to you. Speaking is a great start, but it only gets you so far—at some point, you know most of your talking will come when you're moving the ball down the court. You also see a strong connection between who you are and what you're doing.

3. *You're willing to learn as you go:* You don't need to have all the answers, and you inherently know this. You're willing to figure it out and make the road by walking.

4. *You're resourceful:* You know how to use what you've been given and leverage your knowledge, skills, networks, and opportunities. You see multiple possibilities when it comes to getting things done. You always cultivate new resources even if you're not yet sure how you'll use them.

5. *You're courageous:* Fear does not paralyze you; it inspires you to move. Anything worth doing is going to invite you to grow.

6. *You know how to listen:* You know how to listen to your gut, your team, keep your ear to the ground with your clients, and read the zeitgeist. All of it informs how you serve.

7. *You're up for the challenge:* When things get interesting, you lean forward. Natural curiosity kicks in, and you get energized. You're willing to hang in and try to figure it out when most run for the hills. You make tough calls and hard decisions from a place of motivation, not defeat.

8. *You're resilient:* You keep rising even if you get knocked down. When one door closes, you know another will open. You take the shots and integrate the learning. You use everything that happens to make you clearer, stronger, and more determined. Nothing stops your zest for life.

9. *You focus on what's important:* You focus on vital actions—i.e., things that forward your goals and aspirations. You keep your eyes on the prize and do what matters.

10. *You're results oriented, but . . . :* You deliver. You're clear on objectives and work to achieve them. But they don't define you. You determine when and where they're best used and when they need to change. You bring your best effort and intention to every goal and let go of what you can't control.

11. *You march to the beat of your own drum:* You feel like an outsider because you see things differently than the people around you. You may not fit in, but you know you have something valuable to contribute. Your methods may be a bit unorthodox, but they are effective.

12. *You know your value:* You know the impact of what you have to offer in any given context. You are adamant about ensuring the quality of those benefits. You continuously invest in yourself and in those benefits so you can deliver even more value to those you serve.

13. *You take responsibility for your success:* You have a vision for what success looks like and take full responsibility in achieving what you want. You realize that success is both defined by and up to you.

14. *You know how to inspire others:* You know making things happen is a team sport and requires an ability to ignite the potential for meaningful contribution in others. You know how to be both collaborative and directive.

This list of entrepreneurial attributes really hit home with one of Move The Crowd's first clients, Dana. Because Move The Crowd's mission is to work with those who are purpose driven—meaning those who are passionate about having a positive impact on the lives of others—many of our beloved clients come from the nonprofit world. They are deeply altruistic, but they also know that the current paradigm for most nonprofits isn't sustainable. This was the challenge Dana had. When we first began working together, she was transitioning out of a tumultuous nonprofit position at an organization that sought global conflict resolution; it left her way overworked and far underpaid. She was exhausted and confused, yet proud that she had finally found the courage to leave.

"Whew!" she said when we hopped on the phone for our first session. "I have so much appreciation for the work that I've done in my last organization, and though I do believe we were doing good work, I just don't think it's my work anymore." She took a deep breath and exhaled. "So now, I'm ready to explore what my work is, Ms. Rha!"

I laughed. "So you're ready to find your true calling?" I inquired.

"Yep, so lay it on me!" We both chuckled.

"Tell me more about where you've been professionally and what aspects of the work were most exciting and intriguing for you and why."

"Well," she began, "historically, I've worked in PR, communications, and social media. I know that I'm a writer, so I'd say that I loved some aspects and the writing and I've definitely loved the people part of it."

"Say more," I encouraged. "I love helping someone clarify what their message is and I love helping them build the confidence to share it."

She thought some more. "I also love seeing that message make its way out into the world—so crafting the message and giving it a voice really excites me."

As Dana and I ventured deeper into her dharma, her true nature began to emerge: She was creative, nurturing, quirky, and strategic. And when we started to explore her highest contribution and what an initial offering might be, she said, "I know I want to offer something that nurtures my creativity, while it also helps support a new generation of changemakers. I feel like I could really help them find their voice and clarify their mission and their message, then help them take it out into the world."

"Great, let's start there—for homework I'd love for you to come up with an initial offering that aligns with these passions."

Next, I wanted to encourage an entrepreneurial approach as she thought about this new chapter. "When I say 'thinking more entrepreneurially' what do you think I mean?"

She paused. "I guess it means that I would consider this as a real business and maybe a step up from just freelancing."

"Yes, *and* what I'm referring to right now is less about the formal business structure and more about the mindset that will inform your strategy for developing your offering," I replied. We talked about what it meant for Dana to adopt an entrepreneurial attitude as she pursued her calling. "Thinking more entrepreneurially includes getting laser-focused about the *kinds* of changemakers you want to work with and the kinds of projects you want to lend your talents to. It also means getting crystal clear about the benefits and results you're going to deliver through your work together."

"Ah, okay, this is starting to get really clear for me," Dana replied. When, I walked her through my list of 14 attributes, checking off qualities she possessed and highlighting those she needed to cultivate, that drove it home. "This is so exciting to me!" Dana exclaimed. "Shoot, I want to be an entrepreneur!"

I laughed. "I thought you might see it that way."

"You know, as I look at this list, I realize that everything I've done with my last organizational experience has almost prepared me for this." She took another deep breath. "Wow. I have a lot of gratitude for that experience right now." Her newfound level of appreciation for her past experiences actually freed up a lot of emotional room for her to work on building her new business. Dana had no interest in wallowing in hurt, anger, righteousness, and resentment but was ready to get started on the next chapter of her professional journey.

"Now, let's look at which attributes represent the greatest opportunity for growth," I instructed.

Dana knew that knowing her value was at the top of the list. "In all the years I've worked at nonprofits, I never had to pay attention to the merit of my own contributions," she said. "Everything was about the organization's work and the goal was not to stand out. So, my work was never highlighted within that as being 'the thing' that made the difference." The other part of Dana's growth was confronting head on the fact that she was consistently being underpaid: "Yeah, I have no idea what the market value of my work is, because I've always worked for much less due to the lack of resources on the part of whatever organization I was working with."

These practices caused her to be confused about the value of her offerings. As we dug into this attribute, I gave her an assignment to interview three past clients to get specific feedback on the tangible benefits of her contribution. I also asked Dana to do some market research. I asked her to consider, "When you look at corresponding job descriptions outside the nonprofit sector, and across various industries, what do you see as being the closest to what you do? And which level of compensation appeals most to you?" Finally, I asked her to think about "What is it you really want to make given all the knowledge, wisdom, and experience you bring to the table?" This last assignment posed the greatest challenge of all, because her nonprofit conditioning trained her to believe that wanting more money meant that you had somehow been "corrupted" (Root Cause #3—"I might be changed"). But Dana was adamant about working through this because she understood that to create a new vision for handling her business understanding the value of her services was crucial.

It took three weeks for Dana to finally come back and say, "This is what I want to make!"—and the new number was three times what she'd previously earned. Armed with her new Get Paid vision, she launched an empowerment coaching and communications venture supporting social justice changemakers that increased her income by 50 percent in the first six months—this while working for about 40 percent less than she had at her last job! "Oh my God, Ms. Rha!" Dana earned more money and free time, simply because she was willing to adopt an entrepreneurial mindset and approach to what she was building.

"This is just the beginning, Ms. Dana," I replied. "Just the beginning."

You Are in Business!

Given your new Get Paid philosophy and entrepreneurial mindset, your next step is to embrace the fact that you are in business. Okay, cool! What does that mean?

Being in business means that you have agreed to exchange your talents, gifts, and abilities through goods, services, and experiences for various forms of compensation, including money. And in the True. Paid. Good. formula, it means you've agreed to embrace a new level of stewardship by honoring the values that guide how you participate. You appreciate the trust that you share with your clients, stakeholders, and fellow collaborators, and you contribute in a way that honors that trust. In this section, I'll explain how the current global economy and culture are creating unprecedented opportunities for you to participate in an authentic and values-driven way. Right now, it doesn't matter what your business environment is—nonprofit, corporation, boutique company, or your own venture. What matters is that you understand what the new mandates are for those who seek to have any form of successful marketplace engagement in this new era.

To make real and meaningful strides, know that there are four core tenets for boosting your business goals in the Age of the Citizen: authenticity, transparency, co-creativity, and community. You can't successfully be in business without practicing them.

1. *Authenticity:* This tenet implies that you're genuine, principled, grounded, and real. It also demands that you are who you say you are and don't just espouse a set of values or ideals but work to live by them. This translates into the integrity of what you have to offer. Your credibility in the market relies on your authenticity.

2. *Transparency:* The desire for transparency in business is part of the blowback from the Great Recession of 2008. No more secrecy or trickery. Customers want to see how the sausage is made and be walked through the process, step by step. Another facet of transparency has to do with a willingness to take your audience behind the curtain of your own journey. They want to hear about your struggles even more than your successes. They want to see themselves in you, which allows their own success to feel more tangible and real, which reinforces connection.

3. *Co-creativity:* In exchange for brand loyalty, a customer wants to feel they have a voice in how they're served. They are the

experts on what they will and won't pay for. Your interactions in this new age are more relational than transactional. You and the customer are now in an ongoing dialogue that lets you serve them in a more compelling way.

4. *Community:* Community speaks to our need to feel connected to one another, because deep down, we all feel a little isolated. We live in a time when we're becoming increasingly aware of what's really important to us ("woke" millennials are a prime example), with many finding they no longer have a lot in common with friends and family as they once did. Coming into their own, they look for a home. Finding a community that is like-minded and has aligned values is for them akin to finding an oasis in the desert. Purchasing experiences should help foster this need for community.

The market is clear about this. And so is my client Anu, who came to me with a huge and admirable vision for transforming the way that socially responsible companies did business. Anu is a fierce millennial leader and he wanted to build a venture that not only met the four tenets but also taught other companies how to meet them, too. His original vision was to develop a training course that helped mission-driven companies become more aware of how their practices exploited certain regions and communities (within the United States to start) and reinforced bias—based on race, class, gender, and orientation: "I want to create a certification process to help companies transform those practices." Anu spent serious time and energy honing his idea and reaching out to stakeholders and potential collaborators. Ultimately, he landed on an exciting training product and branded movement called BE MORE.

As Anu brought his vision and product to life, we had very honest conversations about how he wanted to only engage those who understood and respected his values: "I feel like there are a lot of people out there paying lip service to these issues. I'm interested in working with people who genuinely share my passion and who want to see an end to these practices."

Check the box on authenticity right there!

Anu realized that he had to begin piloting the product within an industry that was at least willing to acknowledge it had a problem. After doing significant research and reading an article in the *National Journal of Medicine* that actually measured the impact of implicit bias on a patient's diagnosis and treatment. Given the fact that the industry was willing to be transparent about their struggle, Anu knew where he had to start. "I want to do this work with physicians," he said. "The research is out there and I have connections that would give me access to this community."

"Great! I'd love for you to develop some criteria for your ideal piloting organizations and physicians. So that when you're having these conversations you can determine pretty quickly who's a match and who is not."

"Right!" Anu said. "I want to select people who will give me the kind of feedback and insights that will make the training even better and help inform how we market and sell this product to other institutions." He said, "I'd love for them to become endorsers, and collaborators when we officially launch it in the marketplace." Check the box for co-creativity!

Anu's intention was to begin this work with physicians and expand the offering to Fortune 500 corporations. Anu was clear about his strategic approach, but he needed some additional resources and training to bring all of the pieces together. He reached out to his Move The Crowd network for support; presenting his venture at a recent Mastermind caused a number of his fellow True. Paid. Good. entrepreneurs to step in and lend a hand. Heather knew that Anu needed a compelling story—so she jumped in to help him give voice to the impact that bias and discrimination had on his own life. She helped him prepare for a fellowship interview—one that another entrepreneur in the network nominated him for. Anu got the fellowship for $100K, plus a second major grant that matched his fellowship funding. He then looked at how he would brand his movement, and Ron, another True. Paid. Good. rock star, jumped in to help develop his logo and the branded look for his new website. Anu then turned to our own senior coach and trainer, JLove, to help him expand his platform by developing a subsequent strategy for books, TV, and web content based on his research, unique perspective, and thought leadership. With so much like-minded assistance and support, Anu was able to run a six-week pilot program with thirty physicians from the University of North Texas, Fort Worth, the Institute for Healthcare Improvement, and SUNY Downstate.

"What's been great about doing business in this way has been the trust," he said. "You know, you guys are like my family and I don't have to question your motives or your commitment to me and this work. Everyone knows how important this is and so many people from Move The Crowd have been willing to step in and co-create with me."

"Yep," I replied. "This is the power of like-minded community, my love."

"Indeed," he said. "As BE MORE works to transform leaders, my hope is to build a strong network among them as well, so they can have this kind of support when they begin to take this work into their respective organizations."

Anu is well on his way to building a vibrant multi-seven-figure movement that is #hackingbias and transforming leadership within the corporate healthcare industry. I could not be any prouder of the way he has leveraged this Citizen-era mindset to accomplish all that he has achieved.

As you consider this new age and its values, where are the points of intersection between this moment and your newly defined Get Paid vision? What inspires you about this emerging set of priorities and criteria? Is your professional vision supported by citizen-centric mandates? As you think about your own economy and its values, how does this new era inspire and excite you?

Clarifying Your Values-Aligned Proposition

Once you buy into the core tenets associated with the Age of the Citizen, you have a responsibility to make a valuable contribution to whatever environment you're in. Your contribution, when it's aligned with your values and definition of success, has the potential to not only bring personal fulfillment but make a real difference in others' lives and missions, too—remember, these are all the prerequisites necessary for your calling. Beyond any job description, entrepreneurial thinking requires that you get clear on what I call your unique Values-Aligned Proposition, so that you can become intentional about your contribution in any environment.

A Values-Aligned Proposition is a clear set of specific and measurable benefits that clients or customers receive when they buy your product, service, or experience. The benefits should be considered in some way unique and of greater value than other options in the market. What differentiates a Values-Aligned Proposition from a normal value proposition is the role of your L3. The integration of your values, your unique combination of talents, and your desired impact serves as a central driver for what you want to bring to the world through your Values-Aligned Proposition. This is where the "aligned" part comes in.

Remember, your future clients are seeking more than just transactional benefits. They are looking for radical shifts in their business and quality of life and experience. Authenticity, transparency, co-creativity, and community guide their purchasing decisions. As you plan what you'll contribute to the marketplace, ask yourself, How am I improving my customers' lives or ambitions? How am I fulfilling my calling and forwarding the hopes, dreams, and aspirations of others? Finally, and most important, how does your Values-Aligned Proposition, when it's leveraged in the marketplace, really make a difference? And how can that difference increase the value of what you have to offer?

When a client tells me they're having a hard time making money either at their job or after launching a company, the first thing I address is their belief system and then I move on to their Values-Aligned

Proposition. There are four main areas where I've seen clients repeatedly struggle. First, they aren't clear about who their customer is and why they need to be served. They are also unclear about the direct and tangible benefit they're offering. Remember, in this Age of the Citizen, it's all about your ability to resonate with the daily wants, needs, aspirations, and challenges of those you serve. Getting to know your audience in any context is a priority. Another area where my clients get stuck is that they're unclear about what makes their offering different from or better than what's out there already. Finally, they're not clear about what makes their service timely and relevant.

To address these gaps, I take them through the following process to clarify these areas:

1. KNOW YOUR CUSTOMER: WHO ARE YOU HERE TO SERVE?

Your Values-Aligned Proposition comes to life in the hearts, minds, and spirits of the people you serve. Getting clear about who is your client in every scenario is vital. Sometimes there is a difference between who your client is and who your audience is. Your audience is the people who consume your product: your client is the person who pays for it. When they are not one and the same, you must do the work necessary to understand the realities of both. The more you understand your client/audience, the greater chance you have at making a meaningful connection. Remember, in this Age of the Citizen it's all about your ability to resonate with the daily wants, needs, aspirations, and challenges of those you serve.

2. BE BENEFICIAL: WHAT RESULTS DO YOU DELIVER?

With every product, service, or experience, you must know how your offering either (1) solves an existing problem, (2) simplifies, enhances, and/or improves an existing experience, or (3) achieves a desired aspiration. Let's review all three.

Solves a Problem: If you are solving a problem, you must understand exactly what the problem is and what your customer's "pain point" is—

i.e., why is this such a problem for them? The more frustrating or challenging the problem, the more welcome your solution may be. What's important here is that *they* have to see it as a problem and one that is "painful" enough for them to want to seek a solution—remember, it's all about them.

Take Anu's work with BE MORE for example: He's solving a major issue that affects the quality and accuracy of how physicians diagnose and treat patients who come from diverse backgrounds. This is a major problem and the pain point for patients and hospitals in these instances is very real.

Simplify/Enhance/Improve an Experience: If you are enhancing or improving an existing experience, it is imperative to know where the greatest opportunity for enhancement lies in the eyes of your customer. Again, it's all about them, so what's the most exciting upgrade they'd want you to make? What additional benefits and features would *they desire* enough to pay for?

Take Heather's work with the Million Person Project; her Values-Aligned Proposition is to help leaders connect more authentically to themselves and their audiences so that they can feel more confident onstage and deliver their message in a way that really moves people. This "upgrade" will enable leaders to have real impact on an audience versus just standing up there and giving some canned speech and receiving some canned applause in return.

Achieve a Desired Aspiration: In this Citizen-era economy, consumers are giving voice to their greatest aspirations. If you are helping them be or achieve more, your product needs to clearly demonstrate, step by step, how it supports them in reaching their desired aspiration. The process needs to feel easy and accessible so they have confidence in their ability to achieve their desired result(s).

Take Dante's work with the concept of Nourish as a central part of his Values-Aligned Proposition; he's hitting us stressed-out overachievers where we live. Who doesn't want more joy, creativity, energy, and productivity? Who wouldn't want to feel nourished as opposed to depleted at the end of the day? Those of us with demanding lives who aspire to have a better quality of experience would absolutely pay attention to what he's got to offer.

Dante's also got even greater potential to connect with a wider customer base because his Values-Aligned Proposition actually addresses all three. So if your Values-Aligned Proposition clearly does all three, then you also have a strong proposition!

3. BE DISTINCT: HOW ARE YOU DIFFERENT FROM/BETTER THAN THE COMPETITION?

With every product, service, or experience, it is important to know how you and your venture can innovate and differentiate yourself and your venture. When it comes to creating a unique Values-Aligned Proposition, there are typically three ways to innovate. First is "what" you want to innovate. Here your job is to bring the market, and your audience, an item or experience it has never had before. The second, is "how"; here you serve your market/audience in a way it has never been served before. And third, "who"; here you serve a market/audience that's never been served before.

Now let's look at examples for each of these. I'm gonna go mainstream here to really illustrate the point:

What: An awesome example of a "what" is the television. Created in the late 1930s by Paul Gottlieb Nipkow, this contraption was billed as an electronic box you could plug into your wall that gave you a "window to the world." It was similar to the radio, but better because you could actually see and hear what was going on. This invention was revolutionary because it gave you access to experiences, products, and information without you leaving your home.

How: A great example of a "how" is the concept of fast food. McDonald's was founded in 1940 and mastered the notion of a fast, hot, and cheap hamburger. McDonald's also spawned the concept of the franchise, which became a turnkey strategy for creating a reproducible business model that incorporated a unique philosophy and set of systems, and distinct products could be licensed and sold. If you've ever had food from McDonald's, you know that a hamburger tastes the same in Beijing as it does in Chicago, even though the owners of those franchises are not the same. McDonald's is able to create this product consistency because they use one supplier for each of their food items.

Who: A phenomenal example of "who" innovation goes to L'Oréal and their famous hair color campaign "Because I'm Worth It," launched in 1973. This campaign catered to a new generation of women finding their voices in the feminist movement and fighting for equal rights. L'Oréal brilliantly capitalized on targeting and serving this "newly liberated woman."

4. BE COMPELLING: WHY THIS? WHY NOW? WHY *YOU*?

Being compelling is all about being right and ripe. Right with the offer—and ripe with the timing. It's about the Right place, Right time, Right offering, and Right *you*. Beyond your product or service, what other qualities and attributes do you bring to market that make the customer experience uniquely yours? Your stories, your vibe, your humor, your insights, and your unique experiences and perspective are all part of your secret sauce.

Equally important is knowing who your ideal client is, where your ideal market lives, and when your market is ready for what you are offering, plus knowing which products and services are relevant to their most urgent needs, wants, and desires. All of this sets the stage for creating the kind of urgency that has customers move your way.

One of the greatest examples of a compelling proposition is the famous Apple ad campaign in 1997 that launched a whole new era of leadership, brand positioning, and products for the then-struggling company. Their "Think Different" campaign featured images of Albert

Einstein, Mahatma Gandhi, John Lennon, and Dr. Martin Luther King Jr.—along with the tag line "Here's to the crazy ones." The market went bananas! Apple boldly put its stake in the ground and said, "Like these game changers and visionaries, we're here to think outside of the box!" This super-innovative marketing angle became iconic and easily recognizable as a total brand differentiator for Apple. As such, the integration of technology, culture, and pushing boundaries has caused this brand to stand head and shoulders above the rest. The campaign didn't just turn around a struggling company, it launched a revolution that struck a chord with those who'd become fed up with the status quo. From trendy ads to slick white retail shops, they then built an entire identity around their brand and client experience. They elevated tech to high art and made it cool to be a geek. No mystery why they were the first US-based company to earn $1 trillion in 2017.

Three Additional Ways to Stand Out

It takes a lot to be compelling, with so many options and opportunities out there and all of them vying for your audience's attention. The more you can distinguish yourself, the greater your potential is to stand out. In addition to all the features and benefits associated with your Values-Aligned Proposition, I wanted to give you three additional ways to stand out because they're especially important.

1. UNDERSTAND MARKET TRENDS

Know the current market trends that could positively or negatively impact your industry. Get savvy about major changes in the economy, current events, or new developments. Your ability to anticipate future challenges, opportunities, and needs in your marketplace and beyond puts you in the category of expert, and when you are perceived as having expertise around a particular subject or industry people naturally begin to seek you out.

2. UNDERSTAND WHO AND WHAT ELSE IS OUT THERE

Who's in your competitive and collaborative landscape? Know who the key players are, the pros and cons of their core products and services, and key aspects of their business models (how they earn their revenue, build clients, market products, deliver services, and so on). Learn about their brand ethos, origin story, and the background of their leaders. Use their products so you have a firsthand experience of what they offer to their customers. Also, research their core values and philosophies. When you bring this to the table, you immediately build trust and credibility with those you seek to serve. They see you as thorough and well informed, and as someone who is willing to do their homework. And when people believe you have that hunger for knowledge, they also believe that when it comes to producing results for them, you will go the extra mile.

3. BECOME A TRUSTED ADVISOR

Finally, this is where it all comes together; the quality of what you offer, the skill with which you deliver, the uniqueness of your perspective, the degree of knowledge you possess around trends and landscape all contribute to your Values-Aligned Proposition and give you the potential to make a real difference with your customer. The minute your customer sees you as a trusted advisor, you will have an advantage to deliver great value in a way that is financially profitable and has real impact on those you serve.

Your Call

Are you ready to align your values with the services you have for the marketplace? Over the next three weeks, use these two exercises and two practices to (1) hone in on your Values-Aligned Proposition, (2) find your ideal client/audience, and (3) develop a strategy that enables you to be financially profitable while working in ways that totally align with your Get Paid vision.

PRACTICE 1: MANTRA

Complete this sentence:

I _____ am in business! And my vision for success is _____. Given this realization, I am willing to invest in myself and work toward this vision each and every day.

Use this sentence to create your I Am in Business! declaration. You can also log on to www.movethecrowd.me/TheCalling/resources and download your Business Declaration worksheet so that you can post it on your mirror. Once you've created your declaration, for the next 90 consecutive days recite your Business Declaration into the mirror. If you miss a day, start over at day one!

PRACTICE 2

Once you create your Values-Aligned Proposition (see the following exercise), read it at least once a day over the next three weeks to begin to embody your brand promise. Whether it's for a product you offer or your personal brand, integrate the language of your Values-Aligned Proposition into your speaking. Pay attention to what aspects or attributes connect with and inspire others; use this information to help you strengthen your proposition.

EXERCISE 1: CREATE YOUR VALUES-ALIGNED PROPOSITION

Drawing from your L3, create your Values-Aligned Proposition. If *you* are the central brand, then it should focus on your personal gifts, talents and attributes, and experience. If you're promoting a product or service that has a brand distinct from you personally, then look to the qualities, benefits, features, talents, and attributes of your product or service while considering the talents, attributes, and experience of the team associated with the company. Download your Values-Aligned Proposition Worksheets from www.movethecrowd.me/TheCalling/resources to support your clarity.

MOVETHECROWD

CREATING A UNIQUE, VALUES ALIGNED PROPOSITION

A value proposition is a clear set of specific and measurable benefits that clients or customers receive when they buy your product, service, or experience. The benefits should be unique and of greater value than other options out in the market. When considering your proposition, think about what role your values play in developing and shaping what you offer to the world. Remember, your future clients are seeking more than just transactional benefits. They are looking for radical shifts in their business and quality of life and experience.

Use this statement to target customers who will benefit most from what you and/or your company have to offer. The ideal value proposition is concise and appeals to the customer's strongest decision-making incentives.[1]

PROPOSITION	HEADLINE	DESCRIPTION
Company: Lyft	*Rides in Minutes*	To improve lives by creating the first peer-to-peer ridesharing community and the world's best transportation network.
Person: Martin Lindstorm	*Brand Consultant*	Change Agent. Brand Futurist. Bestselling Author. One of the world's premiere (and toughest) brand building experts.
Product: Bitly	*Shorten.Share.Measure.*	Shorten, brand and optimize your links across devices and channels. Share them via Bitly, API, or partner integrations.

WRITING YOUR VENTURE PROPOSITION

A compelling Venture Proposition should state:

- Who the company is
- What the company promises to those it serves
- Who the company's target market is
- What makes the company unique/compelling

HEADLINE. In one brief sentence, name the end-benefit your company is offering. It can mention the primary offering and/or the customer. Attention grabber.

_____

_____

_____

[1] http://www.investopedia.com/terms/v/valueproposition.asp#ixzz28tbvOeEp

The activities contained in this document are designed exclusively for Move The Crowd, LLC. Copying, duplicating, or otherwise reproducing in any form is prohibited. © 2012 All rights reserved.

 **MOVE**THE**CROWD**

VALUE PROPOSITION WORKSHEET

DESCRIPTION. In 2–3 sentences give a specific explanation of who the company is, what it does, for whom and why is it useful.

_____

_____

_____

DIFFERENTIATOR. What is the company's innovation or competitive advantage?

_____

_____

WRITING YOUR PERSONAL PROPOSITION

A compelling Personal Proposition should state:

- Who you are
- What you do and your promise to those you serve
- Who your target market/audience is
- What makes you (and what you do) unique/compelling

HEADLINE. In one short sentence, name the end-benefit you're offering. It can mention the primary offering and/or the customer. Attention grabber.

_____

_____

_____

DESCRIPTION. In 2–3 sentences give a specific explanation of who you are, what you do, for whom and why is it useful.

_____

_____

_____

DIFFERENTIATOR. What's your innovation or competitive advantage?

_____

_____

_____

The activities contained in this document are designed exclusively for Move The Crowd, LLC. Copying, duplicating, or otherwise reproducing in any form is prohibited. © 2012 All rights reserved.

 **MOVE**THE**CROWD**

WRITING YOUR PRODUCT PROPOSITION

- A compelling Product Proposition should highlight:
- The name of the product
- Main features and benefits the customer will receive
- Who the product is designed for
- What makes it unique/compelling

SAMPLE FEATURES	
New	Modality (live, virtual)
Customized	Guided
Private/Intimate	Comprehensive
Iterative (many over time)	In-depth
Identity specific (industry, gender, culture)	Multi-faceted
Interactive	Easy to follow
Effective	Cost effective
Faster	Delivered to your door

SAMPLE BENEFITS	
Bigger Profits	Greater Strength
Increased Capacity	Increased Stamina
More Confidence	More Beauty
Improved Relationships	Greater Flexibility
More Energy	More Power
Improved Skills (be specific)	Deeper Insights
Greater Knowledge	More Freedom

HEADLINE. In one short sentence, name the end-benefit yout product delivers. It can include your desired customer. Attention grabber.

_____

_____

_____

The activities contained in this document are designed exclusively for Move The Crowd, LLC. Copying, duplicating, or otherwise reproducing in any form is prohibited. © 2012 All rights reserved.

 **MOVETHECROWD**   VALUE PROPOSITION WORKSHEET

DESCRIPTION. In 1–2 sentences describe the product, service or experience, ideal client and why is it useful.

_____

_____

_____

DIFFERENTIATOR. List the 3 key benefits or features.

_____

_____

_____

EVALUATING YOUR PROPOSITION

Finally, evaluate the strength of your proposition by checking the following:

☐ Is it easy to understand?

☐ Does it communicate the concrete results a customer will get from doing business with you and/or purchasing and using your products and/or services?

☐ Does it describe how it's different or better than the competitor's offer?

☐ Does it feel authentic? i.e., avoids hype (like "never seen-before amazing miracle product"), superlatives ("best"), and business jargon ("value-added interactions").

☐ Can it be read and understood in about 5 seconds?[2]

Bonus Tip: Images communicate much faster than words. In brochure or web context, show the product or an image reinforcing your main message.[3]

---

[2]   *Ibid.*
[3]   *http://conversionxl.com/value-proposition-examples-how-to-create/*

The activities contained in this document are designed exclusively for Move The Crowd, LLC. Copying, duplicating, or otherwise reproducing in any form is prohibited. © 2012 All rights reserved.

EXERCISE 2: CREATE YOUR VISION FOR PARTICIPATING IN THE AGE OF THE CITIZEN

As you consider how you'd like to do business in this new age, how can you incorporate the four tenets into your professional/business strategy? Which aspects align most with your own values? How could you engage the marketplace in this new way? Download a worksheet to give voice to your new vision at www.movethecrowd.me/TheCalling/resources.

YOUR NEW VISION FOR DOING BUSINESS

I. As you consider the work you are most passionate about, what industry do you want to participate in? What opportunities or challenges within that industry feel most compelling to you?

II. How would you describe your primary target market/audience? (i.e. the people or organizations you most want to serve).

III. As you consider the four tenets (authenticity, transparency, co-creativity, community), which ones resonate with you and align most with your values? Why?

IV. Given the above, how can you incorporate the four tenets into your professional/ business strategy?

    Authenticity:

    Transparency:

    Co-creativity:

    Community:

V. How can you use the four tenets to engage your desired marketplace in a new way?

The activities contained in this document are designed exclusively for Move The Crowd, LLC. Copying, duplicating, or otherwise reproducing in any form is prohibited. © 2012 All rights reserved.

12

Step #6: Celebrating a New Way
of Doing Business

Once you've cultivated your unique Values-Aligned Proposition, it's time to authentically enter the market. And there is no better way to drive your personal economy and own your power as a conscious creator than to do this in a way that celebrates your Get Paid vision and true calling. Your goal is to summon the courage and commitment to do business in a new way—one that acknowledges your talents and gifts, plus honors and uplifts your values and fosters the kind of economy you want to create and participate in. This is where the rubber meets the road, because monetizing your gifts is what getting paid is all about!

In this Age of the Citizen, consumers are looking for more than just friendly transactions or product benefits. They want radical shifts in their quality of life and experience, too! Think back to the four core tenets in chapter 11: authenticity, transparency, co-creativity, and community. These are what truly guide a customer's purchasing decisions. As you consider what you want to bring to market, ask yourself, *How will I or am I already dramatically improving people's lives or ambitions?* In what way are you fulfilling your mission and forwarding the hopes, dreams, and aspirations of others? How are you honoring your values as you deliver on these? Such are the guiding lights for bringing your unique proposition to life and doing business in a new way.

When it comes to monetizing your products and services, keep a few crucial points in mind. First, know what transformation you're selling—the benefits, results, and why it's important to your audience's quality of life. Also, know who the customer is and what they're willing to pay for it. Speak to why customers need it *now*—what's the nature of their pain that makes their current state intolerable, and how can you alleviate it quickly and easily? Finally, demonstrate why you're the one to do it. What is it about your skills, results, background, journey, aesthetic, process, vibe, and experience that makes them want to work with you?

Each of us has at least one and often many unique gifts that we can bring to the marketplace. If you are cultivating a new idea, your primary focus should be on getting really clear about what your core offering is and what the change or transformation is that your potential client will buy into. If you've already established yourself and your offering either on your own or within another company, your main concern is probably sustainability, or making sure you're able to identify the right market/s for what you have to offer and ensure that you're offering it in a way that's reaching and converting your audience from followers to customers. If you are experienced, your main concern is going to be profitability—meaning, how do you reach *more* people in a way that is even more profitable?

Remember, you can make money as an employee, consultant/freelancer, business owner, or investor—the key is to always have an entrepreneurial mindset. If you work for someone else, this means you'll need to stop thinking of yourself as an employee and start thinking of yourself as a branded collaborator or stakeholder—i.e., someone who has a unique contribution to make, is aligned with the mission, and has a stake in the success of the company.

In this chapter, you'll take your next step toward getting paid for your ideas by showing you how to engage as a conscious creator in the marketplace. You'll learn to recognize which of your talents a client or customer will pay for and how to create a menu of appropriately priced offerings. After all, to make money, you have to hit a few salable points. You must create a product that either solves a problem or creates an opportunity; build trust and credibility; and package your product in a way that's easy to buy, sell, and use. You have to position it in a way that's easy for your ideal client to find and sell it in a way that adds value. Finally, you have to collaborate and partner in a way that expands your reach, with clear criteria for the kinds of relationships that will put the right people in your pipeline. Excellent partnering strengthens your credibility *and* expands your reach. It's imperative to achieving and sustaining financial success.

Last, we'll talk selling. Once you have your audience's attention, how do you convince them to buy? Remember, in this Age of the Citizen engagement is relational; this means that as with any other relationship, you have to establish a rapport and build trust before you can sell anyone anything. (In fact, many people don't even use the world "sell" anymore, preferring "share" or "serve" or "invite"!) I'll also go into the reasons people buy—from trusting the brand and believing in you, to believing you care about them, to trusting that what you have to offer will solve a problem and improve their life and that you are the only person who can deliver their desired result in this way.

Monetizing Your Gifts

When I was developing my own Get Paid vision, I had to reconcile my feelings about monetization. At the time, I was a struggling artist and activist who could barely pay rent. I signed up for a high-priced marketing mastermind (on my credit card) with the hope that I would actually learn how to successfully book my workshops and performances. When our mastermind leader walked us through the definition of "monetization," all kinds of lightbulbs went off. I was floored to learn that you can actually create something, equate a value to it, and then prove that value in the marketplace. It seemed so simple and straightforward as a concept:

make it, describe it, price it, find people who want it, tell them about it, take their money in exchange for your creation, do the money dance! Yet in this workshop, I realized that as an artist, I'd been allowing my clients (i.e., the producers, promoters, and programming directors in the various venues and organizations where I performed and taught) to dictate what I had to offer the world and how much I could charge when some of them had *no idea* what it really took to create the things I was selling. Up until that point, the idea of formalizing my creations in terms of products and services had never really occurred to me. In that moment, I felt completely liberated because I knew that if I could figure out a way to organize, price, and successfully promote my ideas I would have access to unlimited earning potential.

If you think back to Z's challenge in chapter 7, where they felt torn about charging for the true value for their services, I too had to stand for and demonstrate my own credibility and expertise. I also had to get clear on what it really took to create experiences that others would be willing to pay me for. And finally, I had to educate my clients and dictate my value, not the other way around.

Collectively, learning about, and personalizing, monetization took me from being an artist who let everyone else dictate the scope and value of my services to one with a menu of appropriately priced offerings who could then share that menu as a starting point in any prospective relationship. I did this by considering what I could offer that would have value to my prospective clients—from workshops, to performances, to talks—and how much time it took me to create these things. What was the difference between doing an event where I could utilize preexisting material and one where I was asked to write something special? These details helped me distinguish between standard and commissioned content, and then I could price my time and deliverables accordingly. Just bringing a framework like this to prospective clients allowed me to not only quantify my work but also stand firmly in the justification for my pricing. This made every sales interaction empowering for me and the client, because they had a way of understanding the scope of what they were asking. The result? I tripled my income in eight short months! I always left room for negotiation, but I was always the one who led the conversation about my Values-Aligned Proposition and corresponding products and services.

Monetizing Within Someone Else's Company

The concept of monetization is not only reserved for those who own and run a venture; it's just as relevant for those of you who are working inside of a company as well. Remember, even though you may technically be an employee, I'm still going to encourage you to think entrepreneurially. This means: stepping into a leadership role (independent of your title), cultivating a personal brand, aligning with the company's or organization's mission, and then genuinely considering what you specifically have to offer that moves the company closer to its goals and objectives. As you consider your Values-Aligned Proposition within the context of your job description, you'll want to determine first if the two are aligned. If they are not aligned, your work will be to either create that alignment or seek additional opportunities within the company, assuming this company is where you want to be. The second priority will be to access the economic value of what you have to offer to the company that you already work for. What are the duties and qualifications to determine your salary and other benefits? What's your process for distinguishing your unique contribution in the context of a team effort? How can you align your talents with what your company finds compelling? And what can you offer beyond the job description? How will you educate your employer so that you can create innovative opportunities that bring greater value to you, the company, clients, and stakeholders? These may be special initiatives, they may be additional strategies within your existing role, or, as I mentioned earlier, an opportunity to pursue another role within the company, etc. Your bio, résumé, and interview are usually how you make the case for what you have to offer. You may also engage in similar conversations during a performance review, or you may seek to create your own opportunities to have these conversations. Your past accomplishments and bottom-line results are often included. However, if you consider all the aspects of your Values-Aligned Proposition, there may be other contributions you could make that you've never placed a value on. There may be additional training and skills that you've never considered to be a part of what makes you valuable. For example, in addition to your role as a marketing director, you may leverage your major in women's studies and also step up to lead the women's initiative or use your interest in sustainability to move into the area of Corporate Social Responsibility.

According to a 2015 *Forbes* article on underutilized employees, companies engage only about 40 percent of the related talents and skills of their respective employees! If you begin to take a more intentional inventory of "what you bring" drawn from your Values-Aligned Proposition, you'll be able to think more creatively when you engage with companies about how to maximize your contribution.

Monetizing Within Your Venture

As you consider your Values-Aligned Proposition for your own venture, it is imperative to recognize what you have to offer and what it will take to make this compelling to your audience.

What's most important here is to really evaluate what it takes for you to produce your offering—including raw materials, design, packaging, customer service, processing, and delivery—and how much of your time, expertise, and unique intellectual property is utilized. Every single facet of creation costs something—whether it's time, money, or other resources—so you must determine how they factor into your final sale. Map out your process step by step, so you can see all the components that go into what you are creating. Not only does this process allow you to come up with a relevant price, but it also allows you to stand behind your fees because you are now intimately familiar with what it takes to create it. When you are not in the business of widgets, it can feel tricky to turn real interest in what you do into tangible offerings that people will actually pay you for. Sometimes my clients are even afraid to charge because they believe that the monetary exchange adds more "pressure" to the sale—and so, without realizing it, they undervalue themselves and their product. Trust me, it's okay to do what you love *and* charge for it.

Building the skill of designing, organizing, packaging, and pricing your offerings is a crucial part of building an awesome suite of products and services drawn from your Values-Aligned Proposition and an awesome way to create real profitability within your venture.

Before we leave this section, I want to give you a perfect example of what's possible when you are willing to monetize. Another massive breakaway from the Industrial Nonprofit reality happened with our beloved Heather. You remember her from chapter 2—right? Eighteen months into our work not only had Heather significantly transformed her relationship to rescuing, but she'd also unearthed the vision for her new venture.

"Okay, I know what I want the Million Person Project to do. I'm ready to launch it."

But, true to all of her conditioning, as we began to give life to the idea, it was showing up as a nonprofit and Heather was working *hard* trying to raise a modest amount of resources just to get it off the ground. I was supportive of her initial strategy, because I do believe that philanthropic capital can serve as an awesome "angel investment" in an idea. And this concept is one that I believe is so underutilized. However, as I watched Heather chase people down I knew she was getting disheartened.

"Why aren't people calling me back?" she asked in frustration one day—of no one in particular! I could see what was going on and I did not want her launching experience to be riddled with that energy.

In a come-to-Jesus session, I opened the door for a future conversation about the Values-Aligned Proposition of the business: "Heather, you can build this as a for-profit company."

Silence. "Really, you think people would pay us to do this work?"

"Absolutely, you've just got to get really clear about the Values-Aligned Proposition."

"Okay . . . . the what?" I could hear the hesitancy in her voice.

"Everything I know about this work tells me that we're gonna have to raise the money to do it."

"I know," I replied. "But I want you to consider that not only is it doable, but it will be way more empowering, too."

"Uh!" she said. "Boy, do I need that right now. This is crazy; when I look at the budget Julian and I barely have enough to cover our expenses."

Heather did what she needed to do to make the launch work, but as soon as she got back and had a little rest, we reexamined her offerings. "Now, to answer your question, your Values-Aligned Proposition represents the quality of your client's experience and the overall impact your storytelling process has on their lives."

"Oooooh, then we have an awesome Values-Aligned Proposition, because our leaders, I mean clients, are kicking butt with their stories!"

We began with her organizational trainings. I had her walk me through every facet of the experience and probed to help her get clear about what each person walked away with. We looked at how many people she could accommodate and how many trainings she thought she could do. We came away from our session with a clear framework for an organizational product.

Then I gave her the initial assignment that would alter the reality of this business: "Go out now and get five clients for this training."

Two weeks later Heather began our session with, "You are not going to believe what happened! In my first conversation, I booked four trainings for ten K!"

"Woo-hoo!" I said. "Great, now go out there and get four more."

Since that day, Heather has not looked back and now runs a multi-six-figure profitable business that is rapidly growing. She still collaborates with philanthropic partners when it makes sense, but they are not the life or death of her business.

Doing the Money Dance, AKA Handling Your Business in a Whole New Way

Monetizing your gifts is a bit like a dance between you and your client. You have to know when to lead in establishing your Values-Aligned Proposition, when to follow your client in keeping your ear to the ground for their needs, when to add a little sparkle, to make the process shine, enjoy the experience, and build an awesome relationship that comes to life in the back-and-forth. It's a real give-and-take; in the Age of the Citizen you've got to demonstrate that you are as invested in your products and services and the client as they are invested in you.

I often emphasize the importance of building trust and credibility among clients, employees, and even the larger industry as the number one thing you need to do to Get Paid. People buy and do business with those they trust and who have a proven track record of success. How you establish your brand, how you engage with other brands with whom you affiliate, the language you use in your marketing, the way you treat your clients, and your team and what they say about you builds trust and credibility (or challenges it). Integrity is the foundation for prosperity. How you show up in every interaction is a part of your brand and needs to be an integral part of how you build trust in the marketplace.

It's also key to package your product/service in a way that is easy to buy, sell, and use. You want to keep it simple, easy to understand, easy to share, and easy to implement. If your product is a joy to sell, you will want to share it with more people and others will want to pass it along. If people feel confident that users are successful with your product or service, they're far more likely to work with you. And if your sales process is quick, easy, and efficient, clients will equate that positive experience with you and feel encouraged to give you more business.

You also want to position your product in a way that's easy for the ideal client to find. If those who need you most cannot find you or, worse yet, do not even know you exist, you are missing out on tons of revenue. Being in the right place at the right time, with the right offering, is a recipe for success. From how you affiliate to how you syndicate, it is vital that you are where your ideal clients are. SEO, targeted ads and promotions, right affiliation, and right syndication along with thorough client research are the keys to being more accessible to your target market.

You also want to sell your product/service in a way that adds value. One of the best ways to build trust and credibility in a sales process is to give value before your prospect buys anything. This does not mean you should give away everything for free, but you must be willing to build rapport through your work and demonstrate your ability to deliver on the result(s) you promise before clients purchase your product or service. Your willingness to make a difference in the life of a person before money changes hands shows that you care about their success. Your free content, product descriptions, and sales pages all give you an opportunity to be of service and engender greater confidence and comfort around making the purchase.

Finally, be sure to partner in a way that expands your reach. Collaboration with other brands is vital to consistently increase your audience. When partnering, you need to have clear criteria for the types of relationships that will put the right people in your pipeline. Choose those aligned with your values, who have complementary rather than duplicate offerings, who serve the same kinds of clients you do, who operate with high integrity, and who have great products that deliver the intended results. Excellent partnering strengthens your credibility *and* expands your reach. Building relationships with those in your field or industry, and those in complementary fields and industries, is imperative to achieving and sustaining your financial success.

Let's Talk Selling

I'd be remiss if I didn't at least say a word or two about selling. We all know that the marketplace is saturated with all kinds of gimmicks and stunts aimed at getting people's attention, and I'll be the first to admit that in the Age of the Citizen the scrutiny around these kinds of behaviors is at an all-time high. But "selling" doesn't have to be a dirty word or something you avoid because you think it somehow takes away from the difference you want to make. Remember what I said in the last section; you can actually make the selling experience just as transformative and rewarding if you understand what's important to your prospective client.

So, how do you get people to listen to you? And once you get their attention, how do you convince them to buy? After all, this is how you're going to Get Paid *and* Do Good. . . .

There are many reasons people buy, so the more you can understand and address most of these reasons, the greater your chances of making the sale. Remember, buying is an emotional experience. And just as you have a belief system when it comes to money and doing business, guess who else has a belief system they are navigating as well? That's right: your client/customer. After working with thousands of clients over the years, here's what I've found to be the most compelling reasons why they buy.

1. *They trust and believe in you:* Clients believe you are who you say you are. They have a sense of your values/story/history/background, and they've experienced your core offering in some format and received great value from that experience.

2. *They believe that you care about them:* You've demonstrated the kind of generosity that lets them know that not only are you interested in making money, but you are more interested in helping people and making a difference. They can tell from how you interact with them that you actually care about their hopes, dreams, challenges, desires, and aspirations.

3. *They believe you will deliver what you say you will deliver:* You have a demonstrated track record that shows you are capable of producing the desired result again and again. They see your re-

sults and feel your passion and dedication to the task. They also experience the time, energy, and care that you put into everything you do that says you take your promise to them seriously.

4. *They believe you are a person with integrity:* You've demonstrated a combination of 1, 2, and 3, through experiences you've had, through in person or virtual interactions with you, and through the ways that you (or your company) follow up and follow through with them.

5. *They believe that your offering will either solve pressing problems or create a compelling opportunity for them:* They see the value in the offer and recognize how they can apply the solution to their own lives to achieve their desired results.

6. *They believe the result you promise will in some way dramatically improve and/or enhance their quality of life:* They are clear about the *specific* way that your product or service can address their particular challenges, opportunity, and/or aspirations.

7. *They believe that they can't get what you offer anywhere else:* They sense something unique in who you are, what you offer, and the way you've been able to distinguish yourself that lets them know they can't get what you bring anywhere else. This includes a unique combination of talents, gifts, and abilities with your distinct experience, expertise, history, and aesthetic.

8. *They believe they are receiving more value for the price:* When they consider what they're getting, the price feels like a bargain. Value outweighs any sense of "risk" involved.

9. *They buy because the "change" or "transformation" far out-weighs their "do nothing" option:* They know that it will be more painful to continue to do what they have been doing (or not doing) than to work with you and embrace your solution.

10. *They believe they can be successful with you:* The organization of your product, the complimentary support, your style of teaching, and the accountability structure (i.e., the way you keep them on track and motivated) that you create all serve to boost the confidence of those who choose to engage your product or service.

To this point, I remember when Eva, another international client, and I first began working together. At the time, she was running a horse-training company that also taught owners how to ride. Even though this was the company's premise, Eva knew that the real work consistently happened with the owners, more than the animals.

"Teaching people with horses how to communicate with this beautiful animal taught me more about humans than I would have ever imagined. To truly connect with a horse, you must connect with yourself. No chance of hiding. The horse is your mirror," she said.

When Eva approached me, she was interested in evolving from the work she was doing with horses into working directly with people.

"More and more I realize how the horse is merely a 'vehicle' to get people to take a close look in that mirror and that my passion for teaching is actually more about creating space for self-reflection than the actual teaching about the horse."

Eva and I talked about how clients would find her either through social media or through other events they would promote through other collaborations in their community. When I asked her how she felt about taking this new leap she paused.

"I'm not so sure about it—especially the selling part," she replied.

"How do you feel about selling your products and services now?"

"Yuck!" Eva replied.

That said it all.

As we delved deeper, what became clear was that even though Eva believed she was a great teacher, she felt a lot of pressure taking money. In her mind the money created a whole new level of responsibility and she was afraid of not being able to deliver or meet someone else's expectations and these feelings caused her to struggle with owning the value of her services (Root Cause #2—"I am not worthy").

In Eva's industry, the rates were fairly clear; however, once she got out in the personal coaching field, she suddenly had to decide for herself what her rates would have to be. Being afraid she would not live up to the expectations of her future clients, she kept her rates low and put a lot of energy into the coaching sessions. But, after a while, she began to burn out.

When I asked her about why she wouldn't just raise her rates, she talked about the pressure to be responsible for living up to someone else's expectations. I asked her to define what being responsible meant.

"Being responsible means that I have to . . . I don't know, be perfect all the time. But what if I charge all this money and they don't get the result? Then what?" she asked.

"Let me ask you something," I interjected. "Real talk here—have you ever let a client down?"

She gave a nervous laugh. "No . . . my clients are always very happy."

I continued to probe: "So if you are already consistently delivering, why wouldn't you want to honor the value of that exchange?"

She paused. "Funny you should ask me that, because I do notice that when I work with those clients who pay me less, if they put in the full effort, I feel fine. But if I work with a client who can afford to pay me more and they don't put in their best effort, I am exhausted after those coaching sessions. There is definitely an imbalance in the exchange."

"Hmm," I replied. "Very interesting."

She laughed.

"Tell me how you feel when I say this."

"Okay," she said.

"I think you're going to need to raise your rates, not just to sustain your new business, but to maintain your own level of integrity. Money *is* energy. And it's important that every exchange feels honoring—for you and for them."

Eva put her hands over her face, blushed, and then vigorously nodded her head. "I think you're right."

"So, Eva, what should the number be?" I asked.

When Eva thought about a number in alignment with the value of what her clients received, the number was almost double what her current clients paid. "This is the number that feels right to me," she said.

"How did you get there?" I asked.

"Well, when I look at all of the things I've learned that I put into teaching, all of the years of experience I have, including everything I've learned working with horses and people and the way that I give my full presence to supporting those clients, this is what feels like a match energetically."

"Well, my love," I said. "All of this needs to be reflected in your Values-Aligned Proposition and in the way you describe your coaching services." I continued, "Your homework is to update all of your materials to include these additional benefits and features and to speak with every one of your clients and let them know, effective immediately, you are raising your rates."

"Okay!" Eva said as she blushed some more.

True to her word and inspired by a new level of clarity, Eva spoke to every client and doubled her rates.

"How did it feel to do this?" I asked.

"Oh my," she said. "It was very empowering to engage with them in this new way."

We also talked about the design of her new offerings. Rather than booking single appointments randomly, session by session, I encouraged her to create packages that could be discounted if clients purchased them in advance. These two shifts in the business alone had the potential to more than double her teaching revenue across the board and boost her cash flow by 280 percent.

Eva also applied these insights to her horsey business. We evaluated which products made sense to invest in and which did not, and we studied where she could cut back on expenses. Finally, we also addressed the pricing structure for the junior trainers who worked for the company. By the time Eva finished, she'd streamlined the company's product line, reorganized their existing offers, reduced their expenses, and the ultimate result was a 480 percent growth in profit among programs. This body of work enabled Eva to completely step away from the business, which enabled her awesome partner to take the helm.

Eva continues to leverage everything she's learned around owning the value of her work to create profitable coaching programs for people, which represents the evolution of her true calling—she knows it's about more than the money. The money is just a symbol of honoring her worth and the value of her unique proposition.

Your Call

Are you ready to leverage your Values-Aligned Proposition to Get Paid and make a real difference in the lives of your clients? Use these two practices and one exercise over the next two weeks to strengthen your proposition, attract ideal prospects, and deliver awesome results.

PRACTICE 1: MANTRA

Use your Values-Aligned Proposition Worksheet to inspire a one-sentence mantra/tag line that speaks to the value you deliver to every client/customer. This mantra should motivate and inspire you to get up every single day to be of service because it holds your commitment to your calling. For the next two weeks, speak this mantra every day when you get up in the A.M. and when you prepare to interact with your prospects and/or clients.

Here are a couple of examples:

"Empower the Dream." (This is Move The Crowd's internal mantra.)
"Stay True. Get Paid. Do Good." (This is Move The Crowd's Values-Aligned Proposition.)

Other Examples

"Let's Change Lives."
"Help Women's Leadership Thrive."
"Lift Every Voice."
"Give People the Power to Choose."

PRACTICE 2: REVIEW THE TOP 10 REASONS WHY PEOPLE BUY

Every day for the next two weeks, use your Top 10 Reasons Why People Buy checklist to strengthen your sales materials and conversations. Develop a script that supports these reasons and hone in on the ones that feel most challenging to demonstrate.

EXERCISE 1: MONETIZING YOUR GIFTS

Use the Product Development, Ideal Client Profile, and Pricing Worksheets at www.movethecrowd.me/The Calling/resources to create, strengthen, and/or clarify your menu of offerings. If you are just getting started, focus on viability, pick one product, and develop your client profile, product design, and pricing. If you are more established, focus on sustainability and the process of realigning your existing offerings to increase your number of prospective clients. If you are working in an organization, use the guiding questions in the "Monetizing Within Someone Else's Company" section to help you refine and realign your Values-Aligned Proposition to your company.

EXERCISE 2: GET PAID!

Just like Heather, use all of the preceding work to get out there and close at least one new client!

PRODUCT DEVELOPMENT

I.   What is the primary "change" or transformation you are selling in the marketplace? (i.e., What is your core offering?)

Example: Greater Self Love and Personal Confidence

II. How does this product reflect your values and desired impact?

Example: I believe that everyone deserves to be treated with dignity and respect. I am passionate about helping people get the respect they deserve. Building confidence enables them to command that respect.

III. What's the name of this product/service?

Example: More Confidence: Boost Your Self Confidence, Grow Your Following and Blow People Away.

IV. How is this product or service organized/designed?

Example: A six-week online course which consists of: video modules, downloadable templates, and worksheets, etc.

V.   What is the process your client goes through when using your product or service? How does it take the person from point A to point B step by step? (Content and Methodology.)

Content Example: Six-Step Process that: evaluates your confidence level, transforms top 3 limiting beliefs, etc. **Methodology Example:** Interactive journey that includes: recorded training sessions, hot seats, guided reflections, etc.

The activities contained in this document are designed exclusively for Move The Crowd, LLC. Copying, duplicating, or otherwise reproducing in any form is prohibited. © 2012 All rights reserved.

VI. What is the duration of use for your product or service?

Example: 6 Weeks

VII. What kind of results can the person expect in that time if they follow your guidance? (i.e. , What kind of claims or promises are you making with each purchase?)

Example: You'll be able to look anyone in the eye and tell them what you need and/or want, etc.

VIII. What kind of support materials and instructions are included?

Example: Instructional videos, tipsheets, templated scripts, etc.

IX. What additional support or service comes with the purchase of your product or service?

Example: Product orientation, email customer service support, FAQs area, 30-day money back guarantee.

X. What kind of bonuses or special gifts do you offer when they purchase?

Example: Bonus video and downloadable worksheet on how to give a world class signature speech. Bonus video with My Top 5 Quick Confidence Building Exercises you can practice along with at home.

XI. Is there a companion product or more advanced product or service they can purchase once they receive and gain value from your initial product?

Example: Masters of Confidence Program—6-Month Coaching and Mentoring Mastermind Program

XII. If your response to question II was "not really," what are three things you can do to make this product even more aligned with your values and desired impact?

The activities contained in this document are designed exclusively for Move The Crowd, LLC. Copying, duplicating, or otherwise reproducing in any form is prohibited. © 2012 All rights reserved.

 **MOVETHECROWD**

I. WHO ARE THEY?:

Demographic Profile:

If your venture serves individual clients—use the prompts for Individuals (left) to create your profile. If your venture serves other companies, use the prompts for companies (right) to create your profile.

Individual:	Company:
Age:	Size — # of Employees:
Gender:	Years in Business:
Cultural/Ethnic Background:	Industry Focus:
Spiritual/Religious Affiliation:	Products/Services:
Political Affiliation/Views:	Region/Location:
Region/Location:	USP:
Education History:	Target Market:
Professional Occupation:	Ideal Customer:
Career Stage:	Average Price Point:
Income Bracket:	Annual Revenues:
Physical Characteristics:	Stage in Business:
Housing:	Cultural/Ethnic Orientation:
Transportation:	Spiritual/Religious:
Children:	Industry Networks:
Hobbies/Special Interests:	

The activities contained in this document are designed exclusively for Move The Crowd, LLC. Copying, duplicating, or otherwise reproducing in any form is prohibited. © 2012 All rights reserved.

II. PSYCHOGRAPHIC PROFILE:

If your venture serves individual clients—use the prompts for Individuals (left) to create your profile. If your venture serves other companies—use the prompts for companies (right) to create your profile.

Individual:	Company:
Feelings About Themselves:	Vision/Mission:
Core Beliefs/Values:	Values:
Feelings About the Opportunity/ Enhancement You Provide:	Core Value Proposition:
Feelings About the Problem You Want to Solve:	Culture:
Feelings About the Current Marketplace Solutions:	Primary Challenges:
Feelings About Change:	Feelings About Customers:
Core Challenges:	Feelings About Industry:
Core Aspirations:	Core Aspirations:
Big Dreams:	Beliefs About Success:
Core Beliefs About Success:	Beliefs About Money:
Core Beliefs About Money:	
Feelings About this Moment in Their Lives:	

The activities contained in this document are designed exclusively for Move The Crowd, LLC. Copying, duplicating, or otherwise reproducing in any form is prohibited. © 2012 All rights reserved.

MOVETHECROWD

1. What is the biggest problem they face?
2. What is the most important thing to them?
3. When they are sad who do they go to?
4. When they are happy who do they talk to?
5. When they imagine their soulmate what do they see?
6. What kind of environment do they thrive in?
7. If they could solve one major problem in the world what would it be?
8. What do they most want that they don't believe they can achieve?
9. What is the support they've always wanted but never thought they could have?
10. What else needs to be present to support them in feeling comfortable and safe in doing the hard work they need to do?

III. LIFESTYLE PROFILE:

1. What do they do in their spare time?
2. What are the things that they read?
3. Where do they hang out?
4. If they wanted to go have an amazing dinner where would they go?
5. When they imagine their soul mate who do they see?

IV. WHY YOU?

1. Why are they drawn to your offerings (products, services, experiences, etc.)?
2. What are they hoping to achieve by engaging with you?
3. Why are you the perfect company to serve them?

The activities contained in this document are designed exclusively for Move The Crowd, LLC. Copying, duplicating, or otherwise reproducing in any form is prohibited. © 2012 All rights reserved.

 **MOVE**THE**CROWD**

PRICING WORKSHEET

1. What does it cost you to make and deliver this product or service?

2. How does yours compare with similar offerings in the marketplace? What is the most common price point or range?

3. What is most distinct and unique about yours? What additional innovations or value adds does your product contain?

4. What does it cost you to make and deliver this product or service?

5. How does yours compare with similar offerings in the marketplace? What is the most common price point or range?

6. What is most distinct and unique about yours? What additional innovations or value adds does your product contain?

7. How do you assign a market value price to each component or aspect of the product or service? (segmentation/delineation).

8. Are you charging a premium? Can you justify it?

The activities contained in this document are designed exclusively for Move The Crowd, LLC. Copying, duplicating, or otherwise reproducing in any form is prohibited. © 2012 All rights reserved.

MOVETHE**CROWD**

9. How does your pricing align with your brand? (i.e., your mission, your values, your desired market, your desired impact).

10. Do you offer discounts or special promotions?

11. Do you have a clear rationale for when you do and when you don't?

The activities contained in this document are designed exclusively for Move The Crowd, LLC. Copying, duplicating, or otherwise reproducing in any form is prohibited. © 2012 All rights reserved.

Part III

DO GOOD

13

Step #1: Recognizing Your
Power to Do Good

Now that you know how to Get Paid, let's talk about how to leverage your Values-Aligned Proposition to Do Good. There are so many ways to Do Good in the world right now, but your goal isn't just to do something nice for another person. It's to monetize your true calling so all that you are and do is in perfect alignment with who you want to be and what you want to see in the world.

Don't think for a second that you don't have control over what goes on around you—you may have been conditioned to turn away from your calling and play small or hide out. But I guarantee, there's no reason to feel helpless—this is just another form of conditioned victimhood. And we don't do victim anymore—we do conscious creation, remember? Doing good can transform the feelings of overwhelm, apathy, and resignation you may be experiencing. It can embolden you with a sense of power when you see just how much of a difference you can make in the lives of others. This allows you to step into a new definition of what it is to be an empowered citizen—one that leads to your true calling and invites a True. Paid. Good. way of operating in the world.

The thing about doing good is that it doesn't require going out of your way all the time to do little (or big) things to make a difference—you don't have to march every weekend or spend your lunch break signing online petitions. You can if it moves you, but I want to advocate for a more focused, integrated, and big-vision approach. Tens of millions of people every day participate in some form of social good, and because of the Age of the Citizen, we are rapidly becoming a society where this is the norm. Blame it on the hyper-connectivity of social media, or the great millennial invasion, or on the changing multicultural landscape. Whatever the reason, we are in a moment when the call to find a sense of purpose is greater than it's ever been. Don't you want *in*?

Today's social movements are no longer single issue or identity focused, nor are they only nonprofit based. They are more diverse, complex, robust, and far reaching. They represent a combination of ideas and values, and they operate across class, ethnicity, culture, gender, ability, and orientation. They tend to focus on cultural and symbolic issues rooted in our individual and collective identities, like being a woman or a single parent, or even an independent artist. Each is associated with a set of beliefs, symbols, values, and meanings that offer a new set of socially constructed attributes about the meaning of life and a vision for empowered participation.

Similarly, the relationship between individuals and the collective group in these new movements is also blurred, as we've seen with the women's movement. There is a fundamental belief that what is good for one woman is good for all women, including equal pay, extended maternity leave, and flexible hours that support caretaking. We all believe these are important individually and collectively and therefore, as women, we are encouraged to show up for one another. In other words, these new movements center around pursuing a greater quality of life and experience and demand that all people have the right to be healthy, happy, and whole as they aspire to raise their families and reach their full potential in life and in business. These movements are dedicated to a world where all of us can thrive and prosper.

At the end of the day, social impact work relies on a deep and optimistic trust in our innate goodness—the kinds of values, frankly, that my clients access every day to Stay True. Get Paid. Do Good. When it comes to doing good, environmentalist, entrepreneur, activist, and author Paul Hawken said it best:

> When asked if I am pessimistic or optimistic about the future, my answer is always the same: If you look at the science about what is happening on earth and aren't pessimistic, you don't understand data. But if you meet the people working to restore this earth and the lives of the poor, and you aren't optimistic, you haven't got a pulse. What I see everywhere in the world are ordinary people willing to confront despair, power, and incalculable odds in order to restore some semblance of grace, justice, and beauty to this world.

As crazy as it may seem out there, we have far more power than we think when it comes to creating the kind of world we want to live in for ourselves, children, and generations to come. The first step toward becoming an empowered citizen is to address what you believe. And to determine if there is anything right now that is standing in the way of your ability to answer your call. What do you see? Don't judge what comes up—just grab a piece of paper or your journal and jot down all the reasons you've given yourself for why you haven't made your Do Good a priority.

For some of you, like Taylor in chapter 10, you may be doing really good work but not *your* work. If that's the case, I want you to jot down in your journal all the reasons you've given yourself for that, too! For others, you may be in your passion but know you're not playing full out or operating to your highest potential. Why is that? Again, just jot down your responses in your journal without judgment.

The point is, just as you can create your own vision for success and your own empowering economy, you can also create a better world. One of the biggest wounds we're healing as a society is reimagining the term "altruistic," which has a bad rap as too soft or touchy-feely. Having an optimistic view of the world doesn't make you weak or out of touch. It actually makes you hopeful and filled with the potential to make an incredible contribution to humanity.

I'll never forget being invited to give a commencement speech at a small New England college. This institution had developed one of the premiere masters programs in Social Entrepreneurship and was revolutionizing the way students and faculty collaborated to create robust learning experiences. I was honored to be there and enjoying the prospect of being with so many brilliant and heartwarming people. Sipping my water and being introduced around, I connected with a bright young man who'd been invited to the graduation by a friend. We struck up a conversation, and he said, "Man, what's with all this love stuff? The world is screwed up and people are out here trying to pick daisies and run through the fields." I laughed (while shaking my head at God) and said, "That's hilarious. What's your name?" He told me it was Joseph. "Joseph," I asked, "do you really think that's all love is?" He paused, looking confused, and asked, "What do you mean?" I explained, "I actually believe that love, real love, is the hardest work there is." He looked stunned. "I know that some people have this distorted perception," I continued, "that those who claim to be all about love are hippies, sissies, and wusses, but that's not what I see." I told him, "When I think of love, I think of Dr. Martin Luther King Junior, I think of Mother Teresa, I think of Mahatma Gandhi—those are the people who come to mind for me. And I don't see anything 'wussy' about them. They are some of the most courageous people in history. And they *had* to be operating from love. I mean, why else would they knowingly put themselves in harm's way for people they did not know if they didn't feel love for humanity?"

Joseph simply stood still, trying to process what I'd said. I left him with a question. "If love is as soft as you imply," I said, "then tell me, how many people do you know who would literally get out of bed in the middle of the night to leave the comfort of their homes and families to put their life on the line for someone they did not know? Can you name five? Okay, how about three? Okay, let's just say one?" More staring from

J. Just then, the gluten-free pizza arrived, which was my cue. With a loving touch on the shoulder, I said my parting words: "Really great to meet you, Joseph."

In a lot of ways, I could totally understand where Joseph was coming from. So much of what we're fed in the world tells us that love is hopeless. For every awesome thing we watch on the news, we have to endure one hundred terrible things first in order to get there. It's no wonder that people feel like it's useless to raise their voice. It's easy to become overwhelmed just by the demands of your own life, so when you consider what it takes to impact the lives of others, you may not have much left to work with. I hear you. Confronting our own conditioned apathy is hard. But it's also necessary if you're serious about owning your creative powers to Do Good.

In this chapter, I'm going to invite you into the next level of awareness around what you believe when it comes to your ability to make a difference in the world. I'm also going to introduce you to the social impact landscape in a way that will enable you to think about your own passions and gifts in relationship to all that is happening out there. And finally, I'm going to call upon your courage to consider that there may be a much bigger game you're being invited to play when it comes to your True. Paid. Good. that is ultimately your calling.

The Trouble with Being Numb

Technology's seamless integration into our lives means we now have access to just about anything at the swipe of a screen. And while it is amazing, it can also be very taxing. If you're a person who's determined to stay "on top of it" at work, for example, between your phone and computer you can be beeping, dinging, and buzzing all day long. And for as much as those things are designed to keep you in the loop and on track, when you're in a state of flow that's constantly being interrupted it can be stressful. Add to that the layer of family responsibilities also vying for your texting stream and your brain goes into a reptilian state, just by virtue of the sheer overload of information. Shutting down is our body's normal defense mechanism against the onslaught of overstimulation. Rather than frying our neuro-processors, we simply pull the shade down and hit the mute button when it all becomes too much.

Sometimes we try to escape by flipping through our social media stream, and guess what we encounter? Between the cute doggie pics and wacky toddler videos is unadulterated drama, both personal and global—and it all feels so big and daunting that we check right back out. Or even worse, we become totally desensitized to the whole thing. It's like the homeless man on the corner that we pass every day. You've seen him enough that he's now blended into the backdrop.

As much as this kind of response is normal, it's also dangerous, because our inaction has the potential to encourage even more mayhem. It's like a burglar who doesn't stop at the gate. Once he realizes no one's home, he's going to invite himself inside. When we talk about today's issues over our kids' strollers at the park, or at cocktail receptions and dinner parties, nobody's a fan of what's happening, even if they share different views. It's a hot mess out there.

So if all of us feel this way, then why does the state of our world— and, perhaps more relatedly, certain neighborhoods in your town— look the way it does? We're all guilty on some level of not speaking up, whether it's to invite the bully boss to back down or tell a colleague to stop making offensive remarks. It's so much easier to roll the window up and keep backing out of the driveway. The problem is, if we wait until the situations get unbearable, they'll become so much harder to turn around, for ourselves and those most affected by the issues at hand.

Our first job as citizens and your job now as an official True. Paid. Good. entrepreneur is to take back our right to feel. To be connected and care about others and the things that matter to us. And to act in concert with what we genuinely care about. Just like we can create the life we desire and the money that aligns with our truth, so too can we create a vision for our world and work toward that vision through our respective and collective callings with great passion and dedication.

So, What's Out There?

When determining how you'd like to participate in your commitment to Do Good, you've got three main areas to choose from: environmental, economic, and social. The environmental realm deals with issues related to our natural resources, air, water, land, species, and the myriad of initiatives designed to encourage greater ecological preservation and stewardship. Think: Greenpeace and Rainforest Action Network. The economic realm deals with fair markets, corporate governance, sustainable economic systems, supply and demand, values-based goods, products, and services, and community-based wealth building. There are tons of initiatives designed to encourage more compassionate and equitable practices within the realm of conscious capitalism. A few examples are B Corp, Green America, and SOCAP. Finally, the social realm deals with issues of empowerment and development, equal access and opportunity, public health and safety, and social responsibility. Rebuild The Dream, Take The Lead, and the Malala Fund are a few examples. No matter what the focus is, the goal in the social arena is to create a global society where all people can achieve the highest form of their human potential.

So, your first consideration as a True. Paid. Good. entrepreneur is to think about what issue(s) really matter to you so you can identify your area of impact. As I mentioned earlier, this is no longer just happening in the realm of government and nonprofits; major brands, from Airbnb, to Warby Parker, to Dove Soap and Equinox, have positioned or repositioned themselves with marketing campaigns based on values that reflect, on a larger scale, the challenges we all face. In turn, this has created opportunities for employees within those and similar organizations to think more entrepreneurially about what they bring to the table. Socially conscious brands are breaking the zeitgeist. It's become cool to care.

When you think about the difference you want to make, your second consideration among social impact options for your company or venture is the sector. The sector represents a designated segment of the marketplace made up of industries that focus on specific aspects of society, i.e., social, political, and economic, etc. When you are thinking about where you can have the greatest impact, it's important to understand how your efforts fit into the larger scheme of things. I'll give you a hint up front: I'm going to be rooting for your participation in the fourth sector! When you get there you'll see what I mean.

Sectors fall into four main categories. The first is **the social sector** (nonprofit/NGO). Nonprofit organizations focus on uplifting and preserving the human values that contribute to strong, healthy, and vibrant communities. They ensure that people have access to basic necessities and provide opportunities for them to reach their full potential. They protect and advocate for the systems that preserve human, environmental, technological, and organizational capacities and resist those that threaten them. Second is **the public sector** or governmental work. These organizations protect and expand the principles and policies that promote the common good. They provide for common security and build the infrastructure that supports public safety. They mediate civil differences and make decisions that serve the best interest of their society. Third is **the private sector,** or a corporate means of creating social impact. Businesses create and distribute goods and services that enhance our quality of life, promote growth, and generate prosperity. They spur innovation, reward entrepreneurial effort, provide a return on investment, and constantly improve their performance. They draw on the skills, effort, and ingenuity of workers and the resources of shareholders.

Fourth, and finally, you have **for-benefit ventures and initiatives**— and this is where I believe the greatest potential for doing good resides for you, because this fourth sector leverages the best practices of each previous sector to deliver social responsibility *and* fiscal accountability. In addition to blurring lines, the for-benefit sector also uses new models that result in hybrid entities that aim to pursue social, economic, and environmental good using business methods. Great examples would be Tom's Shoes, Eileen Fisher, Tender Greens, Ben & Jerry's, and the Virgin Group, which all integrate a deep commitment to what's known as "the triple bottom line" of people, planet, and profit. For every pair of Tom's Shoes you buy, they give away another pair to a child who needs them. For every gorgeous Eileen Fisher outfit you buy, they invest in the economic empowerment of women and young girls. These commitments are not things these companies do on the side; they are an integral part of their business models.

Seventeen Sustainable Development Goals

In 2015, more than 190 world leaders gathered at the United Nations and committed to 17 Sustainable Development Goals (SDGs) to help us all end extreme poverty, fight inequality and injustice, and fix climate change by the year 2030. They've widely published these ambitious goals with the belief that each of us has a role to play if we're going to achieve the vision of a more prosperous, equitable, and sustainable world.

Now take a moment to revisit your articulated purpose from your L3 (Live.Love.Lead.) declarations in chapter 5. Where does *your* purpose align with these goals? As you consider these 17 objectives, are you inspired by your own Lead Declaration? Do you see and feel a clear connection between what the United Nations has committed to work on and the issues you feel most passionate about affecting? Can you envision precisely what you're contributing to as you answer your true calling? Let me give you an example of how your purpose can come to life in this broader context.

When Priscilla and I began working together she already had a successful events-based business. She curated one of the premiere women's conferences in New York City and was looking to bring all of the elements of her vision together to develop a more cohesive strategy. In our first working session, overlooking the Manhattan skyline in a cool office building smack in the center of midtown, we laid out the grand vision

and tracked key milestones over five-, three-, and one-year increments. As we began to examine these milestones more closely, we were able to discern that an emphasis on corporate partnerships was a pivotal aspect of her growth.

"I really want to deepen my work with corporations. I have lots of amazing relationships that I can build on and we've had an awesome track record partnering with companies and securing financial sponsorship around our annual conference," she said. "I think the next level for us is to develop a suite of offerings that would enable my company to cultivate long-term partnerships."

"Yep," I replied. "And the goal would be to build meaningful relationships that can deliver revenue year after year."

In order to design a robust strategy for engagement, Priscilla had to really tune into the primary change or transformation that her company had to offer.

She said, "I need to move beyond just selling the conference and offer other solutions to drive culture change for gender equality and diversity."

I paused, then asked, "Where is the opportunity to really serve these companies? What are they grappling with that you can help them solve?"

She had to consider and become profoundly connected to the challenge many corporations were facing and how those challenges aligned with her true calling.

She said, "I've been activating change agents in the entrepreneurial and consumer world to lead change. . . . Now I need to activate a new generation of corporate change agents and impact intrapreneurs to drive change through their organizations!" She rose to her feet and began to pace in excitement. "There are so many dynamic corporate women and people who are in positions of influence with passion for diversity initiatives that—if unleashed—could truly accelerate change. I just need to help them see they can lead the change which in turn will also help them advance and break through ceilings."

Just then she grabbed a marker from the table and wrote on the whiteboard: "UN Global Goals—Accelerate Diversity, Equity, and Inclusion to 2030."

Now it was my turn. "Oh my God, yes!!!" I cheered. "Why not invite them to the party? This is so important and these leaders, with your guidance, could do so much good."

What Priscilla found was the perfect storm when it came to engaging and building inclusive leaders. She would be working toward something she was deeply passionate about and providing an incredible service to her corporate clients in the process. As we evolved her partnership strategy, we had to address each of the four considerations I outlined in chapter 11 to create her Values-Aligned Proposition, i.e., (1) Who is she serving?; (2) What results is she delivering?; (3) How is she different from/better than the competition?; (4) Why this? Why now? Why *her*? We understood that getting clear on these considerations would enable her to monetize her unique perspective and the innovative curated experiences she was able to create as a result.

"I don't want to just create cool corporate programming," Priscilla continued. "I want to engage and enroll key corporate stakeholders in a larger movement that places cultivated inclusive leadership at the center."

"A-men!" I said. "Now what's the offering that will help facilitate that?"

She developed multi-level opportunities for collaboration that would allow them to start small and deepen engagement over time, she turned her attention to being in networks and gatherings that increased her exposure to more corporate leaders, and she curated lots of conversations that enabled her to become profoundly related to their varying needs and stages of development. As a result of these efforts, she doubled her corporate partnership revenue, which enabled investment in more resources. Her success with this strategy shifted the strategic priorities of her business and enabled her to find a more elegant way to achieve her desired impact. At Priscilla's closing event later on that year, a number of corporate leaders stood up and spoke about the personal transformation they had undergone through their work with Priscilla.

"She's given all of us a lot of responsibility. We can be stewards of change and I for one am looking forward to partnering with Priscilla and her team to get there."

Priscilla's willingness to push the envelope on her commitment to doing well by doing good gave her a game changer of a strategy that not only doubled her sales but also put her on the path to making her highest contribution. As a result of all of her efforts Priscilla was named a UN Women Champion for Innovation. Woo-hoo!

Now consider your own passion for change: How will your True. Paid. Good. business values, innovation, and impact align with one or more of these 17 goals? If you are working in a company, how might your business, through your efforts, contribute to one or more of these goals? If you own your own venture or are partnering with another venture to build their vision for success, how can you align your efforts with these important calls to action?

Do Good Strategies

Now that you have a clear sense of the social impact landscape and you've got a sense of where you'd like to focus as you consider your purpose, let's look at how your Values-Aligned Proposition can align with these strategies to really crank up the heat on your calling.

Paradigm/Culture Shifting: This is work that aims specifically to transform attitudes, beliefs, perceptions, your language, and behavior associated with a particular issue. Culture-shifting strategies include new messaging campaigns, various forms of media creation, artistic expression, new rituals and customs, training, and education.

Policy/Advocacy: This is aimed at changing laws and policies that affect a particular issue. Lobbying, litigation, petitioning, public education, political organizing, and the creation of corresponding research, propositions, and amendments are included in these strategies.

Capacity Building: This increases the ability of an individual, organization, community, or society to work effectively on a particular issue to achieve a defined outcome. Strategies include building infrastructure, developing leadership, creating associations and networks, forming coalitions and alliances, and providing work-related training, education, materials, and resources.

Frontline Organizing: This seeks to mobilize those affected by a particular issue and those who are empathetic to their plight. It includes educating, coordinating, activating, and engaging everyday people in ways that help them to know their rights, raise their voices, and offer solutions to address their own interests.

Social Entrepreneurship: This work is aimed at developing market-based solutions to address pressing social issues. Strategies include triple-bottom-line benefits that positively impact people, planet, and profit. They incorporate innovations in products, services, processes, workforce development, investment, and profit allocation and distribution.

A World of Opportunities

Over the last 5 to 10 years, there's been a dramatic shift in the business world toward the seamless integration of social mission and revenue-driving impact. Nowadays there is almost a built-in expectation among consumers that if you are in business your efforts must in some way contribute to a positive outcome for the planet and/or the quality of people's lives. As a matter of course, brands continue to reposition themselves with values-based content marketing strategies that embed their propositions into the opportunities and challenges they believe are facing humanity. This is what it means to be in the Age of the Citizen. This global shift has created tons of opportunities for people within organizations to think more entrepreneurially about the kinds of solutions they offer to consumers. Similarly, nonprofits have become edgier—opting for flashier, high-profile campaigns and initiatives that take advantage of marketing tactics traditionally reserved for larger corporate firms. Similarly, celebrities are coming out of the woodwork right now to ensure that you don't just love their art, but you also know where they stand when it comes to the issues they care about and their corresponding strategies for their desired outcomes. In every facet of society now you will find passionate change agents successfully using a more holistic or whole systems-based approach to solving tough issues.

As you consider your own work, identify which of the four sectors you currently reside in. If you are not operating within the for-benefit sector, are there ways in which your venture, company, or institution could be making strides in that direction? Are you actively participating in those efforts? If you are an entrepreneur, is your company helping to drive those efforts? When you consider the kind of impact you'd like to have, are you inspired by the examples you see? I sure hope so!

Confronting the Gap

When you get clear about how you're here to Do Good, you may react in any number of ways. Some lean in and become totally ignited and on fire by their calling. While others run for the hills as all forms of fear and doubt start to take hold! (LOL.) When you consider where you are in proximity to your highest contribution, you may discover that there is indeed a major gap between what you are currently doing and what it is that you believe you are here to do—even if you are doing good work. This is normal and should be expected. The most accomplished and successful people in the world are always confronting the gap, as they seek to consistently take it up a notch in honor of what they want to achieve. Closing this gap is about facing your true calling head on and doing the work necessary to obliterate the distance between where you are right now in your capacity to Do Good and where you really want/ought to be. This is why I wrote this book—to help you, my friend, close this gap!

Now as with any gap, when you face that distance any number of things can come up. Here are some of the concerns my clients have shared:

"If this is really what I'm supposed to be doing in the world, then why wasn't I wasn't encouraged to do it growing up? There must be something wrong with me."

- *"As much as I would love to be doing this, it's just not possible. I need to pay the rent and pursuing this desire does not enable me to do that."*
- *"I don't have the time. I have to be practical and make sure I have a roof over my head. Between family and work, this leaves me little to no time to focus on my calling."*

- *"I'm not qualified to do this. People are going to look at me like I'm crazy: 'Who does he/she think he/she is? Walking around claiming he/she's a [fill in the blank]?'"*
- *"There are so many other people doing this. What could I possibly bring that would be of value and/or different from what others are doing?"*
- *"I don't know anybody who's doing anything remotely like this. Is it even possible? I don't think so."*
- *"Will this really make a difference? I hear people say that it changed their lives all the time, but it sounds more like marketing hype than the truth."*

All of these quotes are born from fear and doubt. If your limiting conversations are similar, your job is to thank this voice for sharing—and then keep inviting your true voice, the voice of your calling, to get louder and louder.

Let me ask you: If money, failure, perfection, or any other concern you have weren't a concern, what would you be doing and why? Who would you be serving? Where would you be making your difference?

Discovering your true calling and recognizing it as your Do Good mission is less about racking your brain for what to "do" and more about allowing yourself to be a vessel for inspiration and activation. Don't overthink it. Simply pay attention to what excites you, to what you have a passion for, to the things that make you *really* emotional. There is something in those feelings and impulses that wants to be expressed.

Your Call

Are you ready to embrace your power to Do Good? For the next two weeks, use these two practices and two exercises to educate yourself about the social impact landscape and start to envision your own contribution and calling in a new way.

PRACTICE 1: MANTRA

"I own my creative powers to Stay True, Get Paid, and Do Good!"
"I can Do Good in a way that's innovative, joyful, and inspiring to me."
"I can answer my calling in a way that's profitable and makes a difference."

Work with this series of mantras daily over the next two weeks and notice what happens in your work. Speak them in the A.M. before you start your day. Say them before you enter into a big meeting or give a presentation. Use these mantras to influence the way you collaborate with your colleagues. Every night take three minutes to journal about what you notice in yourself and in your work as a result.

PRACTICE 2: JOURNALING EXERCISE

For the next two weeks just keep asking and answering these questions: If money, failure, perfection, or any other concern you have weren't a concern, what would you be doing and why? Who would you be serving? Where would you be making your difference? Write down your answers without censoring them. Don't read your responses until the end of the two weeks. When you read them have a highlighter handy—capture any words or phrases that provide clear guidance on what you are being called to do.

EXERCISE 1: GET INSPIRED TO KEEP LEARNING

Now that you have a sense of how this field is organized, become more aware of the broader landscape. For one week, devote twenty minutes a day to a cause-related activity. A few suggestions are below:

- Follow Do Good hashtags like #heforshe or #socialgood or #dogood on Twitter to learn more about the various initiatives and who's involved.

- Check out *HuffPost*'s "Good News" section or flip through *Yes!* magazine.
- Use the UN Sustainable Development Goals to become more aware of what the challenges are on a local, regional, national, and global scale. Learn more about the organizations and movements they endorse (https://sustainabledevelopment.un.org).
- Learn more about the field of Social Entrepreneurship; check out organizations like: the Skoll Foundation, Ashoka Foundation, Virgin Unite, and Social Venture Circle.

EXERCISE 2: HONING IN ON YOUR CALLING

Have a conversation with someone you deeply love, trust, and respect about your insights from this chapter. Maybe share some of the highlighted sections from your journal, or tell them about what inspires you. Just keep engaging with this conversation and letting the insights flow.

14

Step #2: Accepting Responsibility for What You Believe About the World

When you examine the endless procession of shocking and horrific events on most mainstream news and major social media channels, it's not hard to understand why so many people feel overwhelmed and apathetic about the state of our world. Each new day brings yet another scandal, corruption, abuse of authority, out-of-control natural disaster, threat of war, or all of the above. To quote the brilliant economist Naomi Klein in her groundbreaking work *The Shock Doctrine,* we are living in dog years upside-down hyper warp speed times—when countries can be overthrown on Facebook and nations of dissent mobilized overnight on Twitter. All of this breeds a kind of crazy, voyeuristic fascination in us, while simultaneously feeding a sense of insecurity that has us believing that people have lost their minds and the world is going to hell in a hand-basket.

Through either our action or inaction, we make choices about where we stand. No matter what you say, there are really only two routes to go—via love or via fear. And within each of these debates you can either play full out or run for the hills. It takes a lot of courage and patience to attempt to understand what's going on in the world and most people will tell you they don't have the bandwidth or inclination to figure it out.

So, they scan social media streams, sensationalized re-tweets, and prime-time sound bites to feel halfway literate enough to argue with their dim-wit neighbor or gracefully sidestep the inappropriate political banter at the coffee station at work. We pick and choose where we "come out" and lay back as we cobble together hastily found facts to create half-minded arguments. Rarely do we ever slow the conversation down, get real, and tell the truth about how we feel—which is different from what we think (or think we think).

The urge to resort to Binding Behavior here is so overwhelming, you can cut it with a knife. And if you have young children, it all just got 10 times scarier. Facing and embracing the current state of our world is not for the faint of heart, but it *is* necessary if we have any intention of doing good. Which brings us to the million-dollar question: Will you be part of the problem or the solution? What will it be—love or fear?

I feel humbled and honored to support those who've chosen to be on the front lines of love, whether they're talking about gender, race, class, or sexual orientation differences. These courageous souls stand in the hottest part of the kitchen and brave the fire for what they believe in. This is a new generation of leaders incredibly passionate about creating a just and sustainable world. Yet even among the most focused and driven, when we feel wronged the temptation to shame and alienate becomes real. It's so much easier to choose love when you're not met with targeted cruelty. So at every turn, you must ask, Where do I stand? How will I counteract the negativity? And at every turn, you must face your own struggles, which are rooted in what you believe—about yourself, your work, and your world.

In this chapter, you'll examine your Greatest Hits about the state of our world. How do your attitudes, beliefs, and perceptions about the world cause you to make assumptions about yourself, others, and what's possible when it comes to affecting positive change? Where does your information come from? And how does it inform the choices you make when faced with the chaos, hurt, anger, and fear that permeate certain aspects of our society. Who are your greatest influences, and how do they dictate whether you sit down or stand up for what you believe in? And what does it cost you, *and* us, when you don't answer your call?

To put it another way: Are you part of the problem or the solution? Determining your Greatest Hits and influences will either help or hinder your ability to Do Good and pursue your true calling. I want you to get inspired by your vision for the world rather than react to other people's negative perceptions.

Socially, I believe we are finally in a place to have these kinds of tougher conversations with one another, but it requires a certain level of patience and compassion. It also requires discipline to see and own the truth about our own actions or inactions. Taking responsibility for what you believe means confronting every area in which you're resigned and inspired, confused and clear, hopeful and fed up! It is very rarely an either-or conversation but more often both-and for all of us.

Getting Clear About How You See the World

When I decided to take charge of my economy, I had a lot of soul-searching to do. As much as I would have loved to point the finger in the direction of a Bad Guy, I knew that the person I most needed to deal with was myself. I was fortunate enough to have a sense of purpose instilled in me at a very young age, but to only acknowledge the sunny side of life as a creative activist would be irresponsible to my own healing process. There were aspects of my Do Good work that were toxic and debilitating, and I was terrified to confront those behaviors. For all my righteous indignation about "the man," when I really got down to it I was just as much a part of the problem as anyone else.

In 2014, I was asked to give a TEDx talk about my journey from starving artist to thriving CEO, and in the process of preparing for that talk I had to take full responsibility for my own transformation. When I reached a come-to-Jesus moment that enabled me to let go of being a struggling artist, I had to tell the truth about how I saw the world and how much I had idolized my artist/activist community—particularly artists and activists of color. I saw us as victims, with the rest of the world out to get us, undermine us, deny us opportunities, threaten our safety, lock us up, and block our ability to reach our full potential. The devil was everywhere, and my cynicism was well earned.

But a person's story is never that neat, is it? My reluctance to see all the ways I participated in my own disempowerment was fed by a belief that if I acknowledged my own failures and shortcomings, I would somehow be letting these larger, more hostile forces off the hook. Or even worse, that I would prove them right about me and those whom I hoped to serve. When I was finally willing to see the truth, I saw that it was painful and ugly but also liberating, because I sought to understand how I arrived at my current state; I could see all the choices I'd made that had put me there, for better or worse. I had become a victim of my own lack of vision.

Never had my own temptation to resort to those Binding Behaviors—complaining, blaming/judging, justifying, avoiding—been so strong as when I confronted and owned my Greatest Hits. And never had my faith in the goodness of people been so profoundly tested—handing over my martyrdom left me naked and exposed in ways I could not have predicted. But once I let my ego go, I had a lot of room to discover who I really was without a protective cloak, and I had an opportunity to experience the world differently. I gave myself the freedom to laugh more, cry more, and just be human. I released my starving artist/activist, the-world-is-out-to-get-me mentality in favor of a more abundant reality, one that reflected my values and the things I cared most about. I was still myself—that loving, caring, committed-to-humanity me, but with far fewer wounds and less skepticism. This did not mean I turned a blind eye, but it did mean that I consumed less of the hyped-up information that plunged me into anger and fear.

When I brought my concentration, energy, and effort to what I wanted to create—versus everything I was resisting and trying to avoid—the quality of my life shifted. I felt the power to choose what I wanted to have just by virtue of where I was willing to place my energy and attention. And soon my reality began to respond accordingly. I completely rebuilt my activism from the ground up, and I designed it to enable me to do what I knew was my work with people I loved and admired, those who had the capacity to collaborate with me and encourage me to grow; all of this made me feel way more joyful and appreciated. I also became adamant about taking care of myself—mentally, spiritually, emotionally, and financially.

Now, prior to this shift, if I were to list my Greatest Hits, they would have been:

They're never going to respect me, so . . .
We've got to fight for everything, so . . .
Nobody's got our back in this, so . . .
Of course they're not going to pay for this, even though they know it's
    necessary, so . . .
I've got to help, even though I'm tired and broke, so . . .

Every facet of my inner dialogue contained some form of struggle. And I was *angry all the time.* I also felt a sense of urgency that was fed by a scarcity mindset that kept me in survival mode. The world was a dark, cold, and lonely place—and that belief gave me that reality. Such a worldview came with nasty perceptions about The Other, too—you know, rich people, people of a certain hue, those from certain parts of the country, and most men. When it came to creating authentic connections, this took a lot of options off the table! And I'm not even getting into the limiting perceptions I had about myself.

As I re-walked this ground in preparation for my TEDx talk, I cried a lot. I cried for the situations and circumstances that produced these feelings, for all the painful moments I'd witnessed, for the people who reinforced this experience, and for the hurt and hardened person I was. But I also cried tears of joy and gratitude for the insights that enabled me to become more aware of what was happening, for all the steps of learning

I took in favor of who I'd become—not perfect by any means, but way more happy, fulfilled, and free.

Are You Love or Are You Fear?

As you take in my journey, what do you see about your own internal dialogue? What have you believed about the world and how it's affected your ability to be open, loving, trusting, and joyful?

For some, rethinking their activism may look like taking it "down to the studs" like I did and rebuilding their efforts from a new set of beliefs and perceptions. For others, it may look like starting from scratch and learning how to become an engaged and empowered citizen in the first place.

If I ask you, "Are you love or fear?" look honestly at your core. For most, the answer is probably "Both." Use this moment to take an inventory. Tell the truth about what you see. In what ways does love guide your actions or inactions? In what ways does fear do the same?

By "inactions" I'm talking about the times we stand by and allow things to go down on our watch that we know are wrong—or, in the case of love, that we know are just right. Sometimes they are little things like when we see someone's child in the grocery store about to walk into a display that could fall on them and we don't call out to the parent or guide the baby away ourselves. Or we watch someone in our department being treated horribly by coworkers and don't say a peep—to either to the person being treated badly or our coworkers—about their behavior.

Always trying to intervene can be a recipe for exhaustion, but *never* intervening can also wear a person down. No matter where you sit on this spectrum, it's worth noticing. A lack of action may be more about your fear than a lack of desire. If this is you, take the time to examine your inner dialogue and the behavior it produces. What do you see? Is this who you want to be?

I have deep love for my clients, which has become a kind of prerequisite for me at this stage in my work—though Move The Crowd continues to serve thousands of people in various formats every year, these days I only personally coach a very select group of high performers. And when I do, it has to be a love affair. I become deeply vested in their success; each one is special to me. And this is no different from how I feel about my beloved client Micha. When we began working together, I was excited. I met her through a network of spiritual teachers. When I was with these women, a number of younger women would always approach me to ask questions, express their love, or ask about working with me, but I noticed that Micha always hung back. Even so, she was always within earshot. One morning, I arrived at a three-day event after keynoting the day before and everything in my spirit said, *Find her*. I did not know why I felt so compelled to seek Micha out, but I knew to trust it.

As the morning program wound down and we broke for lunch, I looked to my left and there she was. I opened my arms, and she walked right in.

"Girl," I said, "you are so in my spirit right now. Why is that?"

We both sat back down, and in her own quiet way she poured her heart out to me. She was asking big questions about her life's purpose. She had helped a number of teachers become very successful, and she knew her time had come. "When I look at what I think everyone else should do, it's so clear, but that's not the case with me. What am I supposed to be doing?"

In that moment, I opened my mouth and the words, "Be still," fell out. "Take some time away from everyone and everything, so that you can listen to you," I suggested.

Micha promised to figure this out, and five months later, after she'd returned from a trip, she reached out and we scheduled a time to speak.

"The last few months have caused me to really think about what I have to offer," she said. "Traveling caused me to see that I have so much privilege. I have choices that I just take for granted. There are people in this world who just don't have those options." She went on to say that she struggled with how cruel people are to one another online, especially in political debates, and felt a real need to spread kindness. As Micha poured out her soul, my job was to just be there and listen, holding space for these bigger questions that she was grappling with. I wanted to give her room to confront her own apathy, so that she could see everything that was in the way of who she is meant to be and what she is meant to do in this world.

After some time, I finally asked Micha, "When you think about all that you've learned through your work and travels, what is it that you'd really like to share with others who may also be struggling to find their voice?"

Micha instantly knew the answer: "That you are responsible for your life, and your happiness, and there are simple things you can do to bring more joy into your life. You can make the decision to be happy or not—it really is up to you." She went on to say, however, that she struggled with this message because there are so many in the world who struggle to keep a roof over their heads, so who was Micha—a super-privileged white girl who's never had to deal with any of her own struggles—to say this? What could she offer others without sounding out of touch?

To me, the answer was obvious: Plenty of others who come from privileged backgrounds struggle with the same feelings and her transparency about this struggle could be part of what she offers to those like her who have their own insecurities. "I think all of us can find a reason not to lean in," I told her. "Trust me when I say that I don't know anyone who is doing it perfectly, but I do know a lot of people who are willing to exercise the courage to try. So let's not make your race or the addiction to perfection the reason. Let's delve into what you're feeling inspired to share."

Without missing a beat, Micha walked through each insight, and a seven-step protocol began to emerge. What she also discovered was that she had a personal story that corresponded to each step in the process. The more Micha shared, the more we were able to see how her own journey was reinforcing the value of what she'd wanted to offer. Micha also had a huge following, one she was deeply engaged with, and she was able to draw additional correlations and insights from many of those conversations, too. She had her finger on the pulse of something really important. It was just about providing a process that would enable her to express it and giving the kind of encouragement that would allow her to stay with the hard stuff.

As we delved deeper into Micha's core teachings, her desire to speak out and share these insights increased. She co-launched an online product sharing these principles, began hosting provocative conversations about privilege in her community with other prominent thought leaders, and considered working on a book and TV series to chronicle her journey. When we connected a few months later, Micha said, "As much as I could see myself out in the world doing this work, I know that a big part of my work is also in my community." Just a few weeks later, a lone gunman walked into Marjory Stoneman Douglas High School in Parkland, Florida, where 17 students, staff, and faculty were shot dead and 17 others were injured.

The media's student interviews were like nothing I've ever seen. They were devastated, yes, but they had been ignited. I realized that this community was right in Micha's backyard! She reached out to the school, and six months later Micha was on her way to New Zealand to engage in a series of dialogues with a delegation of students from #MarjoryStonemanDouglas and a group of trauma survivors from New Zealand's University of Canterbury. I can't tell you how proud I was of Micha. Once she got back, Micha began working on her book and the TV series, and we are in the process of designing the next level of her strategy—all of which aligns perfectly with her True. Paid. Good.

Taking Stock of Your Major Influences

Just as you've examined your inherited influences around money and success, it's time to now look at who your major influences have been when it comes to your perception of how you see the world—and, therefore, how *you* view what's possible when it comes to making a difference. Just as you did in chapter 2, let's go all the way back. What is your earliest memory of what you felt about others you didn't know? Can you identify a specific story or event that demonstrated this perception? What about your earliest perception of the outside world? What did you witness, or what stories were you told and by whom? Get specific about these incidents and corresponding players. What do you notice about the people who were involved? How did they respond and how did their behavior influence you?

When I ask clients these questions, many people return to very painful childhood experiences. They play back memories of being bullied or even physically violated because of how they looked, where they lived, and how they spoke. And whether you were the one bullying, being bullied, or watching it all go down, those experiences stay with you and feed your cynicism about your own humanity and that of others. If these feelings go unaddressed, they can greatly diminish your capacity to truly open your heart and empathize with your own experience. And when you can't feel empathy for yourself or others, you're in trouble. You must identify with great precision what you may want and need, to be healed and released in the next chapter.

In addition to what you may have personally experienced, you also have to acknowledge the media as a massive player in how you perceive the world. What gets highlighted as news can be quite disturbing, to say the least. The negative, fear-based nature of these narratives, combined with the endless inundation of traumatic messages and images, can make anyone want to stick their head in the sand. How it is that so much information can contribute to so much ignorance is beyond me. But that's kind of where we are. These machines are powerful, and the values and code of ethics they live by influence the kind of "information" you receive. There are all kinds of debates going on about the state of journalism right now and whether one can truly be impartial when reporting. I believe these debates are important for helping to strengthen the field and its commitment to fairness and accuracy—now and in the future.

Then, there are some things, as difficult as they may be, that we do need to see and experience. And this is where it gets hard, because unless we are able to confront certain realities, we may never awaken to the true callings of our soul. Just as Micha's calling came to a head through the Parkland shooting, the same can be said of the death of Trayvon Martin, or the hurricane in Puerto Rico, or Katrina in New Orleans, or the devastating war in Syria, or the collapsing of the economy in England or Venezuela. I believe these events, by their very nature, are designed to shake us up and wake us up—and, in that way, become profound gifts that ultimately bring us back to our humanity and drop us right in the center of our calling if we allow it.

In August 2017, a disruptive challenge/opportunity arrived on my office's front doorstep and drove a wedge right through the center of my team. On August 11, a group of Unite the Right protestors gathered in Charlottesville to voice their outrage about the removal of a statue of Gen. Robert E. Lee; pretty soon after they arrived near the campus of the University of Virginia, a group of counterprotestors began to gather. The exchanges became heated, and sadly, angry words turned into physical blows. In the midst of all the chaos, a young man drove his vehicle right through the center of the counterprotestors line, killing one young woman and injuring 19 others, 5 of them critically. One of the members of my staff grew up in this area and actually lived on the street where the vehicular attack occurred. She was devastated as she watched her community ripped apart, and as the events became the center of a national debate on the issue of race and the importance of preserving or taking down historical landmarks. Other members of my team who held deep roots working around issues of social justice and equity struggled to empathize. We suspended our work for two afternoons to engage in a series of provocative conversations about our own personal journeys and levels of awareness around race, class, and privilege—and yes, the impact of America's bloody history. The conversations were tough and very revealing. We held public forums on Facebook and shared snippets of these conversations on YouTube. We wanted to help inspire others to engage in these kinds of provocative conversations, and we wanted to own the fact that though it might get messy, the conversations were possible and a greater understanding among different perspectives could be reached.

This process was a defining moment for me as a leader because it challenged everything I believed in my newly developed perception of the world. It was humbling and excruciating to see people I loved and respected struggle so profoundly with themselves and one another. I felt like we were on the front line of the debate and absolutely represented a microcosm of what existed in our larger society. Perceptions about who's right and wrong can run deep and waking up can be terrifying and disorienting. I wish I could tell you that the final outcome was rosy—it was not. However, I learned so much through this process about myself as a leader. My vision for my team transformed through this process, and my determination to stand for a world where we can actually see and hear one another is stronger now than it's ever been.

Genuine heartfelt dialogue across all forms of difference is one of the most important Do Good practices we can employ if we are committed to a world that works for all. Sometimes it's hard to know all that's shaping your world view until that view is tested. Engaging in conversations that let you explore the nature of your own experience and the experiences of others is vital. The more we can share our journeys with one another, the faster we will arrive at the insights that inspire us to be more loving, compassionate, and solution-oriented citizens.

The Price of Your Inheritance

I know I've challenged you a lot in this chapter, and I want to thank you for going here with me. I believe our callings and aspirations represent the most underutilized resources on the planet. However, up until very recently I don't believe we've felt the level of urgency necessary to seize our moment and rise in our individual and collective power to be a part of the solution. We have so much more capacity to create the kind of world we want than we give ourselves credit for.

When you don't stand for what you believe in, you don't get the world you want and neither do we. In other words, if you don't bring what you've been called to bring, then we as a world don't get to receive the benefit of your full gifts—and that's our loss. But it's also your loss, because it means that the people you care most about will inherit a world that is largely cynical, polarized, and disconnected. We lose the richness and our access to the full range of possibilities for evolution and growth as a human family. The imperative here is clear: Realizing your full potential and achieving your true calling is what drives your genuine fulfillment. Let's do this—you can be that change!

Your Call

Are you ready to take responsibility for what you believe about our world and stand up for being part of the solution? Use these two practices and two exercises over the next two weeks to examine your inheritance and create a new commitment to your participation.

PRACTICE 1: MANTRA

"This is my world and this is my watch."
"I'm ready to take my rightful place and be a part of the solution."
"Watch out, world! I'm moving from fear to love."

Speak this mantra series daily for the next two weeks. Notice how you feel when you say it. Say it in the A.M. when you first wake up, say it when you're feeling disillusioned or angry about an issue or incident, and say it when you see something that inspires and motivates you.

PRACTICE 2: STEP UP, STEP BACK

Depending on your natural tendency, choose one of the following practices for the next two weeks. If you are generally soft spoken and uncomfortable raising your voice, your practice is going to be to Step Up. If you usually have a lot to say, your practice will be to Step Back.

Step Up

Over the next two weeks, make a concerted effort to speak up. Say what's on your mind for a change. Speak your truth. It may be messy; you may not have the perfect words. That's okay. It's time to get your voice into the mix. When you engage with those in your life and community, let them know how you feel. And when you express yourself, don't apologize! Just say it and let people respond in whatever way that they respond. You don't need to attack, but you don't need to cower either. Practice finding a "sweet spot" as you start to speak your mind.

Step Back

Over the next two weeks, make a concerted effort to listen more when you are in conversations with the people in your life and your community. Try not to come from a place of already "knowing" what they're going to say. Sit back and don't dominate the conversations. When you do engage, ask questions and be curious. Commit to learning something new about the people in your life that you did not know before. When you feel the urge to speak or argue, listen some more. Practice exercising the muscle of listening.

EXERCISE 1: MEDIA FAST

For the next two weeks, try to minimize how much negative media you consume and how much media you consume in general. If you're someone who watches television all the time or scrolls on your phone all day, I'm going to ask you to take a break. Limit yourself to no more than one hour a day. From the evening news to your Facebook or Twitter feed, try your best to bypass the drama and only engage in messages that are positive and uplifting for the next two weeks. This includes any negative movies or shows where there is lots of violence and drama. (It's just two weeks—you won't die, I swear!) Notice at the end of the two weeks if there is a shift in your demeanor.

EXERCISE 2: GET REAL ABOUT HOW YOU FEEL

In the next 24 to 36 hours, set aside about an hour to answer these questions in your journal: When you consider all your own experiences, how would you define the current state of our world—are you hopeful, doubtful, inspired, resigned? What are your biggest influences right now on where you think we are as a human family? When it comes to fear and love, where are you standing? What do you believe is possible, and what would it take for you to remain hopeful in these times? Reread your answers at least once a day for the next two weeks. Feel free to add, refine, and amend them—let these swish around and find a place that feels good in your soul.

15

Step #3: Forgiving Your Fear, Ignorance, Apathy, Guilt, and Resignation

When you aim to Do Good in your life and business, you have the golden opportunity to set a whole new agenda for how you want to impact the current state of our world. You can't do everything and save everyone—and that's okay!—but you can contribute to the greater good by committing to the values you hold dear. Your first step in making progress is to let go of the limiting beliefs and false perceptions that keep you: (1) paralyzed or in a reactionary state of victimhood, (2) overcompensating in a state of misguided martyrdom, or (3) totally resigned and basically checked out.

In order to move to a more authentic and loving place—one that aligns with your true calling—you've got to get honest with yourself, not only about how much you're able to contribute but also, more important, where and how you'd like to contribute and what is the highest and best use of what you have to offer. I've made the case for a Values-Aligned Proposition in all businesses, because I don't believe that traditional, nonprofit-based charity as we've known it is sustainable. I also don't believe that all charitable solutions work, and if I really go there, some charitable solutions actually make the problems worse and perpetuate the very things they're trying to eliminate. For example, studies have shown that traditional aid as a response to chronic poverty is not the answer; unless you are building the capacity for some level of agency and autonomy, people are left crippled when the resources run out—and the resources do run out at some point. Organizations that are dedicated to ending poverty are starting to realize this and adopt more innovative entrepreneurial approaches that actually include teaching entrepreneurship to those they seek to serve. Developing an ecosystem that has the potential to replenish itself is far more solution oriented than just giving Band-Aids. Give the Band-Aid to stabilize if you have to, but then go to work on rehabilitating that arm or leg—because if you do, it will come back so much stronger than if you keep that limb, or person, or community, or nation dependent on a crutch.

In this chapter, I'll encourage you to let go of any debilitating conversations that ultimately hold you back and hinder your ability to get inspired about the change you plan to initiate, so that you can move the needle on what matters most to you. To be clear, I'm not here to tell you what to do with your time and energy; I'm here to help you figure out what you'd like to do so that you can design a concrete strategy that inspires and fulfills you as you prepare to make your desired impact. My aim in this chapter is to help you forgive anything that causes you to question who you need to be, what you need to do, or how you need to do it in order to be worthy of doing good. This may seem like a strange way to use the term, but giving up and letting go is what forgiveness is all about. This includes forgiving all the ways you've been unconscious, apathetic, and resigned about affecting change. This means forgiving the ways you've held judgment about yourself and others that's also kept the status quo in place (yes, this may include your unconscious biases and prejudices). Perhaps this has impeded your ability to Do Good and pursue your calling, because as long as you engage in a false perception about yourself or anyone else you're limited in what you can do. You'll also aim to forgive the times that you've leaned on misplaced guilt or altruism as you've attempted to Do Good (I know there's a lot of you grappling with your privilege and whether or not you even belong in some of the places you are drawn to); my job is to encourage you to be in your full power—so you can embrace your calling with joy, excitement, and love.

Moving from Reactive to Proactive, from Victim to Visionary

I can't tell you the number of times I've heard a client, fellow dinner party guest, or stranger say, "I really want to get involved, but I just don't know how." Or, "If I had the time, I'd really like to give back in X way, but I'm just too busy." Or, "It's all just such a mess out there, but I don't think there's anything I can really do about it." And listen, I know I'm not the only one!

Though each of these statements seems a bit different, they all stem from the same core—victimhood. In other words, we've allowed our rationalizations to get in the way of our power to lead the solution. These rationalizations are often driven by our external world—but we have the power to choose what we want to create over our excuses. And though each of these statements seems common enough, they represent a limiting conversation or perspective that keeps you from fully realizing your purpose and, more important, the world from receiving your full contribution. What makes these statements even more of a challenge is when you feel like you have to defend your position, i.e., your fear, your guilt, your ignorance, or your apathy about a particular issue. Once you feel put on the defensive, you then start to "dig in" and place more importance on having your point validated than anything else. When you find yourself in moments like these, notice if you feel tempted to engage in any of the Binding Behaviors, aka the famous four—complaining, blaming/judging, justifying, and avoiding. This will let you know if your Greatest Hit also known as your primary limiting belief is in the vicinity.

I've watched these four dynamics play out as clients' internal struggles or even arguments over the Thanksgiving dinner table—and as you can imagine, none of it is pretty. However, when I ask the person making these statements to expand on these ideas, I actually find that their perceptions are driven by the societal conditioning that constantly places limitations on our perceived ability to Do Good. Here are the three root causes; see if any of these resonate with you.

ROOT CAUSE #1: "DOING GOOD HAS GOT NOTHING TO DO WITH ME"

Somehow, whatever you are doing in your life or work is actually separate from what is happening or not happening in the world. Meaning that you live your life "over here" and whatever is going on in the world is happening "over there." Which sounds like this: "It's a shame what happened to that young man. Someone in that community really needs to do something about it."

ROOT CAUSE #2: "DOING GOOD IS A LUXURY"

This leads to the second limiting conversation or misguided perception, that being part of the solution somehow requires extra effort and there is a scarcity of whatever that required effort is. In other words, you see doing good as extracurricular activity rather than integral to how you live your life. "I'd like to do more to 'give back,' but who has the time? I mean, I don't even know where to look if I wanted to get involved."

ROOT CAUSE #3: "DOING GOOD IS HARD"

Most of us have been conditioned to believe that putting a dent in any of the world's challenges is almost impossible. You also get labeled "altruistic" or "naive" when you share your hopes and intentions of making a difference. Or you believe the flip side of this, where the bar for making a difference has been set so high that unless you're capable of becoming the next Al Gore or Oprah, you're not sure you can Do Good at all: "I think it's so great what those celebrities are doing—using all that money, power, and influence to 'give back'—thank God they've got the resources and willpower to do it. I sure don't."

Forgiving yourself for the reasons you've hesitated to Do Good becomes easier when you can recognize all the places where those limiting perceptions may have come from the limiting perceptions of our larger society. Most of us have not been conditioned to make "making a difference" a priority, yet so many of us yearn to Do Good and know that our efforts matter. This is why each of us feels that tug and pull toward our calling.

Now if you're a millennial and you're reading this, you may be shaking your head. Because your generation, almost as a whole, already sees doing good as integral to your success. I mean, one of the greatest innate contributions you've already made as a generation is holding all of us to a higher societal standard of social engagement. You've used your entrepreneurial and purchasing influence to demand that brands demonstrate their awareness and commitment to being part of a solution. Making a difference is as ingrained in your sense of ambition as making your first $1 million.

If you are a millennial who does feel like doing good comes with the territory, then your forgiveness work should focus on shifting any perceptions about yourself in relationship to your calling. You will need to stop viewing yourself as "separate" or "inadequate," "delusional" or "unentitled," so you have a greater chance of reaching the Do Good goals that you set for yourself. You have the vision; now it's time to develop the confidence to get out there.

On the other end of the spectrum are those who've sacrificed themselves, their relationships, health, or financial stability due to a distorted belief that suffering makes you more noble, righteous, or more special—and this too deserves some forgiveness. Such scarcity-based conditioning forces you to believe that you have to trade on what contributes to your well-being, and you need to heal that; doing good should not be painful—just the opposite, actually. If you operate out of shame or guilt, those feelings can dramatically hinder your contribution. Sadly, this conditioning has been an integral part of the field of traditional activism, but it is also changing. Masterful organizers are recognizing that they cannot build sustainable or profitable movements if the very fiber of their lifeforce and communities is stretched beyond reason.

One of the saddest reminders of this, for me, came at the expense of one of my dearest friends and colleagues, who passed away far too soon. Lizzie was a brilliant strategist, organizer, and thought leader— one of the most dedicated humans I have ever known. She helped architect movements that shifted policies and positively impacted the lives of millions of everyday hardworking people. Born in South Carolina, Lizzie was bold, funny, quiet, and mischievous in the best ways and extremely effective at building coalitions and shaping social-good agendas. Young people were her passion, and at the time, in the mid-nineties, they were in crisis all over the nation. Because of her unique perspective and expansive Rolodex, Lizzie stayed in high demand. And because of her humble upbringing and the urgency of the time, she found it very hard to say no. This meant 26 days out of 30 on the road, with back-to-back 16- to 18-hour days—not to mention, the high-stress nature of her work and a steady diet of quick burgers and fries. Together, it became a recipe for mass destruction. By the time Lizzie received the final three-alarm warnings from the doctors, her blood pressure and cholesterol were through the roof and the prognosis was not good. She had to either slow down or face the consequences of a potential heart attack. Lizzie heard the warnings, but she was so entrenched in the launch of a new initiative that she found it almost impossible to slow down. I remember one of our last phone calls together; after we talked strategy around an upcoming conference, we shifted into girlfriend mode. I heard the ever-confident tone in her voice soften, as she asked me about how to shift her eating habits. She knew I'd just finished a cleansing fast and wanted to know if I'd seen any benefit. Little did she know, another dear friend had already told me that Lizzie had received a medical directive to slow down. I shared my best tips and "cheats" to make things taste good. We laughed and moved into a comfortable silence afterward.

"Well, my sister," she said, "let me get on up out of here." It was 9:00 P.M. and she was still in the office—typical Lizzie.

"Love you," I said. "And I'm here if you need me for anything, including cooking lessons!" We laughed and hung up. Two weeks later another dear friend called to say that our beloved Lizzie had died from complications related to her heart at the tender age of 40.

Transforming Your Greatest Hit(s)

No matter which of the preceding scenarios resonate most with you, it's time to let go. Use this four-step forgiveness ritual to help you shift out of victim mode and into visionary mode.

FORGIVENESS → AS AN ACT OF RE-MEMBERING

Take a moment to consider your Greatest Hit and determine which of these root causes earlier in this book may be operating in your current reality, causing you to say, "I don't know how," or I'm too busy," or, "It's too much," or "I'm not good enough," or "It's not enough—I have to do more." What do you see? Can you pinpoint a specific interaction or incident where this conversation has recently played out? What was the result? Is there any place where you want or need to take responsibility? What part of you needs to be nurtured and cared for? Are you ready to reclaim your power? Are you ready to stand up for your highest vision? You are whole.

FORGIVENESS → AS AN ACT OF COMPLETION

As you consider the impact that interaction or incident may have had on you, see if you can identify the feelings associated with that experience—let yourself feel them fully, without judgment—is there an important lesson here? What would support you in being able to let go once and for all? Do you need to write about it? Or take it into some other form of creative expression? Or have a conversation with the person (live or via letter)? What supports you in being able to fully let go? Remember, the aim here is to go forward. You are complete.

FORGIVENESS → AS AN ACT OF LIBERATION

Now that you've released all of that old, debilitating energy, and given yourself a clean slate, what would you like to explore in your Do Good vision? Free from any of the previous restraints, you can develop and nurture your calling in a whole new way. Feel your capacity to create from a place of pure inspiration instead of old limitations. What would you like to affect? You are free.

FORGIVENESS → AS AN ACT OF SELF-LOVE

In this last step, I'd like you to see all of the ways that you already have done good. All of the things you've done to bring more love, joy, peace, beauty, and inspiration into the world. From the smallest of acts to the largest. See the contribution that you've already made and know that it is just the tip of the iceberg. Honor yourself for all of the courage you've shown and the wisdom you've gained. As you embrace all you've done and been through, see the abundant possibilities before you as the next step. You are love.

Honoring Real Limitations, AKA Having Boundaries

Now that you've begun to forgive and release the limitations that have hindered your ability to make your highest contribution, you must consider the importance of honoring those limitations that actually support you. What do I mean by supportive limitations, you ask? The truth is there are only so many hours in a day and you do only have so much energy to devote to what really matters to you. So, when it comes to creating a viable strategy for doing good, it's vital to set a few standards and criteria to help you pursue your highest contribution. Given all the work we've done in the previous two chapters, you now have the freedom to decide which factors enable you to honor your unique talents and gifts, your own standard of excellence, and really be effective at what you do. Setting healthy boundaries is a necessary part of creating sustainability and longevity in your contribution. Knowing when you need to step back and rest, knowing when and where to balance the work and your quality time with family and friends, and knowing when you need to laugh are imperatives for bringing your best.

No matter how important your work is, it's vital to not become consumed by the challenges your work presents. Creating a high-quality Do Good experience allows difficulties to inspire and enliven you; it lets you give more without feeling drained in the process. A big part of letting go of the old paradigm of contribution is recognizing that you deserve and are entitled to a whole life and that the more healthy, happy, and vibrant you are, the more you can bring to your Do Good.

When I think about what it takes to honor a happy and healthy commitment, once you're free of the limitations you've chosen to forgive, I think of my client Dr. Jen. Dr. Jen came to me after seeing me keynote at a gathering for women entrepreneurs in the health and wellness space.

Tall, statuesque, and gorgeous inside and out, she ran up to me and said, "I'm supposed to work with you, Rha; I just know you're going to help me transform the field of medicine."

Her humility, coupled with her clarity and conviction, instantly won me over. We set up a time to speak shortly after. As I listened to all the pivotal moments in her story, I could easily see the potential for her to go from caring for young children and their families as a pediatrician to reimagining how, as a culture, medicine is practiced in the United States. Dr. Jen was the ultimate student when it came to doing the research to support her commitment. She devoted hundreds of hours to exploring various aspects of Eastern and Western medicine and listened to many of her colleagues discuss the challenges of building and sustaining their practices while providing quality care to patients.

The struggle was real, and Dr. Jen knew this from her own experience. She'd been on both sides of the stethoscope: first as a patient when she battled through multiple miscarriages, then as a physician managing her own budding practice and making the tough decision to only accept certain forms of insurance. The first part of our work together was about bringing Dr. Jen's current commitments into alignment with the highest and best use of her talents and gifts and providing more room to support the growth and evolution of her calling.

When I asked her about what she was here to do, this is what she said: "I firmly believe that I am here to help other physicians heal."

"Oooh, say more. . . ."

"The stress and pressure of dealing with a broken healthcare system is taking its toll on my colleagues. I know what they're dealing with because I had the same issue before I completed my residency." She could see all of the ways her colleagues began to practice medicine from a place of fear rather than from a place of compassion and love.

Her first step in that work was to revamp her practice and organize her visits with children and families in a way that freed up more of her energy to devote to this new calling. We redesigned Dr. Jen's offerings and helped revamp her assistant's role so that Dr. Jen spent more time with patients and families. This simple move freed up tons of mental, spiritual, and emotional space for Dr. Jen to devote time to developing a plan that would ultimately support her vision to spend 70 percent of her time working with "healing warriors," as she called them.

Now that the practice was running smoothly, I asked her, "What else is on your plate that needs to be repositioned?" That's when she told me about her nonprofit organization. She'd developed this nonprofit in collaboration with a local business leader who was also passionate about children's health and well-being. Dr. Jen's nonprofit created healthy meal plans for kids and provided crucial information to parents of children who struggled with various food allergies. She *loved* this organization, yet when she looked at the existing team and board configuration she knew the role she'd been playing as co-director did not reflect her greatest talents and skills.

She was torn about what to do because she did not want to abandon the mission or the team. But the more we looked at what was needed versus what would be the best way to utilize her knowledge and skills, the clearer it became that she needed to transition out of the co-director role and into that of a more forward-facing mission ambassador. This would cut Dr. Jen's time commitment to the organization by about 75 percent!

"Ugh! This is so hard," she said. "I don't want to abandon this mission, or the people who've devoted so much of their time and energy to getting it off the ground." This is often where the rubber meets the road for those who are doing really good and important work but not doing *their* work, or work that is better aligned with the highest use of their talents and skills.

"Letting go is so hard!" she cried.

"I know," I replied. "But if you don't let go, then neither one of you will be free, not you and not the organization. And in both cases you could be blocking a lot of good that wants to happen for you and for them."

Dr. Jen and I spent a lot of time working through the guilt she felt around this and forgiving herself and others for overextending themselves in ways that actually limited the potential of the organization. This dynamic is far more common than you would imagine—many caring people stay in not-so-good Do Good situations far longer than they should. Dr. Jen held on with the best intentions—because she really did want to see the organization succeed.

After six weeks of real truth-telling, Dr. Jen began to put her plan into place. This included shifting out of her role, which made her feel lighter, on fire, and ready to devote everything to her true purpose and aspirations—helping her "healing warriors" return to the real reason they began practicing medicine in the first place. When I asked Dr. Jen what the ultimate impact she desired was, she said, "If physicians can reconnect to that original spark and reclaim all of their gifts, along with their excitement and inspiration, then we have the potential to heal the healthcare system." She continued, "Which would result in more compassionate and healing experiences for their patients."

"This is so good, Dr. Jen," I replied, "and it's an awesome reason to want to get freed up. We need this. Thank you for your courage."

Healing Collective Trauma

One of the most profound challenges that we grapple with as a society is the way we're being forced to confront the chaos of our world. As I mentioned in chapter 14, technology has been a total game changer in giving us a front-row seat to realities that we would otherwise know little to nothing about. Beyond syndicated media, we now have access to just about anything that happens in the vicinity of a cell phone. This has proven to be both a blessing and a trial. Confronting what little we know about human rights violations and even our basic everyday inhumanity toward one another can be shocking and deeply disturbing. It can also cause us to wrestle with a wide range of emotions from guilt, to sadness, to rage, and everything in between. All of this, of course, becomes even more daunting when those experiences hit home—an item in the news that affects us or someone we know, or simply feeling a connection to a tragic event. I don't know anyone who was not moved and deeply affected by the 2012 Sandy Hook shooting. Random mass homicides are difficult to take in general, but when it involves small, innocent children it's even harder. When it comes to this never-ending procession of experiences, we must learn how to care for ourselves, not only how to comfort ourselves through the wealth of emotions that arise but also how to heal the blows to our faith in our fellow man. It's hard to prevent ourselves from going numb. So much attention in the media can cause us to get hooked on all forms of social engagement, the circumstances almost beg us to overcommit, yet as we consider what is most aligned for us we have to recognize what is our best contribution in any situation.

How do you find a connection between what the world needs and your true calling?

Every empowered citizen has to grapple with this dilemma as they consider what it means to be awake and aware. When you make the choice to Do Good and pursue your calling, you also say yes to meeting your moment, and for every single person reading this book, I assure you: Your moment is now and the call to serve is urgent and great. Your ability to bring more love, kindness, and compassion into the world matters. And the love, kindness, and compassion you're willing to extend to "strangers" matters even more.

What I know from experience is that with every loving interaction, you're healing apathy and resignation, other people's and your own. When you answer your call, you are being the light and the change— the transformation you seek in a world that often forgets how to care for itself and others. With every consciously creative step you take, you are forgiving the past and rebuilding trust for a future world that you want to see as a global citizen. One that would be worthy to pass down to our children.

When I think about what it means to restore faith in humanity, I think of my beloved client Rachel. When Rachel first approached me about working together, she was looking for support in taking her awesome movement for moms to the next level. Already a brilliant content creator, thought leader, and community engager, Rachel was preparing to launch a new book and wanted to use this opportunity to both deepen and expand her impact through more paid in-depth offerings. Her mom movement was centered around encouraging moms to take a more holistic approach to who they were and hence take better care of themselves, mentally, spiritually, physically, emotionally, and professionally.

"It's like we don't stop being people just because we have children," Rachel shared. "We have dreams, gifts, wants, needs, and aspirations like anybody else." She continued, "But nobody is encouraging us to explore those talents, desires, or aspirations, nor are they encouraging us to think more holistically about ourselves and what makes us really happy." She paused. "We are more than just diaper bags and strollers. We are CEOs, artists, badasses, and visionaries."

I love this woman! Rachel's passion was palpable.

As we turned to wrap up our initial consultation early one November morning, Rachel paused and added, "Oh, I guess I should also mention that I have these other businesses, too."

"Really?" I asked. "Tell me more."

"Well, I have these properties and these buildings upstate, and they include a number of industrial rental properties, some storage facilities, and an airport."

An airport? Who casually drops this into a conversation? Like . . . "Oh, and ah . . . by the way, I'm a #Mogul!"

"It's all very complicated, but it's mine." Rachel sighed—audibly.

"Huh!" I said. "Sounds like there's a lot going on around this."

"Oh, sister, you don't know the half of it." She continued, "I inherited these businesses from my dad. He passed away eleven years ago in a plane crash."

"Oh, Rachel, I am so very sorry," I replied.

"Thank you. He was a brilliant inventor and creative risk-taker and also very complex—hence the complexity of all these businesses."

"And do you have a vision for these businesses?" I probed.

"Well, I bring it up because as we think about the expansion of my movement for moms, I'm considering if there is another way that I might utilize the properties that I have upstate more."

"Okay," I said, "I'm making a note to revisit this when we come together. I'm curious about how these additional assets might support this new vision. As a matter of fact, I'd love for you to start thinking about this as part of your homework."

Though I did not have all of the specifics, I could tell from the shift in energy on the call that there was a lot here and somehow it was definitely connected to her sense of freedom and full self-expression.

A few weeks later, we arrived in New York City for her half-day retreat and in the check-in portion of the agenda she immediately began to describe the physical manifestation of this disconnect between her current venture and all of those other businesses.

"I feel like there is this separation between the right half of my body and the left half of my body right now. The left side of my body is in serious pain and I can feel it from the top of my neck all the way down to my hip. Whereas the right side of my body is fine. It's like I have two separate bodies that are operating totally differently," Rachel shared after our grounding meditation.

"What do you think this pain all along the left side is about?" I asked.

"I think it has something to do with what I'm not saying about what's going on with these businesses." She paused and I could feel her checking in with herself. This was difficult to express, I could tell.

"It has to do with a dynamic within my family that revolves around a certain person and how they are choosing to handle things right now in the businesses."

"So there is a family member running things right now?" I inquired.

She nodded. "But it goes deeper than just how things are being run in the businesses. There have been things that have been said and done in the name of protecting me that have not been cool. Like, things that have been said to other members of the family about some of the choices I've made about my life, my business, and *my* family. Boundaries have been crossed and I've tried to find a way to keep this very delicate situation from exploding."

"Wow." I could feel the gravity and tenderness of the situation in every word she spoke.

"In the beginning, this person was incredibly helpful to me; as a matter of fact, I don't know what would have happened to all of those businesses if they hadn't taken over. But over the years, I've noticed things that I don't think are as helpful and I've not been as proactive on calling them out as I should be. I think it's getting to a place where the situation may actually be more harmful than helpful. I think this whole thing is taking a massive toll on me and it has everything to do with my own clarity, authenticity, and responsibility."

"Absolutely," I agreed. "Any time any of us are not in our full voice about something we can feel all kinds of things, including physical pain in our bodies."

"Well, okay then. I guess we have to look at this, too—huh?" She said this sheepishly.

"Yes, ma'am, somehow, all of this is connected," I assured her.

I could feel her courage, determination, and compassion for herself and for the situation.

"Things are not on the up-and-up. Even with the best intentions, I think there are some things happening that don't feel quite in integrity. But what's also true is that a lot of things have been done that, quite honestly, have been a godsend to me—because I don't think I've wanted to come to terms with what it really meant to run all of these businesses, maybe even up until now. And the truth is, I'm still not sure I want to take all of these businesses on."

I paused to really let what she shared sink in—for both of us.

"What do you think taking on all these businesses would mean?"

"Making a lot of people angry and uncomfortable. That's for sure."

So began our journey into the depths of what was an extremely complicated dynamic that existed within a family and series of businesses that represented Rachel's inheritance in the best and most challenging ways possible. In order to untangle these loaded interactions she was having around these businesses with staff and family, what was required was a lot of truth telling.

Especially hers.

It also required Rachel to create a compelling vision for her life, her life's work, and her leadership. So that this truth telling could be in service to something greater. Something that would motivate and inspire her, even when it was hard.

When we got to the bottom of it Rachel began to see that she had to reevaluate her relationship with every single member of her family and make a clear stand for her own power, and her own voice, and her own right to make the choices in her life and in her business that she felt were best. It was time to get free. And in order to do that, we had to support the cultivation of her truth as a practice and a discipline, so that she could see when she was honoring herself versus when she was succumbing to the pressure of those old perceptions about who she was as this fragile little girl who lost her dad rather than who she was now. At a fundamental level, this was about Rachel now stepping up and growing up in the eyes of her family. It was time to own her womanhood and her CEO-ness. This meant taking full responsibility for the kick-ass leader she already was.

Each of these were huge bodies of work unto themselves. But even more impressive and vital for her was to do it in a way that honored everyone's humanity. There was so much individual and collective trauma that was shared among the staff and the family, it could feel debilitating at times. Some days we'd speak and she'd begin or end with, "All I want to do is cry."

In the end, it became very clear that on a personal level, healthy boundaries needed to be set. And within the businesses, a family member who had been in charge and fought the good fight all these years to the best of their ability needed to step down. It was time for Rachel to move into her rightful place of leadership. Which meant taking the helm of the day-to-day operations of all the businesses and leading an evolving team into a new era of possibility—one that reflected Rachel's distinct values and convictions.

We prepared diligently for that important conversation. Rachel was thorough in researching, observing, asking questions, enlisting the right support, doing everything she could to ensure that this important family member was honored in the process. Rachel also became adamant about healing other key relationships and laid the groundwork for that potential, too. I remember our last conversation as she was packing to head up to have the meeting.

"It's time," she said.

"You got this!" I replied.

And she did.

Rachel is now leading these businesses with so much grace and dedication. It has not been easy, but she has been rising to meet each challenge. As for her relationship with the family member, that situation is more complicated—Rachel is open but unsure of what the future holds. What she does know is that she did what she had to do and she has handled it all, as my beloved team member Mari would say, #LikeABoss.

Forgiving and Releasing the
Greatest Societal Myth of All

There is a famous quote by Margaret Mead that I love: "Never doubt that a small group of thoughtful, committed citizens can change the world; indeed, it's the only thing that ever has."

I remember reading this quote almost daily when I worked as a conflict resolution facilitator and trainer. It spoke to me because I wanted to always act in ways that took into account the ripple effects of my efforts that I might never see. I think of Dr. Martin Luther King Jr's. famous last speech, which included the words "I may not get there with you"— and the fact that we stand on the shoulders of other people's grand efforts every single day. It's cool to also realize that someday someone will stand on ours. When you surrender to your calling, inspiring others is a daily event that makes it impossible to track all the ways you're having an impact. And while sometimes you'll be able to see your efforts, sometimes you won't.

The biggest myth to forgive here is the one that says that one person cannot make a difference. It's simply not true. Often, when someone is called to a big vision you hear the phrase "It isn't about you," which is a nice way of inviting them to edge their egos out of the way. Because of the unfortunate, long legacy of self-neglect that exists within many forms of activism, I've actually amended this phrase to become "It is bigger than you *and* it includes you—you do have a role to play." This is how I help clients recognize and own their power, while not being totally overwhelmed

and consumed by the magnitude of what they may be wanting to transform. As I share this philosophy, my hope is that it gives you greater capacity to make your contribution. It is important to experience the power of your own efforts while also recognizing that you are part of a larger movement where your efforts are being leveraged in concert with the efforts of so many others. Don't forget, too, about how all those efforts combine with the universal forces that become activated through your actions for positive change to occur. When you appreciate your role, while also appreciating the whole, you get a more empowering way of seeing yourself in the world and acknowledging the strength of your own contribution.

Your Call

Are you ready to let go of anything that stands in the way of your highest contribution? Over the next two weeks, use these two practices and two exercises to invite in a new level of freedom, clarity, and confidence as you pursue your calling.

PRACTICE 1:

"I release and let go my [negative feelings] about the state of our world."
"I'm ready to embrace my rightful place as an empowered citizen."

Work with these two mantras over the next two weeks as you transform limiting perceptions about the difference you can make in the world. Set aside five minutes in the morning to speak these two statements while looking in the mirror. Also, keep these mantras on hand as you encounter any challenging events in your community and/or the media. Take three deep breaths before speaking these words. Keep repeating the series until you feel your energy shift to a more expansive place.

PRACTICE 2

Over the next two weeks, practice saying no to anything that does not totally align with what matters to you. Notice if you have more energy for the things that do matter as a result.

EXERCISE 1

Use the four-step forgiveness ritual in the "Transforming Your Greatest Hit(s)" section of this chapter to transform your Greatest Hit(s) and any underlying root causes you may have about your ability to be a part of the solution. You can download this worksheet at www.movethecrowd .me/TheCalling/resources.

EXERCISE 2

Find the image of someone who inspires you to pursue your calling. They can be living or deceased, old or young, someone you personally know or someone you've read about. Place that image on your phone or in your work area. Any time you feel discouraged, take a look at that image and imagine that person is cheering you on.

16

Step #4: Visualizing and Redefining What It Means to Do Good in the Age of the Citizen

Now that you've cleared the obstacles away, it's time to lean into what it means to be an empowered citizen dedicated to doing good in the world. Your participation in this Age of the Citizen is an invitation into a new brand of citizenship. One that will enable you to be a vibrant, thriving, consciously contributing member of society. An active shaper of the person you want to be and the world you want to see. I fundamentally believe that no matter where we come from or what we've struggled through, we all want to do good and we all have been given everything we need to make our own unique contribution. Even if our "world" only consists of the people we are immediately responsible for, there is a desire to ensure that those we love are taken care of. So whether it's Super-Mom or Super-Mogul, now's the time to give voice to your vision.

Given all of the ways to make a difference, you'd think it would be easy to choose where to dive in. Nope! One of the biggest challenges I see every day is people trying to figure out where they belong when it comes to their calling. For some of you, your vision may take you in a whole new direction—meaning you are newly discovering what your work in the world is—and it may be vastly different than what you are currently doing right now. For others, it may simply be the next evolution of what they've always known. Maybe it's bigger platforms or stages or more interesting collaborations or new and improved offerings.

In this chapter, I'll show you how to step up and give voice to the difference you want to make. I've already shown you how to articulate your vision, mission, and purpose (L3) and how to create a unique Values-Aligned Proposition and I've shown you how to monetize that proposition. In this chapter, I want to help you bring it all together as you consider where your proposition, guided by your purpose, can have the greatest impact. My aim as you put all of this on the court is to have you experience what it means to be a part of the solution, creatively, consciously molding and shaping the world you want to see day in and day out.

From Dharma to Vision

Let's revisit your homework from chapter 13. Were you able to give voice to your calling? Could you see the elements of your desired contribution starting to take shape as you allowed yourself to respond to the question: If money, failure, perfection, or any other concern you have weren't a concern, what would you be doing and why? If you are clear about what you're being called to do and are already acting on it, then your work may be focused on how to give it even more life—so that you are doing it more often, with greater precision, and reaching more people with your gifts. Often, when I speak to people who are clear about their calling, the work is how to align their proposition in a way that invites more profitability and impact.

If you are still ruminating on what your calling may be, don't worry, just pay attention to where you feel called right now, in this moment. When you look at the things that make you happy, pique your curiosity, or ignite your passion, your dharma is right there. What has your attention? Where do you feel a desire to lean in and make a difference? What additional information or practice are you being inspired to pursue?

Remember, in the evolutionary process, every step you take toward those impulses moves you closer and closer to where you ought to be.

The articulation of your highest contribution may not look like a job description: it may come in as a very broad but very specific mandate. Use this opportunity to revisit your Love declaration from your L3 as your mission statement is a great place to draw from. For example, when mine came through I heard my highest contribution as follows:

> *Help people discover the truth of who they are in service to their highest calling and contribution.*

In other words, my dharma came as a directive to help other people find their dharma and act on it. Now, there are a million ways I can do this and there are many ways that I have already done it—as an artist, an executive director, as an organizational development consultant, as a creative producer, and currently as social entrepreneur, coach, and professional mentor. So you see, my work has taken shape and form through lots of professions. But my commitment has always been the same: to help people find their truest self and their highest calling.

As you move through each stage of personal and professional evolution, you may find yourself expressing your highest contribution in various ways and through any number of vehicles. Your practice with each transition is to keep coming back to the original vision, essence, and nature of your calling.

There is a great saying by one of my beloved mentors, David Gershon: "Stay true to the impulse, but be flexible about the form." I cannot tell you how many times I've had to remind myself of this sage wisdom as I've leveraged my highest contribution in many different arenas. And especially as I've built my own company. I want to give you permission right here and now to nurture your vision before you put all of the "pressure" on it to have to support your family.

Write it down, talk it out, draw symbols, figures, phrases, whatever it takes to allow the idea to be born in you. If you are looking to give your calling more life take the time to get it down on paper using the strategies above and vividly express what that looks like.

Recently, I was in conversation with a brilliant serial entrepreneur, someone who has built and sold businesses for the last 25 years, and he happens to be working on a new idea. What I *love* is that with every email he sends me I can feel him nurturing and fine-tuning the concept. He's still got lots of questions *and* he knows from experience that it is perfectly okay, it's just part of the process.

Casting Your Pearls

Now, as much as I'm encouraging you to write it out and talk it out, I'm also going to be a stickler for recommending that you do this work in environments that are conducive to nurturing new ideas. Many of the anxieties the entrepreneurs I serve face have stemmed from sharing their ideas with people who just don't get it *and* who have more words of caution for them than encouragement. Or from sharing their ideas in environments that are negatively competitive.

When you are in the early stages of an idea, be mindful about where and how you share.

I always ask the question, "Would you just let anyone hold your baby?" Whether you are a parent or not, my guess is your response would be the same: "Hell no!" Well, you've got to bring the same level of loving conviction to your idea. Your vision for your work should be given lots of water and sunlight in the early stages. It should be given space and time to crystallize. As you become more confident in the idea, then you can begin to think about what form it could or should take.

If you are on your way and seeking to give your calling more life, you also want to be mindful of when and how you are putting forth your vision. If the environment feels welcoming to your voice and ideas then by all means speak up, but if you are not sure take the time to feel the space out and build authentic supportive connections before you delve into sharing your dreams.

This piece of advice comes from hard-earned experience, let me tell you! I remember meeting Myla at an awesome new co-working space in the city that was dedicated to supporting women entrepreneurs. At the time, co-working spaces were popping up all over the place and this new wave of spaces that focused on women or creatives or tech start-ups was beginning to catch on. I connected with Myla because I was looking to rent space for an upcoming event. She was an active member of the community and sometimes helped bring in various kinds of programming. It was from this perspective that she began to inquire about who I was and what I did.

"Wow. So, like, you help people live out their dreams while doing good?" she asked.

"Yep. That is exactly what I do," I replied.

We wound up going with a different space, but Myla and I stayed in touch and any time we were hosting an event I would invite her. She finally made it out one chilly night in January and I could tell that she was blown away by the community. The mix of people, the range of industries, the quality of work they were doing in the world, all of it inspired her in a pretty big way.

At the end of the evening, Myla came up to me and said, "I think I'm ready to talk to one of your coaches."

I smiled and said, "Awesome."

A few weeks later, I'd reached out to Myla to make an introduction and asked if she'd scheduled her consultation with one of our coaches yet.

"Nope," she said, "I've been too busy." As we talked more she began to backtrack. "Actually, I've been really scared, that's the truth." When I asked her why, she said, "As much as I know it's time to do something different, nobody in my immediate circle understands what I'm trying to do, and these are really smart people." She continued, "If they don't get it then maybe it's just not worth pursuing."

"Hmph," I said. "Is that what you think?"

She paused to gather her thoughts. "No, I think there is something here. But it's hard to have faith in it when the people around you, those you really respect, can't see your vision. Or worse yet, they think you're weird for coming up with it."

Really? I thought. "I'd love to hear it; what's the idea?"

She jumped up from our video call and said, "Hold on," and she went and closed the door. "So I've been imagining this two-day retreat for women in social impact where we use various forms of creativity and art to help them get to an idea for something they want to pursue." She leaned into the video screen. "They would all spend two days working on the idea—or at least the articulation of the idea. At the end, each woman would present and then the group would decide which idea they would support and each woman would get very specific about what she'd offer to help get the idea off of the ground."

"Sounds really interesting," I said. "So what part didn't your friends/ colleagues get?"

She sighed. "They couldn't understand why any of the women would support the others. They felt like everyone would only want to support and promote their own idea and so the whole thing won't work."

"Hmph," I said. "Well, hopefully you'll have an opportunity to pilot the idea so that you can see for yourself what does and does not work."

Another sigh. "Yeah, I guess so—it's just I was planning on going to my friends for support and if they don't get it they probably won't support it." She continued, "That's what I loved about being in the room with your community; it's seems like everyone really supports each other. I mean, it's clear that everybody's got their own thing, but they're not afraid to extend a hand to one another without it having to be about them all of the time."

"Yep," I said, "so, when is your consult?"

Even when you are enrolling your best friends, take the time to understand where they are coming from before you dive in. Your vision is sacred . . . pay attention to who's receiving it.

Connecting the Dots—Your Highest Contribution

Now that you have a working statement for your calling, let's look at how your passion, commitment, and unique proposition come together to actually form your highest contribution.

In this Age of the Citizen there are so many ways that you can be doing good in the world right now. Remember, in chapter 4, you worked to cultivate a new self-narrative drawn from defining moments in your life, moments where you were able to see your most authentic self in motion; similarly, in chapter 11, you got to reimagine your offering to the marketplace based upon your unique combination of values, talents, gifts, and abilities. Both of these insights should be supporting how you express your work in the world. And now, as we revisit your Lead declaration from your L3, we get to look at where and how you want to leverage your amazing skills to have real impact.

When it comes to creating a clear focus for your contribution, I like to use the social impact framework I laid out in chapter 13. Let's organize your preferences into the categories of area, sector, objective, purpose, strategy, idea, and vehicle. This will allow you to parse out your thoughts and options a bit more clearly. To begin this process, think about the work you most want to be doing and how it fulfills your highest contribution. For instance: Let's say that you have a passion for working with stressed-out professionals and you want to help them make better choices around the way they take care of themselves while they work in demanding environments to achieve their goals. The first thing you want to understand is how helping stressed-out professionals speaks to your highest contribution. Think back to Priscilla's example in chapter 13; she believes that having more women in positions of leadership will lead to more compassionate organizations and bringing more compassion to the world is her calling. For the purposes of this example I'm going to assume that you want to help stressed-out professionals because you know that if they take better care of themselves they'll do better work and if they do better work they'll be more satisfied and if they are more satisfied then they will be more inclined to foster a more joyful work environment and you know that a more joyful work environment will encourage other people to bring their best and the company as a result will become more joyful and ultimately successful at what it does. And if we assume that this company is doing good in the world, it means that they now have the capacity to do even more good. And if your purpose is to bring more joy to the world then you are right on track with this contribution.

Now let's break down how your preference to work with stressed-out professionals fits into each of the categories of impact I listed previously:

Area: Social—because self-care is a form of empowerment.

Sector: Business or for benefit—I'm going to go out on a limb here because I want to encourage you to bring a more entrepreneurial approach to your Do Good vision.

Objective: Good health—when I look at the 17 UN goals this fits perfectly with promoting a greater sense of well-being for all.

Purpose: Bring more joy—increase the capacity of others to do good—this is your true north.

Strategy: Paradigm/culture shifting—new rituals, practices, beliefs. I could also make a case for capacity building—because more joyful professionals naturally bring more capacity to achieve their goals.

Idea: Teach stressed-out professionals how to take better care of themselves.

Vehicle: Professional wellness company that delivers programs on how to reduce stress and boost all forms of well-being.

Highest Contribution: Teach various forms of mindfulness (i.e., yoga, meditation, breathwork, conscious eating, etc.) to stressed-out professionals.

When it comes to your highest contribution here's where your specific talents and gifts in the form of your Values-Aligned Proposition are leveraged to achieve your purpose. I call this your Do Good framework. As you walk through this example, take a few moments now to jot down in your journal how this process would apply to your contribution.

Now, what if the audience you most want to serve doesn't have the means to afford your services? This is a question that often arises when I'm working with clients. It may mean that you've got to devise a different strategy for your monetization. Here I want to remind you of the difference between your audience and your client. The most popular examples of where clients are leveraged to serve a desired audience would be Tom's Shoes and Warby Parker. In both cases, these companies have chosen to create one-to-one matches for the purchasing of their products or matching donation initiatives. Meaning that for every client who purchases their products a member of their "audience" receives either a matching product or corresponding donation to support key initiatives that the company is passionate about.

When it comes to developing interesting models for monetizing impact, I think of the beautiful Dara and her work building community wealth through the BronXchange. I met Dara at a training I was brought in to deliver in Atlanta for a national fellowship on social change innovation with the Nathan Cummings Foundation. Dara was co-director of the Bronx Cooperative Development Initiative, a regional nonprofit that was looking to create a robust revenue-generating strategy as part of their vision for sustainability and economic democracy in the Bronx. Dara was utilizing her fellowship to work with local nonprofits, business leaders, and a social impact investor to envision the strategy for a tech start-up. After the daylong training, Dara reached out to me to continue working with her on this initiative. The vision for the BronXchange was to build an online platform that would enable large "anchor" institutions within the Bronx to utilize local, mission-driven vendors—the majority of them women and people of color—for everything from building services, to printing and marketing, to catering, to IT support. These local vendors would be featured on the site and have access to new contracts from large institutional purchasers that weren't previously available to them. A nominal percentage of each contract booked through the portal covered operating costs and eventually would generate a surplus to support equitable business and economic development in the Bronx. The primary intention of the exchange was to encourage greater investment in the local economy on the part of larger corporations that usually looked outside of the city for similar resources—thereby generating community wealth for Bronx residents and businesses. Dara enlisted my support in helping her step into the next level of leadership, which for her meant transitioning from a nonprofit management role to launch the new social enterprise. Components of the concept had been successfully modeled in other cities and there were a number of stakeholders at the table guiding the vision and strategy, all interested in investing resources to support the launch. There were various facets of the enterprise that she was lifting at once and our work was to help her get crystal clear about all of the ways the BronXchange could make money and then prioritize which aspects of the business model should be rolled out first. In addition to hosting the vendors, the BronXchange would provide wraparound services that would not only enable the vendors to build strong referral pages but would also walk them step by step through a process of securing and onboarding major institutional clients and provide access to financing to remove barriers. Dara and the Bronx Cooperative Development

Initiative saw an opportunity to enlist anchor institutions in a fee-based service that would not only give them access to the portal but also facilitate curated matches based on certain criteria so that purchasers could minimize the time needed to arrive at their top candidates and do business with them online. In this way, the institutions were able to achieve a triple-bottom-line impact—demonstrating their mission-driven values by supporting their local community through good business decisions. As we dove deep on the design, I encouraged Dara to think about all of the ways the portal could be leveraged to provide awesome opportunities for both longtime local business as well as up-and-coming entrepreneurs and how it could foster a deeper connection and greater sense of commitment on the part of large entities that were often in the community but not of the community. According to Dara's research, there were billions of dollars spent in procuring products and services currently leaking out of the Bronx that could instead be redirected to support local entrepreneurs, provide good jobs for residents, and improve health outcomes in the community. The clearer she got around the business model, the more able she was to execute the vision and move it from concept to action. In our last conversation, Dara was in the final stages of launching the beta site and feeling proud of the core revenue model she'd created in collaboration with the team. She knew who her customers were and she was ready to go get them.

I'm sharing the examples of Tom's Shoes, Warby Parker, and the BronXchange because they are becoming more popular in this Age of the Citizen and because I want you to know what's possible when it comes to your contribution.

Missing the Mark: 20 Feet from Stardom

As you become clear about the potential of your own contribution, I want to encourage you to bring a high level of rigor to this process. Why? Because your old conditioned mind may want to creep back in here and challenge you around what you can or cannot monetize when it comes to your highest contribution. The key to the connecting the dots exercise and Do Good framework in the previous section above (i.e., Area, Sector, Objective, Purpose, Strategy, etc.) is to find true alignment so that you feel like you're being the person you most want to be while making the contribution you most want to make.

In Stephen Cope's celebrated book *The Great Work of Your Life,* he talks about the fact that most people spend their lives hanging out in the "vicinity" of their dharma and never quite make it to the center of their own stream. Part of why I believe this happens is because we are deeply conditioned to trade—time, joy, freedom, authenticity, etc., in exchange for money or success—I've talked a lot about this in this book.

It takes courage and rigor to find the center of your own stream and to remain unwavering in your commitment to live and express from that place. Chögyam Trungpa speaks of it in the Shambhala Warrior tradition as being disciplined in remaining "genuine" in everything that you do.

When I first met Sarah, I was immediately impressed by her focus and dedication to her new role as head of a women's initiative in a large marketing and branding company. In addition to her duties on the client-facing side, Sarah had stepped up to lead a new company-wide commitment to help recruit and advance more women within her organization. Sarah had lots of ideas about how she wanted to approach this new role and I was one of a number of thought leaders who had been brought in to help push her thinking. "I want this to mean something," she said. All of us knew that sometimes, even with the best intentions, companies announce initiatives that wind up being more like mini–PR campaigns than true efforts that actually shift culture and change behavior. Sarah wanted it clear from the beginning that she meant business. As she walked us through her research findings, we began to see where some of the greatest opportunities resided. As we looked at the company's track record in this area, there had been some awesome achievements over the years and some places where things languished. We were all aware that this moment would be about leadership—Sarah's to be exact. As she laid out her plan there was a lot of emphasis on the external strategy and the way the company hoped to demonstrate this commitment in the marketplace. I thought that emphasis felt really clear; however, when I posed questions around the internal strategy, Sarah agreed that they had an opportunity to bring a new level of engagement to those within the company. Over the course of six months, we met in various configurations to help bring fresh new language to the initiative. As Sarah began to implement changes, the roadblocks started to arrive. This was normal and to be expected. Any time a new initiative is launched, big companies are tested around their capacity for change. Sarah knew she'd have to bring other leaders on board to be able to realize the full vision and she began having very candid and important conversations among key senior-level executives.

As Sarah leaned deeper into this process, she began to question whether or not the company was ready. The more she attempted to push forward, the more other colleagues began to question her role and authority. I remember having a late-night conversation with Sarah after a particularly challenging week when the company politics was at an all-time high.

I asked her, "What do you believe is your work here?"

She paused, then asked me, "What do you mean?"

I replied, "I know that it can be very tempting to get caught up in the politics, but I know that's not why you took on this role; you took on this role because you wanted to make a difference. Remember?"

"Ohh, now I get what you're saying."

"Why don't we come back to that?" My aim here was to keep reminding Sarah that she had a purpose and a vision for the change she wanted to bring to her company. She loved her company and felt committed to its success—but somehow in all of the back-and-forth around what was possible and what was not, it became easy to lose sight of what was most important for her. We took it one leader and one conversation at a time, and suddenly Sarah began to feel movement. She was asked to take the stage at a major global event to talk about the initiative; she was invited into key meetings with the board to share the vision she'd worked tirelessly to create. She was asked to speak to incoming women about her journey and their role in this new vision. The more she began to own this commitment, the more her vision for her own leadership began to expand. And at some point, it became very clear that she was being called to something even greater than her role at the company. As a result of the initiative, she'd talked to literally hundreds of women. And it was clear that her company was not alone in its need to bring more women into the fold.

"This is about the way we lead and do business everywhere," Sarah reflected back in one of our conversations. "Maybe it's time to talk more about that—about what needs to happen for all of us to lead differently." As Sarah started to feel her own conviction, she knew that her calling was about to move her into totally uncharted waters. She was terrified and excited as she came to this realization. No matter what Sarah ultimately decides about her role, one thing has become supremely clear: She is ready to embrace what feels most aligned and genuine for her, no matter where that commitment takes her.

When it comes to having passion, purpose, and profitability occupying the same space many of us are skeptical—can I really do this? Will they (whoever they are) let me? Will I starve if I strike out on my own? I've watched many of my clients in the early stages actively manage these concerns And as difficult as it feels in the moment, it's important to know that times are changing. Every day we become aware of yet another example where someone has found a way to bring passion, purpose, and profit together—and companies are also starting to recognize the imperative to get on board—it's why I'm so excited about the Age of the Citizen, because I believe that each of us, not matter what structure we choose to occupy, will finally get to answer the call in our own way.

Your Call

Are you ready to define what doing good means on your terms? Over the next week, use these two practices and exercise to get super-clear about our own specific calling and contribution.

PRACTICE 1

"I know who I am and I know what I bring."
"I'm ready to make my highest contribution: I'm ready to do good."

Use this set of mantras to inspire you as you embrace your vision for doing good. Speak them in the mirror in the A.M. when you first wake up, then any time during the day when you take a break from being immersed in your work. Take a deep breath just before you say each phrase—feel your dedication and commitment with each word.

PRACTICE 2

Revisit your Love declaration from your L3 over the next seven days—notice how this statement connects to the statement of your highest contribution? Use this exploration to refine each statement as desired.

EXERCISE 1

Using the Do Good framework I outlined in the "Connecting the Dots—Your Highest Contribution" section (i.e., Area, Sector, Objective, Purpose, Strategy, etc.), create the blueprint for where you believe you want to make your highest contribution right now. Remember, there can be many options available to you. Select the one you feel most passionate about in this moment. Do the work to ensure that it aligns with your True. Paid. Good. You can download your Do Good Strategy worksheet from www.movethecrowd.me/TheCalling/resources.

 **MOVETHECROWD**

CREATING YOUR DO GOOD STRATEGY

I. Select Your Primary Area :
My Area is:

sustainabledevelopment.svg
Move The Crowd supports the Sustainable
Development Goals

II. Select Your Primary Sector.
My Sector is:

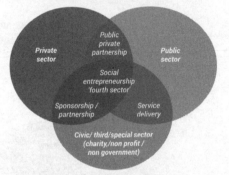

III. Select Your Primary Objective:
My objective is:

*Figure by Tania Ellis, The Social
Business Company*

**IV. What's Your Purpose? (Hint—revisit your
L3 Declarations)** Your Lead Declaration
should be used here and potentially refined
given your insights from above. The ultimate
question is what is the impact you most
want to make?

UN Sustainable Goals
www.unsustainabledevelopmentgoals.un.org

The activities contained in this document are designed exclusively for Move The Crowd, LLC. Copying, duplicating, or otherwise
reproducing in any form is prohibited. © 2012 All rights reserved.

sustainabledevelopment.svg
Move The crowd supports the
Sustainable Development Goals

Figure by Tania Ellis,
The Social Business Company

UN Sustainable Goals
http://unsustainabledevelopmentgoals.un.org

V. Describe Your Idea: What do you want to specifically work on as your social change idea? Your idea represents the strategy you will employ in order achieve your desired impact.

VI. Describe Your Company, Organization or Initiative: (Hint—revisit your Value Proposition) Your initiative represents the vehicle through which you'll make your desired impact. It can be one you create yourself or one that already exists that you choose to join.

VII. Describe Your Highest Contribution: (Hint—revisit your Value Proposition) As you consider your idea, what are the specific and unique talents and abilities you can bring to help make this happen?

VIII. What Is The Necessary Capital You Need In Order To Make This Contribution?

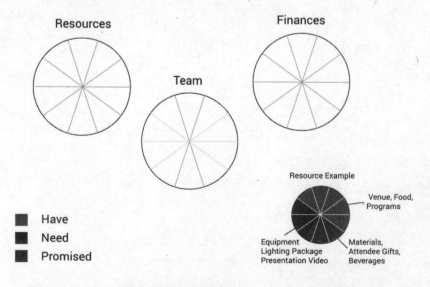

The activities contained in this document are designed exclusively for Move The Crowd, LLC. Copying, duplicating, or otherwise reproducing in any form is prohibited. © 2012 All rights reserved.

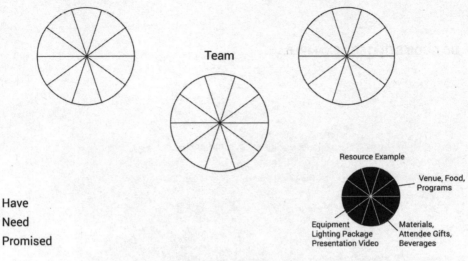

Resources

Team

Finances

Have
Need
Promised

Resource Example

Venue, Food,
Programs

Equipment
Lighting Package
Presentation Video

Materials,
Attendee Gifts,
Beverages

Move The Crowd, 2012

DO GOOD STRATEGY EXAMPLE:

Area: Intersection of Social and Environmental

Sector: For Benefit—revenue-generating mission-based initiative

Objective: End Hunger

Purpose: Create a world that is more agriculturally sustainable

Idea: Teach young people sustainable farming practices

Vehicle: ReVision Urban Farm

Highest Contribution: To restore ancient practices that nourish and uplift humanity by acquiring mastery in these practices and teaching them to young people throughout the state of Massachusetts.

Needs: Community partners who can provide students, financial partners who will help underwrite student stipends, a developed 6-week farming curriculum, etc.

The activities contained in this document are designed exclusively for Move The Crowd, LLC. Copying, duplicating, or otherwise reproducing in any form is prohibited. © 2012 All rights reserved.

Needs

Highest contribution

Vehicle

Idea

Purpose

Objective

Sector

Area

Move The Crowd, 2017

17

Step #5: Aligning Your Power
with Your Movement

Now that you've gotten clear about the contribution you want to make, it's time to take it up a notch! The term "movement" is very hot right now. But it has a long history within the realm of doing good. Often, when we hear this word we think of rallies and thousands, if not millions, of people holding up signs, chanting, or following a specific leader who is teaching a specific doctrine. As I shared in chapter 13, the way that we think about movements over the last 10 years has shifted considerably. Those traditional strategies of organizing and engaging still exist, but now they are joined by a whole new set of agendas, tools, and strategies. Moreover, as movements have evolved and become more multi-faceted, movement leaders have discovered multiple ways to engage a wide array of constituents—some even without leaving the comfort of their living rooms. Just as we've taken back economy, I want to give you the same permission to embrace the concept of movement and to create a clear vision for your participation that totally aligns with your calling.

So, first of all, what is a movement? For the purposes of this conversation a movement is defined as a group of people who are aligned to advance shared philosophical, political, social, cultural, or economic ideas. Given this definition, your first pushback might be "I'm not a group. I'm just an individual trying to find my truth." And I would say yes *and* you are not the only one seeking. Just take a moment to imagine, all of the other people out there who are searching to find their truth, too. Now I want you to imagine the effect that your collective searching is having on the planet. In what way does your aspiration to connect with your true self influence our society? The Age of the Citizen was birthed from this kind of collective energy and intention. Meaning that you may not know who the other people are in your movement, yet, but what you do know is that as a conscious creator, you are working with a particular kind of intention and—guess what?—other people are, too. And the power of that collective energy and intention is what causes things to move—ideas get generated, conversations get instigated, and solutions get created: this is how it works. Take the practice of meditation for example. You have a commitment to reduce the stress in your life, and everywhere you turn, people are talking about the negative effect that stress has on the body; next thing you know, there are all of these experts emerging, talking about how you can reduce stress, and one of the most consistent solutions they mention is meditation. As you take in this information, you make a commitment to meditate, then you start meditating and, seeing the benefits, you begin to share this information with others in your life and they begin meditating as well. Next thing you know, there are meditation centers sprouting up all over the place; heck, you can even get a meditation app on your phone. So your movement, whatever it is, comes to life through your intention to speak, live, and work in a way that aligns with the intention and efforts of others and advances the issues and opportunities you care most about.

For some of you, just having this knowledge and showing up every day to make your contribution will be enough. However, for others of you, when you consider your vision for Doing Good, you do see yourself in a position of leadership and influence—one where you are working consciously to engage and align the efforts of others.

In this chapter, I'm going to invite you to claim your movement and explore how your highest contribution aligns with some of the most important social, environmental, and economic efforts of our time. I'm also going to show you how your intention and aligned right action actually do have the potential to move the needle on the things you care most about. Once you've identified your movement, you need to make a plan. I'll explain how to create a sustainable and innovative strategy that brings your true self, Values-Aligned Proposition, and desired contribution to life. It should be supported by a strong philosophical framework and set of guiding principles drawn from your L3. This can be an ambitious effort, like launching a purpose-driven venture, or a smaller one, like doing daily acts that align with your values—or both. In the end, you'll have created a strategy that reflects your own unique brand of contribution, which is what the Age of the Citizen is all about.

If any of this sounds intimidating, don't worry. I'll show you how to come at it with a realistic and accessible approach. Your goal isn't to change the whole world tomorrow; it's to make your highest contribution in a way that is integral to who you are, aligns with your calling, and reflects the quality of life and experience you want to have. This is the heart of the True. Paid. Good. proposition. There's a frustrating and all-too-common myth out there that says only sweeping and grandiose actions will make a dent in global issues. But I can assure you this is in *no way* true. In fact, small, consistent, deliberate, and sustainable actions made over time are those that repeatedly deliver the greatest impact. If more people understood how valuable simple acts are, so many more of us would actively participate in creating change. Your ability and power to Do Good have little to do with the size of your actions, but the clarity of your intentions and how that aligns with everything you do in service to your calling.

What's *My* Movement?

No matter how you define your role, your movement lives at the intersection of where your true calling and highest contribution meet the greatest opportunities and challenges that exist in the world. It's the place where you have the potential to achieve the greatest impact and leave a legacy of positive change in the process.

Your movement could be a long-term goal that may seem initially impossible because the vision is so grand; just remember that all movements embody those collective actions I referred to earlier on a massive scale, so you really aren't alone in this. In fact, there are tens of millions of others working right alongside of you. You may each go about your work differently, but there is a common thread that runs through what you do that bonds you to the work and one another.

As you consider the Do Good framework for defining your highest contribution presented in chapter 16, you'll notice that every facet of your definition points to an opportunity to engage with a broader community and align your efforts with others.

If I bring back my original example:

Area: Social—because self-care is a form of empowerment.

Sector: Business or for benefit—because I want to encourage you to bring a more entrepreneurial approach to your Do Good vision.

Objective: Good health—when I look at the 17 UN goals this fits perfectly with promoting a greater sense of well-being for all.

Purpose: Bring more joy—increase the capacity of others to do good—this is your true north.

Strategy: Paradigm/culture shifting—new rituals, practices, beliefs. I could also make a case for capacity building—because more joyful professionals naturally bring more capacity to achieve their goals.

Idea: Teach stressed-out professionals how to take better care of themselves.

Vehicle: Professional wellness company that delivers programs on how to reduce stress and boost all forms of well-being.

Highest Contribution: Teach various forms of mindfulness (i.e., yoga, meditation, breathwork, conscious eating, etc.) to stressed-out professionals.

You have a myriad of opportunities to define and align your contribution with various fields and industries from personal growth and empowerment, to health and wellness, to mindfulness and spiritual transformation (that's the joy work!), to do-good or for-benefit companies that not only teach wellness but promote wellness as an integral part of their culture. All of these are movements—and have millions of people working toward a happier and healthier and more ethically aligned society. As you revisit your highest contribution, drawn from your homework assignment from chapter 16, take a moment now and identify all of the potential movements that you might align your efforts with. Take two minutes right now and just jot them down in your journal. If you need a cheat sheet, use the diagram from the UN 2030 Sustainable Development Goals in chapter 13 to help inspire you.

Just identifying with these efforts as you do your work puts you on the court of your movement. But again, if you want to go bigger (and I sense you might) then begin by highlighting the uniqueness and innovation of your contribution.

I mentioned the for-benefit approach in chapter 13, which offers a terrific opportunity to not only blur the lines in how you create change but also leave room for innovative ways to market and position that change. The field is wide open when it comes to pursuing unique solutions that improve the quality of life and experience for the people you're serving. Engagement here can be as top-down as the White House's Office of Social Innovation and Civic Participation (created during the Obama

Administration) and as bottom-up as the #BlackLivesMatter movement. It's a recent and exciting shift that's encouraged those who wouldn't traditionally consider themselves to be "activists" to put their ideas to work and participate in ways that make them part of a solution.

What makes today's social movements so exciting is that you get to construct every facet of how you engage, on your own terms. In traditional movements, organizations liked to create specific calls to action, or catchy phrases that drive people to show support, that were in line with that movement's agenda. In other words, they chose the objective, purpose, and strategy—and you followed the script. Now calls to action are more accessible, flexible, and inspiring and they give tons of options for how to engage but also leave space for you to create your own point of entry. The greatest opportunity you have as a conscious citizen is to create *exactly* how you want to participate.

I began working with Jericho after being a major fan of her work for three years. We met through a social venture organization and became fast buddies. Jericho was fierce, no-nonsense, and all about repping the South. She was particularly dedicated to helping African-American entrepreneurs gain access to the same kind of financial resources she observed other founders receiving in the social impact space during the start-up phases of their enterprises.

Jericho was masterful at being able to articulate her vision and attracted a number of heavy hitters to the table almost immediately. We all know the phrase "be careful what you wish for." Jericho's passion set the wheels in motion, and as her idea began to take flight, the work expanded in ways she could not have imagined. Building a movement for investment parity for African American entrepreneurs was one of those things that a lot of people aspired to in language, but it was a whole other thing to actually try to get it done.

Jericho wasn't just lifting an incubator; she was attempting to deliver on the concept of community wealth building by leveraging entrepreneurial innovation, incubation, and acceleration into targeted regions of the country. This meant she not only had to create the incubators and develop the investment tools but also had to build the infrastructure to make it all come together.

When she arrived at our retreat rendezvous in midtown Manhattan, she had basically given up on sleep just so that she could stay in the communication loop with all of her collaborators.

Things were going really well, but she was fried. Her team was awesome, so our work was to help her to step out of the fray and get super-clear about the articulation of her movement and her own role as a leader. What was the highest and best use of her genius?

"There are a lot of things I could be doing that absolutely need to get done," she said. "But should I be the one doing them? That's the real question."

We laughed, because we both knew just how stretched she was. In order to get really clear about what was the highest and best use of her talents and gifts, I guided her through the milestones and dharma exercises. Her history was fascinating. She'd been working in service to under-resourced and under-engaged communities almost all of her life. However, the commitment to economic development and community wealth came to a head for her post–Hurricane Katrina.

"Watching the way the African American and poor communities were treated, especially in the aftermath, set a fire under me that I can't even explain. I was on the ground working on behalf of these amazing foundations, but no one had enough financial capacity to fully close the gap. I knew then that the key to changing the poverty narrative lived in leveraging of capital through business—particularly in a way that empowered communities *and* generated resources."

As I listened to her story, the values of empowerment, self-determination, history, culture, and personal narrative as a way to understand and engage with others surfaced over and over again. How could these values live at the center of this new movement? Jericho initially had been resisting telling her story, because she wanted the movement to feel more expansive and inclusive.

"The personal is universal," I explained. "People must have something to hold on to in order to really understand why this matters."

"Well, I know how to tell this story!" she replied.

"You absolutely do," I concurred, then continued, "Your story is vital because it also speaks to your values and convictions—which is a central part of what is driving your vision."

"Yes!" At this point she was sitting up and leaning forward.

"Now, there has to be a process that enables your collaborators to align with this vision and these values. They've got to see where their calling and their work align with this greater opportunity." I paused, giving her a moment to jot down a few notes.

"And I need to be the one to lead them through this process," she added.

"Yep." I paused again.

"So, it looks like one of my roles in this initiative is to be the voice of the vision." She took the note, then looked up. "Is that enough?"

There was so much implied in Jericho's question. She and I both knew how it traditionally worked. It is ingrained in us as activists that we don't have the luxury of highest and best. It's our job to do what needs to be done. The circumstances are just too dire. Self-sacrifice, well, that just comes with the territory. But if this vision was really going to thrive, Jericho had to spend her time in the places where she could make the greatest, sustainable impact. Key word—"sustainable."

"Do you believe that telling your story and giving voice to the vision is the highest and best use of you right now? Is this role *your* calling?"

I could see Jericho thinking, we both knew that the full answer would not arrive in that moment, but she now had a point of entry for starting to figure it out.

My parting words were simple: "Be rigorous here."

"Yes, ma'am!" she replied.

Branding Your Contribution

Once your movement has been identified, you get to apply everything you've learned in the previous chapters to architect your own profitable triple-bottom-line strategy and make your desired contribution. Regardless of the vehicles you choose, the commitment should be to build an innovative and sustainable approach that is supported by a strong philosophical framework and set of guiding principles.

This formalized interest in making our own personal form of contribution is what is also now fueling the field of personal and professional development, hence the reason why you are holding this book. The Age of the Citizen lives in every individual expression that is aimed at being part of the solution.

In my work with clients over the years, to really hone in on their movement and highest contribution I've developed a framework drawn from the evangelical lineage of mission and movement building. This model is as old as Jesus (and probably older) but still has a power and potency when lifting any mission and message into the world. This model was used by Susan B. Anthony and Dr. Martin Luther King Jr. and it's also been adopted by personal and professional development experts like Tony Robbins and the amazing Brendon Burchard and world-class marketers and branders, too.

I've used this frame to support my clients in being able to become very explicit about their own unique form of contribution. Drawn from the traditional models for building brands and movements, this frame enables you to construct your personal and/or organizational strategy from the ground up.

As we move through each aspect, you'll have an opportunity to draw on everything I've taught you in this book to bring your branded contribution to life.

It begins with your **core philosophy**—drawn from your L3, your philosophy gives voice to the values, conviction, and principles that govern

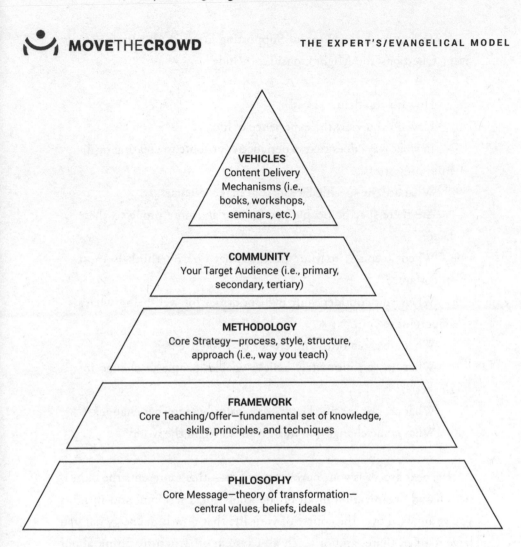

The activities contained in this document are designed exclusively for Move The Crowd, LLC. Copying, duplicating, or otherwise reproducing in any form is prohibited. © 2012 All rights reserved.

how you see the world, and your vision for the kind of world you want to see. What also lives at the heart of your philosophy is what I call your theory of transformation, also known in organizing circles as your theory of change. This speaks to what are the specific things that you believe make a difference in the world and in the lives of other people as you consider what matters most.

If We Stay with the Work of Supporting Stressed-Out Professionals, Some Questions You Might Consider Include:

How do you define stress?

How do you view the experience of life?

In what ways does that experience contribute to creating or diminishing stress?

What are the specific factors that make it worse?

Are there specific people you believe are more prone to these factors?

When it comes to your health, what do you think is most important?

When you consider your own priorities for well-being what's important to you?

What are the mottos and credos that you live by?

What do you ultimately believe enables people to change for the better?

What are the specific factors that contribute to that change?

What is the change you most want to see in the world?

The next aspect is your **core framework**—this represents the culmination and organization of all of the knowledge, wisdom, and insights you've amassed over the course of your life that now influence what you have to offer, share, and/or teach as a system or structure. Think about your milestones exercise back in chapter 4 and how each pivotal moment has contributed to your wisdom. Consider all of the things you've studied and all of the ways you've applied that learning. This framework may be expressed in a product or service or even in an experience. For example, if you teach yoga the framework for this experience consists of 84 primary asanas (postures); there are a myriad of types and styles, but the concept and framework represent this teachable distillation of knowledge.

Some Potential Questions to Support the Creation of Your Framework

When it comes to the issue/opportunity you want to address, what is the primary information that you wish to share with others?

What are the bodies of knowledge that inform that information you most want to share?

What are the principles, techniques, skills, and insights you have amassed that enable you to share this information?

What have been the greatest lessons and/or insights associated with what you want to share?

Is there a process or set of protocols associated with what you want to share?

What is the most logical progression associated with the information you want to share? (In other words, in what way does each piece of information build on or strengthen the previous piece of information?)

The next aspect is your **core methodology**—I describe this as your aesthetic, pedagogy, or approach. This is the way that you actually bring your knowledge, wisdom, and insights to life, or the way that you integrate, own, embody, and deliver the various forms of knowledge that you have assimilated over time. Your Values-Aligned Proposition created in chapter 11 draws on all of the above. If I stay with the yoga example, you can recognize that even though there are only 84 asanas there are many yoga teachers in the world and they each bring their own way of embodying and expressing this knowledge. Moreover, there are other things they bring that are integrated into the way they design their teaching and learning experiences—and these are both implicitly and explicitly expressed.

Some Questions You Might Consider Include:

What are the key elements that enable you to deliver the information you want to share?

Are there creative (and unique) elements that you (want to) integrate into how you share this information?

Is there an approach to sharing this information that you think is better or more effective in your experience?

What aspects of your personality or character also influence the design of your approach?

Are there other factors that influence this design?

If you had to describe your "style" or unique way of presenting this information how would you describe it?

Then there is **your community**—this represents who you most want to engage with your knowledge and insights. And, drawn from the Age of the Citizen, who you most want to co-create with. When I engage my clients in this exploration, we are often looking at primary, secondary, and tertiary audiences—this helps them think about the ripple effects they want to influence as they share their philosophy, framework, and methodology with the world. The co-creation aspect of community is vital because movements in their truest sense are about these collective and collaborative efforts. Even the greatest teachers are influenced by their students and the same is true for the greatest leaders. I also believe that Age of the Citizen leading is about fostering a whole new level of engagement that invites a more dynamic role for those who buy into the change or transformation you are offering.

Some Questions You Might Consider Include:

When you consider this body of knowledge, who do you think can benefit most?

What are the primary challenges and/or opportunities they face?

In what way would this offering help them?

Why is it so important to you to serve this audience in this way?

Why do you believe they would be interested and invest in your solution?

Finally, there are **your channels and vehicles**—this speaks to all of the ways that you share your philosophy, framework, and methodology with your community. Again, these can be products, services, and/or experiences, and if we stay with the entrepreneurial for-benefit commitment all of these should be driving profitability and impact.

Some Questions You Might Ask Include:

What do you think are the best formats for sharing this information?

Why do you think your audience would gravitate toward this format?

In what way does this format support you in making your desired impact?

How does this format(s) enable you to grow?

Your responses to these questions will enable you to cultivate a strategy that reflects your own unique brand of contribution, which is what the Age of the Citizen is all about. You don't have to do it any particular way; you can bring your unique flavor to anything you want to create. Now that you have the most important insights, frameworks, and tools, you are free to explore and arrive at your own signature offering(s).

What attracts people to you is resonance. The way that their values, commitments, challenges, opportunities, and convictions align with the problem you're giving voice to and the opportunity or solution you are offering. The more you lean into your commitment to be a part of that solution, through the various channels and vehicles you select, the more your community will respond positively and your movement and venture (i.e., organization, company, initiative, etc.) will naturally expand.

The Greatest Opportunity

What makes the concept of individual and collective branded movements so exciting is that you literally get to construct every facet of how you engage on your own terms. What matters more than any path you take is the values and level of integrity you bring to these strategies and insights. If you are not answering your calling by leaning into your highest contribution, it won't matter how effective these strategies are. You will not be fulfilled. Having the courage to keep returning to your core impulse as you build is the primary thing that will enliven *and* distinguish you.

One of the greatest examples of staying true to one's calling comes from another beloved client. I met Denise while speaking at another event for women entrepreneurs who were deeply committed to making a difference in the world.

She approached me with fire in her eyes and said, "I have a massive vision and calling, but I'm hiding out and I know it. I'm hoping that you can help me."

By now you know that I'm a sucker for genuine conviction, and

Denise had it—big-time. There was something about her combination of calm, power, and fortitude that told me that she had a story to tell and, for sure, a contribution to make. We got on the phone soon after, and Denise shared a bit of her journey with me. She'd made a fortune very early in her life as a savvy entrepreneur and franchisee for a megabrand. Though she achieved incredible success, it came at a price to her well-being and she wound up battling with a severe anxiety disorder as a result. At the point when she hit rock bottom, she sold her companies and set off on a journey to heal herself and break free from this gripping disease. Through her quest for solutions, Denise stumbled upon the practice of meditation. This was long before the practice went mainstream. Denise spent the next 10 years studying, practicing, and working in various spiritual communities. She became a sponge absorbing the teachings of spiritual gurus, pioneering change agents, and human rights leaders, which laid the foundation for her ultimate calling to teach.

"That was over fifteen years ago," she told me, "but somehow in this moment, I feel like I may have lost my way." Denise had established a nonprofit organization to support her work five years after she became a teacher. When I asked about the work the organization was doing, I discovered that the biggest part of their work centered around bringing in and highlighting other teachers.

"I've gotten so wrapped up in promoting everyone else's thing that I've lost sight of my own voice and desires. There is so much more that I'm here to bring."

"Say more," I interjected.

"Well, when I look at what's going on in the world right now, I feel a strong impulse to speak up about issues of violence, abuse, and injustice. Not just toward women, but all people who are being passed over and rejected—in our society."

As Denise and I delved deeper into this conversation, she realized that when it came to her organization, she'd basically given her power away. She'd also surrounded herself with a team that was not in a position to support this new direction. Moreover, the organization was losing far more money than it was making. Denise stepped into working with me and we mapped out a whole new plan that supported the vision and direction she really wanted to move in. The original impetus for the organization was to cultivate her unique voice and share her innovative approach to mindfulness and her radical approach to self-love and empowerment.

"It's time to get back to that," Denise said.

Denise also had some local projects in her community that were near and dear to her heart and she wanted to do more to support those kinds of opportunities: "I also want to ignite the women in my community to get way more active."

Finally, we got to the elephant in the room, her team. "You've gotta take back your CEO-ness," I told her. "You are the leader and this is your vision."

"Agreed," she said.

Denise emerged from our retreat ready to go back home and make the necessary changes that would lay the foundation for her new vision. Let's just say that it was easier said than done. Denise, like many compassionate leaders, battled with her sense of loyalty, until one day it all came to a head with an event that she'd agreed to produce with another wellness teacher. Though Denise had made a significant financial investment, the teacher had backed out of the event due to poor ticket sales and it looked like Denise was going to be left holding the bag. She texted me and we jumped on the phone to talk through her strategy.

"This is not about the money," I offered. "This is about you taking back your voice and your power."

"You're right," she said. Now, we'd had this conversation before, but this time I could hear the fire in her voice. "Enough is enough." Forty-eight hours later, Denise had personally stepped in to cancel the event, handled the negotiations with the venue and other stakeholders, and then proceeded to completely clean house.

When we got back on the phone for an update the following week in our normal session, Denise was like, "Done, done, and done."

"I am so proud of you."

She laughed. "Me too. And now that I've cleaned house, I'm ready to rebuild this organization my way."

We leaned into her 5-, 3-, 1-year vision with a passion and Denise is now leading one of the most compelling movements on mindfulness and social change in the world. In collaboration with her amazing daughter and a brilliant marketer/family friend, she has amassed millions of followers and boosted their revenue and is pushing the leading edge on bridging the gap between overresourced communities and a whole new generation of young agents of change. I could not be any prouder of the work she's done—to realign her mission, message, and movement on her terms.

If more people understood the value of simple acts it is my belief that they would be inclined to actively participate in creating their desired world. Moreover, if people could engage in those simple acts as an integral part of their everyday societal contribution, then we would rapidly approach the kind of world we want to see. This is the call in the Age of the Citizen, to leverage all of our individual and collective gifts to re-create every facet of our society that does not lend itself to greater well-being for the planet and for us all.

Your Call

Are you ready to own your power and claim your movement? Use the following practice and exercise to give voice to your own brand of change and identify where and how you'd like to play.

PRACTICE 1

Drawn from the exercise in the "What's *My* Movement?" section, complete this sentence:

My movement is _____.

And for the next two weeks, keep giving voice to what you believe your movement is. Don't worry if the words keep changing; this is part of the refinement process. Also, notice when you share how people respond, is it clear? Do they get excited? Do they ask you interesting questions? (Remember my advice to you in chapter 14—share in a nurturing setting with trusted advisors, peers, and confidants.) Stay in this experience until you feel like you've honed it down to a powerful sentence that really inspires you.

EXERCISE 1

Use the Evangelical/Expert's Model (i.e., your core philosophy, framework, methodology, community, and channels/vehicles) to help you create and identify your role in your movement. You can download the worksheet from: www.movethecrowd.me/TheCalling/resources.

THE EXPERT'S/EVANGELICAL MODEL

VEHICLES
Content Delivery
Mechanisms (i.e.,
books, workshops,
seminars, etc.)

COMMUNITY
Your Target Audience (i.e., primary,
secondary, tertiary)

METHODOLOGY
Core Strategy—process, style, structure,
approach (i.e., way you teach)

FRAMEWORK
Core Teaching/Offer—fundamental set of knowledge,
skills, principles, and techniques

PHILOSOPHY
Core Message—theory of transformation—
central values, beliefs, ideals

The activities contained in this document are designed exclusively for Move The Crowd, LLC. Copying, duplicating, or otherwise reproducing in any form is prohibited. © 2012 All rights reserved.

 **MOVETHECROWD**   YOUR TRUE.PAID.GOOD. STRATEGY

THE EXPERT'S/EVANGELICAL MODEL WORKSHEET

I. Philosophy -> Core Message:
Your unique perspective (POV) on your related fields of endeavor: theories of change, values, principles, standards, beliefs. (i.e., life, health, business, success, spirit, the world, opportunity, etc.)

I Believe . . .

II. Framework -> Core Teaching/Offer:
The fundamental set of knowledge, principles, techniques, skills and/or insights you seek to organize and share with others.

I Teach/Provide . . .

III. Methodology -> Core Strategy:
You unique style, process, structure, approach to delivering the information you seek to share.

My Methodology Consists of . . .

IV. Community -> Your Target Audience:
Those you desire to engage and can most effectively reach (i.e., primary, secondary, tertiary).

I Seek to Engage . . .

V. Vehicles -> Content Delivery Mechanisms:
Format, design, and structures of your content-based offerings. (i.e., books, workshops, seminars, etc.).

My Primary Vehicles Are . . .

The activities contained in this document are designed exclusively for Move The Crowd, LLC. Copying, duplicating, or otherwise reproducing in any form is prohibited. © 2012 All rights reserved.

18

Step #6: Celebrating Your Next Level of Contribution

Now that you've developed your True. Paid. Good. strategy, it's time to take it out into the world. One of the books that changed my life is called *The Science of Getting Rich* by Wallace D. Wattles. It is a small book that contains big wisdom on the principles and characteristics that breed abundance. In it, Wattles points out how crucial it is to work in ways that make everything around you better. He calls this "being advancing." He says: "No matter whether you are a physician, a teacher, or a clergyman, if you can give increase of life to others and make them sensible of the fact, they will be attracted to you and you will be rich." In other words, no matter what you do, if you commit to enriching the lives of others and they actually experience that enrichment, you will prosper, because they will continue to come back for more, thereby contributing to your success.

If you think about anything you've ever been passionate about in any area of your life and how it made you feel after achieving it—whether it was running a marathon for charity, giving advice to a friend, or teaching your child the ABCs—I'll bet it was driven by a deeper desire to give "more life" to those around you. Now just imagine profiting from this same generosity that is now deeply rooted in your life's work. This is the promise of True. Paid. Good., if you apply the lessons and principles I've given you. You have enormous potential to live a fulfilling, prosperous life and make a difference in the lives of others—to be advancing in every sense of the word.

As you move into the final chapter of this book, I will explain how all three aspects of this equation come together as a whole proposition, so you can wholly apply them. My wish is to inspire you to take everything you've learned and make it real in your own life and out in the world. My hope, through our time together, is that you've felt, seen, and thus been able to see yourself in a whole new way, that you've explored your passions and touched your greatness, that you've discovered there's more than what you're settling for and that you're now inspired more than ever to go for it.

As you bring your True. Paid. Good. commitment to life you may find that there are a number of radical changes you'll need to make, or you may discover that it's just about making a few minor tweaks to what already exists. Whatever the case may be, I want to urge you to take it one step at a time and one day at a time. Achieving the goals and culti-vating the new habits that support this new commitment will take some time, but if you remain strong in your intention and consistent in your aligned actions and practices, then this new reality is yours.

Answering the Call at Home

Now that you are clear about your calling, how does that translate to your most intimate relationships? Your L3 is your moral compass wher-ever you are. Use these declarations as a guide for helping you determine who you want to be for those you love. For some of you, the call may be to take a more active role in the lives of your children; for others of you, it may be to actually take a step back and let family members work it out on their own; for still others, it may be to just bring a renewed and refreshed commitment to what you're already doing. Whatever the case, I want you to take the time and create a clear vision for what you'd like to create and manifest here. Are there specific conflicts that need to be resolved? Are there relationships that need to be healed? Are there things you need to say to your parents or your siblings or your spouse that you've never said before? What are the daily, weekly, and monthly practices that support your vision and calling when it comes to caring for your home? Use this opportunity to move to a whole new level of love and contribution with yourself and with those you love.

Answering the Call at Work

Your greatest opportunity and challenge here is to activate your personal economy through how you acquire and invest your resources. How does every facet of your work align with your highest contribution? What changes or shifts need to happen in the context of your work that will move you into greater integrity with this commitment? You must begin with your Values-Aligned Proposition. What do you want to offer to the marketplace? Whether you choose to work for a company or organization or to create/grow your own venture, your clarity around your proposition and contribution is vital to establishing the value of what you bring. For some of you, it may be time to transition out of your current job and either find a new, more aligned position or step out on your own; if this is the case, your focus may need to be on a transition plan—taking the time to clarify your vision for your work and then identifying what the steps are to support moving you in that direction. I highly recommend that you set a date for when your desired transition is complete so that you can keep this intention in front of you as you take consistent action to bring it to life. For others of you, you may already be leaning into your highest contribution; therefore, the focus may be getting the knowledge, skills, and experience that will enable you to expand and make your current passion even more profitable. Drawing on all of the learning in part II, become adamant about your Get Paid vision. Also, stay connected to your motivation for wanting to achieve your money truth. What does this level of financial resource enable you to do? Does it support a particular quality of life and experience? Does it enable you to leverage and invest your resources toward the things you really care about? Remember, the financial resources that you attract through your Get Paid vision should be a symbol of the incredible value you give to those who engage your products, services, and experiences. If your vision is guided by making a certain amount of money or having a certain amount in the bank, consider what the key milestones might be along the way. The more opportunities you can give yourself to celebrate here, the more encouraged you will be to keep going. Remember, your work is love made visible.

Answering the Call in the World

This is where you get to evaluate how your highest contribution really moves the needle on the things you care about. In every dimension of your life you have the chance to contribute to the person you want to be and to the world you want to see. From how you relate, to how you consume, to how you serve, each decision, choice, and action matters. When you hold the intention for doing good, every effort you make and every interaction you have can contribute toward that commitment. The more you give voice to your Do Good vision and align your actions with that image, the more you will feel a deep sense of connection to not only your own efforts but also the efforts of all those millions of people who are sharing that commitment with you. Every day, take a moment to feel that connection—how will you show up for your calling today? What is the difference you will strive to make today? Whose life will you make it your business to touch today? What will you leave better than you found it today? The more specific and explicit you are about these intentions, the more impactful your efforts will be.

In each of these dimensions you have an opportunity to set a standard. One that not only activates your calling but also can serve to inspire those around you to step back and consider *their* purpose. You are not alone in your quest for a greater, more aligned and prosperous life, and just as you need to know you're not alone, others do, too. Your Do Good is personal because it embodies your values and aspirations, but it's also universal because you have the potential to become a role model by sharing your knowledge, wisdom, expertise, and journey in a way that inspires others.

From Doing to BE-ing

Mastering your True. Paid. Good. commitment is far less about doing and much more about BE-ing. We live in a world that is so hyper-focused on doing that, and when though action has its place, when it comes to your calling the ultimate aim and desire is get to the point where you are simply BE-ing and your purpose, contribution, and impact are just flowing from you. This takes me back to my original definition of dharma, i.e., your true nature *expressed* as your highest contribution and calling. This definition should take on a whole new meaning for you now that you've had the chance to go deep on who you are and on what you're ultimately here to provide to the world.

Your conscious creating power at its best shows up in your presence. And your presence is the part of you that carries all of the things you encompass and embody—in other words, your presence is the cumulative impact of everything you are, everything you know, everything you desire, and everything you've been through—it is an energy that becomes palpable when you dedicate yourself to cultivating a life that is guided by your True. Paid. Good. Your personal development, the strengthening of your knowledge, skills, and expertise, the ownership and expansion of your hard-earned wisdom, and your vibrant commitment to a better world are all of the things that live in your BE-ing. And when you show up with your full presence, i.e., your full intention and attention, your highest contribution invariably shows up with you. It becomes almost an effortless expression of who you are. When you get to this level of mastery, you don't even have to think about your calling—your calling will be present simply because you are just BE-ing you!

So how do you get to this level of ingrained contribution? Practice, practice, practice—my friend! At the end of chapter 6, I introduced you to three vital practices that were designed to strengthen and enliven your new Stay True reality. They are *stillness* (quietude and deep listening), *subtle body observation* (internal access to joy, peace, love, and well-being), and *conscious, courageous choosing* (decisions made from a heightened state of awareness and devotion). These three practices strengthen your presence because they keep you connected to your True. Paid. Good. commitment and remind you that anything you want to have, do, be, or create starts from within.

One of my favorite examples of cultivating an empowering presence comes from working with another one of my amazing international clients, Terri. I remember the first time Terri and I spoke, she'd come to the Move The Crowd site through an online program focused on spirituality and business. From the word go I loved her energy and her honesty.

"I've built a number of successful businesses, but I'm being called to do something totally different than what I've ever done before." Terri had many past lives, as an award-winning hairstylist, top real estate agent, and, most recently, renowned chef and restaurateur. "I'm being called to teach the tools of transformation."

Not being one to sit on the sidelines, Terri was already in action even before she reached out to me. She had made a list of what she needed to do and was checking things off left and right. That wasn't the issue. When I asked her about why she hadn't stepped out there fully and started promoting, she began to share about all of the fears and limiting conversations she held around her brand: "People are going to think I'm just all over the place."

"You mean, people are going to want to know why you are *successfully* all over the place?" I added. She laughed; we could both see that

Terri's challenge had nothing to do with not taking aligned action but, rather, had to do with who she was BE-ing, and who she was BE-ing was "too scared to put herself out there." My job was to help her shift her BE-ing so that it was in total alignment with all of the great work she'd already done. We dug deep on the milestone exercise, which gave her a vivid experience of her journey and how far she'd come. Terri had overcome living in deep depression and being reliant on drugs, she'd made it through the severe sickness of her youngest child, she'd persevered through the dark side of "instant stardom" as a reality TV show contestant, and through all of these challenges she built not one but three successful careers—I wanted her to see this. I introduced the conversation of dharma and evolution and the way that brands (and callings) evolve over time—because I wanted her to give herself permission to change. Together, we identified her true nature and the common thread moving throughout all of her work: which was to live by example, to nurture, uplift, and empower people and show them that they were capable of far more than they imagined. We dug into her core philosophy, her framework and methodology, to really zero in on what she was here to teach and why. And the more Terri could hear herself, the more confident she became. As the elements of her brand and offerings began to take shape Terri had a total freak-out moment and reached out in desperation.

"I don't know why I have so much fear about this, but I do," she said. "There are all of these opportunities coming to me if I just stay with what I'm doing rather than take the harder path and answer my calling."

This is a common dynamic; Terri's freak-out is something I see all the time. Just when people get really close to stepping onto the path of their true calling all of their fears and insecurities arise and they freak out.

Terri and I got on the phone and I asked her, "What do you perceive your calling as the hardest path?"

She sighed. "I don't know; I just keep thinking about what other people are going to think. It's easy to stand behind a company brand, but this is the first time I'm coming out there as just me."

As much as Terri could see the value of her contribution, those old conversations about being good enough "just as me" were standing in the way. We needed to confront them head on.

"Terri, I want you to allow yourself right now to feel those feelings, to not run from them, or hide from them, but to face them head on and just breathe through them right now."

"Okay," she said with a trembling voice.

"Keep breathing and just keep talking."

"I don't know," she started. "I think about some of the people around me who have always criticized me, saying things like 'I can't believe you got this opportunity' or 'How come they picked you?' It's like they don't want me to succeed—especially because of where I come from, you know, humble beginnings."

As Terri poured out her soul I just listened and encouraged her to listen, because at the end of it all she was going to have to choose. Was she going to live for her jealous neighbors or was she going to follow her heart and answer her calling? Once Terri completed the preceding exercise, I added in the three practices; *stillness, subtle body observation,* and *conscious, courageous choosing.* She took on a daily practice of stillness and meditation. In our conversations, I kept urging her to tap into her emotional body—so that she could observe her fears—and notice the vast and subtle shifts in energy from when we began a conversation until the point we ended. And finally, I gave her the assignment to log and track her choices—to notice when she was coming from a place of scarcity and fear versus when she was coming from a place of creativity and love. As Terri engaged these practices, her voice actually began to change—it became deeper, warmer, and more resonant. As she embraced her evolving brand, she also embraced the next level of confidence.

"I'm choosing to follow my dreams," she said matter-of-factly in a subsequent session, and the new concepts and ideas began pouring through. Finally, Terri was ready to get back out there and call in her ideal clients and collaborators. She created a gorgeous new landing page that told her story by drawing on from our milestones work and she created coaching packages and started attracting new clients almost immediately. "People are just finding me . . ." she said. "It's like they know that I'm ready for them."

I laughed and replied, "Yes, indeed!"

The True. Paid. Good. Movement

When I considered the primary aim for starting my own venture, I knew exactly what I wanted my company to do. I've always been passionate about helping people see and achieve their greatness, so that part was easy. But a fundamental question remained for me as I considered our business model, which was *how* we would ultimately be successful. In other words, what would be my primary motivation for success and how would I define it? There is so much entrepreneurial mythology out there about everything you're supposed to give up and risk in order to prove yourself worthy of the quest. Now I understand that this imagery excites a lot of people, but for most of us, it's terrifying.

And the question "What will people think?" often tops the list.

When I was earning my unorthodox MBA sitting in all those entrepreneurial and professional development trainings, there was this unspoken mandate that you should gamble in ways that were just not healthy. Balls to the wall is one method, but it isn't the only way. It was painful for me to watch people make crazy financial decisions jacked up on somebody's sales conversion strategy. Or to watch fellow entrepreneurs risk their kids and marriages to pursue "the dream."

Each of us owes it to ourselves to determine what we want to be the driver for our success. I've never been afraid of hard work, nor am I shy about taking calculated risks. But I knew that I had no interest in trading my well-being (mental, spiritual, or emotional) for anything. I was interested in whole success. Not "Pyrrhic victories," as my beloved mentor Lisa Nichols would say.

When I was creating Move The Crowd, it was important to me to have the philosophy behind this company be just as precise as my goals and objectives. I knew what we wanted to do, but who would we BE in order to get there? How would we live the values in the day-to-day? What would we practice? What was our L3? As clear as I was about the mission, there was a part of me that still doubted whether or not I could successfully build this company and maintain the values that were most important to me. And it was in Wattles's fifteenth chapter on being advancing that I finally got the answer I needed to build this company, make it successful, *and* be *me*.

When I look at anything that I have ever been passionate about in my life, and all of the things I've done as a result, I see it has been driven by the desire to give "more life" to everything and everyone. It has been my experience that people gravitate to others who inspire and enliven them. People need to be inspired and encouraged, especially as they meet the challenges of their everyday lives. What you choose to give doesn't have to be money; it can be other kinds of resources and/or information or really useful advice. Sometimes you can even enhance someone's experience just through the nature of your very presence.

As you consider your own definition of success, how can a central part of your motivation be rooted in creating opportunities for others? This doesn't just apply to your clients. How can you consider this commitment at every stage and in every facet of your life and business? At home, at work, and in the world, as I've encouraged earlier.

I believe my success lives fostering the success of everyone around me and this is what Wattles touched with the notion of being advancing. I am someone, at the very core, who roots for the greatness in others. If you took everything away from me I would still be that person. This is who I have always been and who I always will be. And this is what fuels my True. Paid. Good. branded movement.

In all my years of sharing the True. Paid. Good. philosophy with clients and audiences, I've helped lift up a new generation of courageous leaders and everyday citizens who are changing the game and bringing more life to others. Some are world renowned and others are just quietly doing their thing. Whatever the case may be, the relationships I've built go beyond "programs" and "packages"; they are bonds that last a lifetime, whether we are actively working together or not.

Over the last 11 years I've had the joy to bear witness to one amazing journey in particular that fills my heart every time I think about it. And that is the incredible journey of my beloved Gabby. Gabby's story is so special to me because I remember the passionate young woman who sat across from me in a cozy Brooklyn restaurant all those years ago.

"I am a teacher," she said. "And I have a message that I want to bring to the world."

Even then, her conviction was palpable. Gabby came to me initially seeking my counsel around a particular relationship challenge she was having, but what evolved from that challenge was the creation of a foundation that enabled her to find her truth. And once Gabby found her truth, the next step was to strengthen her courage to speak it, honor it, and care for it. She boldly stepped away from the relationship and went to work full-time on cultivating a whole new level of self-love and appreciation. She began to see the connection between her life and her work and there was an integrity that naturally started to emerge as a result. She said, "I'm a teacher."

I said, "Actually, you're a world leader."

The first time I said it she just looked at me. "Huh!" she replied.

I could feel this broader foundation resonating with her. One afternoon in a working session, we began to talk about her story.

"I've heard you tell your story, but I think there is so much more there."

"You're right," she said.

"You gotta take us there," I said. "People are going to be broken open by what you share."

"Damn right!" she said.

I am always fascinated by the questions I get about how Gabby's become so popular. It is no mystery to me. Over the years, we have worked in every facet of her life and business and she has brought the same level of willingness and surrender to transforming anything that has stood in the way of her purpose. "She's always had conviction and she's always done the work" is always my reply. She has wanted to transform in honor of her calling more than she's wanted anything else and that burning desire has made all of the difference. Gabby has truly practiced everything she teaches and the resonance in the lessons is undeniable to her students. They know she's been there and that she's got a story to tell and some insights to offer. And through those three vital practices, *stillness, subtle body observation*, and *conscious, courageous choosing,* Gabby has become so profoundly connected to who she is and what she's here to do that it just pours forth from her being. We worked together to shape her vision, monetize it, and reach as many people as possible—and at every turn, we've surpassed our goals and objectives. What moved me then, and still blows me away today, is how Gabby's generous spirit and drive to "give an increase of life" expands as she does. This is the rocket fuel that's led to multiple *New York Times* bestsellers and sold-out speaking venues around the world. What's even more amazing to me is that not only does Gabby live the True. Paid. Good. philosophy, but the souls she's here to serve are also taking the world by storm because of her teachings—Spirit Junkies are making their mark in every corner of the globe. She's an incredible force that's built more than just a profitable venture; she's built a movement and is on her way to cultivating a legacy that will continue affecting millions of lives long after she's gone.

In my work, I am called many things, but who I am is a professional champion, encouraging you to rise to meet your calling. I am in the business of creating a loving army of True. Paid. Good. change agents just like Gabby, with the hope that we can positively transform and uplift every facet of our society.

My desire to be there for you is a legacy I've inherited from my parents because this is who they were and who my father, specifically, was for me. He was always there to cheer me on, lovingly caution me, and tell me I mattered and that my happiness was important. He shared his wisdom and hard-earned lessons, hoping I wouldn't suffer, the same as all great parents do.

It is humbling to be loved in that way, and I believe that's why I seek to be that for others. Helping you live the True. Paid. Good. philosophy is my way of rooting for you, too.

When I was growing up, my father had a favorite saying that gave him courage and strength, and though I never fully understood it as a kid, I sensed it was his way of soldiering on no matter what he faced.

"It's a great life," he'd tell me, "if you don't weaken." When my father passed away, I had the honor of writing his obituary, which sent me hunting for the source of this quote. It actually comes from the Scottish author John Buchan's 1941 novel called *Sick Heart River* (it was renamed *Mountain Meadow* for US publication). It's the story of one man's quest against the tough northern Canadian terrain, which serves as a greater metaphor for man's struggle against himself. We've been grappling with our ability to know, and ultimately love and accept, ourselves since the dawn of time. This may be why True. Paid. Good. has resonated with thousands of clients. It's a philosophy that has helped them and will help you become the keeper of your own destiny—regardless of any imperfections, obstacles, and distractions in your way. In so many ways, my father's mantra is about *not* turning away from your truest self and your divine duty to grow and serve by any means necessary. Any one aspect of the True. Paid. Good. philosophy will certainly improve some corner of your career or sense of self when done in isolation. But to really transform your whole life and give you a solid foundation for making a difference in the lives of others, all aspects must seamlessly work together and inform one another.

French writer, philosopher, and political activist Simone de Beauvoir once said, "That's what I consider true generosity: You give your all, and yet you always feel as if it costs you nothing." This kind of generosity speaks to a natural expansion of self—an effortless extension of your purpose, values, gifts, and energy that flow from a place of earnest desire and unconditional love. This is the reward for bringing your true calling to life. This is what my clients who work, live, and dream by the True. Paid. Good. philosophy come to embrace and celebrate every single day.

Taking the vow to be True. Paid. Good. is tantamount to saying, "I will walk my own path and be my own person. And I will thrive and prosper." Each of us deserves the right and opportunity to explore the depths of what that means. Whether it comes as a gentle kiss on the mouth or as a swift kick in the you-know-what, rest assured the call to your greatest self will come. We are all here to live a great life, but we must be strong enough, courageous enough, loving enough, and aware enough to answer.

Your Call

Are you ready to bring it all together and activate the True. Paid. Good. promise in your life and out in the world? Use these practices and exercise to bring your True. Paid. Good. commitment to life.

PRACTICE 1

Revisit the three vital practices.

Create a morning and evening practice of **stillness.** Even if you begin with just two minutes each day, start that practice now!

PRACTICE 2

Schedule two- to three-minute **subtle body observation** breaks throughout the day to just tap into how you are feeling. Notice what emotions are present, notice your level of energy, notice what activities and interactions inspire and motivate (i.e., raise your energy, rather than drain and deplete it), and write down what you observe daily.

PRACTICE 3

Slow down and begin to pay closer attention to your **conscious, courageous choosing** in every moment. Not just the big decisions, but those micro-choices that you make unconsciously throughout the day. Your conscious courage is needed and can be the difference between achieving your objectives and missing the mark. Keep looking at where you can move into greater alignment—remember, this is the work of true success and this is the practice that supports it.

EXERCISE 1

Use the guidance I offer in this chapter called Answering the Call at Home, Answering the Call at Work, and Answering the Call in the World, to give voice to your whole self and whole success life vision. This will become your blueprint for how your True. Paid. Good. commitment comes alive in your life and in the world.